THE

CANDLE OF THE LORD

And Other Sermons

BY THE

REV. PHILLIPS BROOKS

RECTOR OF TRINITY CHURCH, BOSTON

———◆———

NEW YORK

E. P. DUTTON AND COMPANY

1881·

UNIVERSITY PRESS:
JOHN WILSON AND SON, CAMBRIDGE.

CONTENTS.

———◆———

SERMONS.

———•———

I.

THE CANDLE OF THE LORD.

"The spirit of man is the candle of the Lord." — PROV. xx. 27.

THE essential connection between the life of God and
the life of man is the great truth of the world; and that
is the truth which Solomon sets forth in the striking
words which I have chosen for my text this morning.
The picture which the words suggest is very simple.
An unlighted candle is standing in the darkness and some
one comes to light it.   A blazing bit of paper holds the
fire at first, but it is vague and fitful. `It flares and wavers
and at any moment may go out.   But the vague, uncertain, flaring blaze touches the candle, and the candle
catches fire and at once you have a steady flame.   It
burns straight and clear and constant.   The candle gives
the fire a manifestation-point for all the room which is
illuminated by it.   The candle is glorified by the fire
and the fire is manifested by the candle.   The two bear
witness that they were made for one another by the way
in which they fulfil each other's life.   That fulfilment
comes by the way in which the inferior substance renders
obedience to its superior.   The candle obeys the fire.
The docile wax acknowledges that the subtle flame is
its master and it yields to his power; and so, like every

1

faithful servant of a noble master, it at once gives its
master's nobility the chance to utter itself, and its own
substance is clothed with a glory which is not its own.
The disobedient granite, if you try to burn it, neither
gives the fire a chance to show its brightness nor gathers
any splendor to itself. It only glows with sullen resistance, and, as the heat increases, splits and breaks but
will not yield. But the candle obeys, and so in it the
scattered fire finds a point of permanent and clear expression.

Can we not see, with such a picture clear before us,
what must be meant when it is said that one being is
the candle of another being? There is in a community
a man of large, rich character, whose influence runs
everywhere. You cannot talk with any man in all the
city but you get, shown in that man's own way, the
thought, the feeling of that central man who teaches all
the community to think, to feel. The very boys catch
something of his power, and have something about them
that would not be there if he were not living in the town.
What better description could you give of all that, than
to say that that man's life was fire and that all these
men's lives were candles which he lighted, which gave
to the rich, warm, live, fertile nature that was in him
multiplied points of steady exhibition, so that he lighted
the town through them? Or, not to look so widely, I
pity you if in the circle of your home there is not some
warm and living nature which is your fire. Your cold,
dark candle-nature, touched by that fire, burns bright
and clear. Wherever you are carried, perhaps into regions where that nature cannot go, you carry its fire and
set it up in some new place. Nay, the fire itself may have

disappeared, the nature may have vanished from the earth and gone to heaven; and yet still your candle-life, which was lighted at it, keeps that fire still in the world, as the fire of the lightning lives in the tree that it has struck, long after the quick lightning itself has finished its short, hot life and died. So the man in the counting-room is the candle of the woman who stays at home, making her soft influence felt in the rough places of trade where her feet never go; and so a man who lives like an inspiration in the city for honesty and purity and charity may be only the candle in whose obedient life burns still the fire of another strong, true man who was his father, and who passed out of men's sight a score of years ago. Men call the father dead, but he is no more dead than the torch has gone out which lighted the beacon that is blazing on the hill.

And now, regarding all this lighting of life from life, two things are evident, the same two which appeared in the story of the candle and its flame: First, there must be a correspondency of nature between the two; and second, there must be a cordial obedience of the less to the greater. The nature which cannot feel the other nature's warmth, even if it is held close to it; and the nature which refuses to be held where the other nature's flame can reach it, — both of these must go unlighted, no matter how hotly the fire of the higher life may burn.

I think that we are ready now to turn to Solomon and read his words again and understand them. "The spirit of man is the candle of the Lord," he says. God is the fire of this world, its vital principle, a warm pervading presence everywhere. What thing of outward nature can so picture to us the mysterious, the subtle, the quick, live, productive and destructive thought, which has always lifted men's hearts and solemnized their faces when they have said the word GOD, as this strange thing, — so heavenly, so unearthly, so terrible, and yet so gracious; so full of creativeness, and yet so quick and fierce to sweep whatever opposes it out of its path, — this marvel, this beauty and glory and mystery of fire ?   Men have always felt the fitness of the figure; and the fire has always crowded, closest of all earthly elements, about the throne on which their conception of Deity was seated. And now of this fire the spirit of man is the candle. What does that mean ?   If, because man is of a nature which corresponds to the nature of God, and just so far as man is obedient to God, the life of God, which is spread throughout the universe, gathers itself into utterance; and men, aye, and all other beings, if such beings there are, capable of watching our humanity, see what God is, in gazing at the man whom He has kindled, — then is not the figure plain ?   It is a wondrous thought, but it is clear enough.   Here is the universe, full of the diffused fire of divinity.   Men feel it in the air, as they feel an intense heat which has not broken into a blaze. That is the meaning of a great deal of the unexplained, mysterious awfulness of life, of which they who are very much in its power are often only half aware.   It is the sense of God, felt but unseen, like an atmosphere burdened with heat that does not burst out into fire.   Now in the midst of this solemn, burdened world there stands up a man, pure, God-like, and perfectly obedient to God. In an instant it is as if the heated room had found some sensitive, inflammable point where it could kindle to a blaze. The vague oppressiveness of God's felt presence becomes clear and definite. The fitfulness of the impression of divinity is steadied into permanence. The mystery changes its character, and is a mystery of light and not of darkness. The fire of the Lord has found the candle of the Lord, and burns clear and steady, guiding and cheering instead of bewildering and frightening us, just so soon as a man who is obedient to God has begun to catch and manifest His nature.

I hope that we shall find that this truth comes very close to our personal, separate lives ; but, before we come to that, let me remind you first with what a central dignity it clothes the life of man in the great world. Certain philosophies, which belong to our time, would depreciate the importance of man in the world, and rob him of his centralness. Man's instinct and man's pride rebel against them, but he is puzzled by their speciousness. Is it indeed true, as it seems, that the world is made for man, and that from man, standing in the centre, all things besides which the world contains get their true value and receive the verdict of their destiny ? That was the old story that the Bible told. The book of Genesis with its Garden of Eden, and its obedient beasts waiting until the man should tell them what they should be called, struck firmly, at the beginning of the anthem of the world's history, the great note of the centralness of man. And the Garden of Eden, in this its first idea, repeats itself in every cabin of the western forests or the southern jungles, where a new Adam and a new Eve, a solitary settler and his wife, begin as it were the human history anew. There once again the note of Genesis is struck, and man asserts his central-

ness. The forest waits to catch the color of his life.
The beasts hesitate in fear or anger till he shall tame
them to his service or bid them depart. The earth under
his feet holds its fertility at his command, and answers
the summons of his grain or flower-seeds. The very sky
over his head regards him, and what he does upon the
earth is echoed in the changes of the climate and the
haste or slowness of the storms. This is the great impression which all the simplest life of man is ever
creating, and with which the philosophies, which would
make little of the separateness and centralness of the
life of man, must always have to fight. And this is
the impression which is taken up and strengthened and
made clear, and turned from a petty pride to a lofty
dignity and a solemn responsibility, when there comes
such a message as this of Solomon's. He says that the
true separateness and superiority and centralness of man
is in that likeness of nature to God, and that capacity
of spiritual obedience to Him, in virtue of which man
may be the declaration and manifestation of God to all
the world. So long as that truth stands, the centralness
of man is sure. " The spirit of man is the candle of the
Lord."

This is the truth of which I wish to speak to you
to-day, the perpetual revelation of God by human life.
You must ask yourself first, what God is. You must
see how at the very bottom of His existence, as you
conceive of it, lie these two thoughts — purpose and
righteousness; how absolutely impossible it is to give
God any personality except as the fulfilment of these
two qualities — the intelligence that plans in love, and
the righteousness that lives in duty. Then ask yourself

how any knowledge of these qualities — of what they are, of what kind of being they will make in their perfect combination — could exist upon the earth if there were not a human nature here in which they could be uttered, from which they could shine. Only a person can truly utter a person. Only from a character can a character be echoed. You might write it all over the skies that God was just, but it would not burn there. It would be, at best, only a bit of knowledge; never a Gospel; never something which it would gladden the hearts of men to know. That comes only when a human life, capable of a justice like God's, made just by God, glows with His justice in the eyes of men, a candle of the Lord.

I have just intimated one thing which we need to observe. Man's utterance of God is purely an utterance of quality. It can tell me nothing of the quantities which make up His perfect life. That God is just, and what it is to be just — those things I can learn from the just lives of the just men about me; but how just God is, to what unconceived perfection, to what unexpected developments of itself, that majestic quality of justice may extend in Him, — of that I can form no judgment, that is worth anything, from the justice that I see in fellow-man. This seems to me to widen at once the range of the truth which I am stating. If it be the quality of God which man is capable of uttering, then it must be the quality of manhood that is necessary for the utterance; the quality of manhood, but not any specific quantity, not any assignable degree of human greatness. Whoever has in him the human quality, whoever really has the spirit of man, may be a candle of the Lord. A larger measure of that spirit may make

a brighter light; but there must be a light wherever
any human being, in virtue of his humanness, by obedience becomes luminous with God.   There are the men
of lofty spiritual genius, the leaders of our race.   How
they stand out through history!   How all men feel as
they pass into their presence that they are passing into
the light of God!   They are puzzled when they try to
explain it.   There is nothing more instructive and suggestive than the bewilderment which men feel when
they try to tell what inspiration is, — how men become
inspired.   The lines which they draw through the continual communication between God and man are always
becoming unsteady and confused.   But in general, he
who comes into the presence of any powerful nature,
whose power is at all of a spiritual sort, feels sure that
in some way he is coming into the presence of God.
But it would be melancholy if only the great men could
give us this conviction.   The world would be darker
than it is if every human spirit, so soon as it became
obedient, did not become the Lord's candle.   A poor,
meagre, starved, bruised life, if only it keeps the true
human quality and does not become inhuman, and if it
is obedient to God in its blind, dull, half-conscious way,
becomes a light.   Lives yet more dark than it is, become
dimly aware of God through it.   A mere child, in his
pure humanity, and with his easy and instinctive turning of his life toward the God from whom he came, —
it is one of the commonplaces of your homes how often
he may burn with some suggestion of divinity, and cast
illumination upon problems and mysteries whose difficulty he himself has never felt.   There are great lamps
and little lamps burning everywhere.   The world is

bright with them. You shut your book in which you have been holding communion with one of the great souls of all time; and while you are standing in the light which he has shed about him, your child beside you says some simple, childlike thing, and a new thread of shining wisdom runs through the sweet and subtle thoughts that the great thinker gave you, as the light of a little taper sends its special needle of brightness through the pervasive splendor of a sunlit world. It is not strange. The fire is the same, whatever be the human lamp that gives it its expression. There is no life so humble that, if it be true and genuinely human and obedient to God, it may not hope to shed some of His light. There is no life so meagre that the greatest and wisest of us can afford to despise it. We cannot know at all at what sudden moment it may flash forth with the life of God.

And in this truth of ours we have certainly the key to another mystery which sometimes puzzles us. What shall we make of some man rich in attainments and in generous desires, well educated, well behaved, who has trained himself to be a light and help to other men, and who, now that his training is complete, stands in the midst of his fellow-men completely dark and helpless? There are plenty of such men. We have all known them who have seen how men grow up. Their brethren stand around them expecting light from them, but no light comes. They themselves are full of amazement at themselves. They built themselves for influence, but no one feels them. They kindled themselves to give light; but no one shines a grateful answer back to them. Perhaps they blame their fellow-men, who are too dull to see their radiance. Perhaps they only wonder what is the matter, and wait, with a hope that never quite dies out into despair, for the long-delayed recognition and gratitude. At last they die, and the men who stand about their graves feel that the saddest thing about their death is that the world is not perceptibly the darker for their dying. What does it mean? If we let the truth of Solomon's figure play upon it, is not the meaning of the familiar failure simply this: These men are unlighted candles; they are the spirit of man, elaborated, cultivated, finished to its very finest, but lacking the last touch of God. As dark as a row of silver lamps, all chased and wrought with wondrous skill, all filled with rarest oil, but all untouched with fire, — so dark in this world is a long row of cultivated men, set up along the corridors of some age of history, around the halls of some wise university, or in the pulpits of some stately church, to whom there has come no fire of devotion, who stand in awe and reverence before no wisdom greater than their own, who are proud and selfish, who do not know what it is to obey. There is the explanation of your wonder when you cling close to some man whom the world calls bright, and find that you get no brightness from him. There is the explanation of yourself, O puzzled man, who never can make out why the world does not turn to you for help. The poor blind world cannot tell its need, nor analyze its instinct, nor say why it seeks one man and leaves another; but through its blind eyes it knows when the fire of God has fallen on a human life. This is the meaning of the strange helpfulness which comes into a man when he truly is converted. It is not new truth that he knows, not new wonders that he can do, but it is that the unlighted nature, in the utter obedience and self-surrender of that great hour, has been lifted up and lighted at the life of God, and now burns with Him.

But it is not the worst thing in life for a man to be powerless or uninfluential. There are men enough for whom we would thank God if they did no harm, even if they did no good. I will not stop now to question whether there be such a thing possible as a life totally without influence of any kind, whether perhaps the men of whom I have been speaking do not also belong to the class of whom I want next to speak. However that may be, I am sure you will recognize the fact that there is a multitude of men whose lamps are certainly not dark, and yet who certainly are not the candles of the Lord. A nature furnished richly to the very brim, a man of knowledge, of wit, of skill, of thought, with the very graces of the body perfect, and yet profane, impure, worldly, and scattering scepticism of all good and truth about him wherever he may go. His is no unlighted candle. He burns so bright and lurid that often the purer lights grow dim in the glare. But if it be possible for the human candle, when it is all made, when the subtle components of a human nature are all mingled most carefully, — if it be possible that then, instead of being lifted up to heaven and kindled at the pure being of Him who is eternally and absolutely good, it should be plunged down into hell and lighted at the yellow flames that burn out of the dreadful brimstone of the pit, then we can understand the sight of a man who is rich in every brilliant human quality, cursing the world with the continual exhibition of the devilish instead of

the godlike in his life. When the power of pure love
appears as a capacity of brutal lust; when the holy ingenuity with which man may search the character of a
fellow-man, that he may help him to be his best, is
turned into the unholy skill with which the bad man
studies his victim, that he may know how to make his
damnation most complete; when the almost divine
magnetism, which is given to a man in order that he
may instil his faith and hope into some soul that trusts
him, is used to breathe doubt and despair through all
the substance of a friend's reliant soul; when wit, which
ought to make truth beautiful, is deliberately prostituted
to the service of a lie; when earnestness is degraded to
be the slave of blasphemy, and the slave's reputation is
made the cloak for the master's shame, — in all these
cases, and how frequent they are no man among us fails
to know, you have simply the spirit of man kindled
from below, not from above, the candle of the Lord
burning with the fire of the devil. Still it will burn;
still the native inflammableness of humanity will show
itself. There will be light; there will be power; and
men who want nothing but light and power will come
to it. It is wonderful how mere power, or mere brightness, apart altogether from the work that the power is
doing and the story that the brightness has to tell, will
win the confidence and admiration of men from whom
we might have expected better things. A bright book
or a bright play will draw the crowd, although its
meaning be detestable. A clever man will make a
host of boys and men stand like charmed birds while he
draws their principles quietly out of them and leaves
them moral idiots. A whole great majority of a com-

munity will rush like foolish sheep to the polls and vote for a man who they know is false and brutal, because they have learned to say that he is strong. All this is true enough ; and yet while men do these wild and foolish things, they know the difference between the illumination of a human life that is kindled from above and that which is kindled from below. They know the pure flames of one and the lurid glare of the other ; and however they may praise and follow wit and power, as if to be witty or powerful were an end sufficient in itself, they will always keep their sacredest respect and confidence for that power or wit which is inspired by God, and works for righteousness.

There is still another way, more subtle and sometimes more dangerous than these, in which the spirit of man may fail of its completest function as the candle of the Lord. The lamp may be lighted, and the fire at which it is lighted may be indeed the fire of God, and yet it may not be God alone who shines forth upon the world. I can picture to myself a candle which should in some way mingle a peculiarity of its own substance with the light it shed, giving to that light a hue which did not belong essentially to the fire at which it was lighted. Men who saw it would see not only the brightness of the fire. They would see also the tone and color of the lamp. And so it is, I think, with the way in which some good men manifest God. They have really kindled their lives at Him. It is His fire that burns in them. They are obedient, and so He can make them His points of exhibition ; but they cannot get rid of themselves. They are mixed with the God they show. They show themselves as well as Him. It is as when a mirror mingles its own shape with the reflections of the things that are reflected from it, and gives them a curious convexity because it is itself convex. This is the secret of all pious bigotry, of all holy prejudice. It is the candle, putting its own color into the flame which it has borrowed from the fire of God. The violent man makes God seem violent. The feeble man makes God seem feeble. The speculative man makes God look like a beautiful dream. The legal man makes God look like a hard and steel-like law. Here is where all the harsh and narrow part of sectarianism comes from. The narrow Presbyterian or Methodist, or Episcopalian or Quaker, full of devoutness, really afire with God, — what is he but a candle which is always giving the flame its color, and which, by a disposition which many men have to value the little parts of their life more than the greater, makes less of the essential brightness of the flame than of the special color which it lends to it? It seems, perhaps, as if, in saying this, I threw some slight or doubt upon that individual and separate element in every man's religion, on which, upon the contrary, I place the very highest value. Every man who is a Christian must live a Christian life that is peculiarly his own. Every candle of the Lord must utter its peculiar light; only the true individuality of faith is marked by these characteristics which rescue it from bigotry: first, that it does not add something to the universal light, but only brings out most strongly some aspect of it which is specially its own; second, that it always cares more about the essential light than about the peculiar way in which it utters it; and third, that it easily blends with other special utterances of the universal light, in cordial sympathy and recognition of the value which it finds in them. Let these characteristics be in every man's religion, and then the individuality of faith is an inestimable gain. Then the different candles of the Lord burn in long rows down His great palace-halls of the world; and all together, each complementing all the rest, they light the whole vast space with Him.

I have tried to depict some of the difficulties which beset the full exhibition in the world of this great truth of Solomon, that "the spirit of man is the candle of the Lord." Man is selfish and disobedient, and will not let his life burn at all. Man is wilful and passionate, and kindles his life with ungodly fire. Man is narrow and bigoted, and makes the light of God shine with his own special color. But all these are accidents. All these are distortions of the true idea of man. How can we know that? Here is the perfect man, Christ Jesus! What a man He is! How nobly, beautifully, perfectly human! What hands, what feet, what an eye, what a heart! How genuinely, unmistakably a man! I bring the men of my experience or of my imagination into His presence, and behold, just when the worst or best of them falls short of Him, my human consciousness assures me that they fall short also of the best idea of what it is to be a man. Here is the spirit of man in its perfection. And what then? Is it not also the candle of the Lord? "I am come a light into the world," said Jesus. "He that hath seen Me hath seen the Father." "In Him was life and the life was the light of men." So wrote the man of all men who knew Him best. And in Him where are the difficulties that

we saw.? where for one moment is the dimness of selfishness ?   O, it seems to me a wonderful thing that the
supremely rich human nature of Jesus never for an instant turned with self-indulgence in on its own richness,
or was beguiled by that besetting danger of all opulent
souls, the wish, in the deepest sense, just to enjoy himself.   How fascinating that desire is.   How it keeps
many and many of the most abundant natures in the
world from usefulness.   Just to handle over and over
their hidden treasures, and with a spiritual miserliness
to think their thought for the pure joy of thinking,
and turn emotion into the soft atmosphere of a life of
gardened selfishness.   Not one instant of that in Jesus.
All the vast richness of His human nature only meant
for Him more power to utter God to man.

    And yet how pure His rich life was.   How it ab-
horred to burn with any fire that was not divine.   Such
abundant life, and yet such utter incapacity of any living
but the holiest ; such power of burning, and yet such
utter incapacity of being kindled by any torch but God's ;
such fulness with such purity was never seen besides
upon the earth ; and yet we know as we behold it that
it is no monster, but only the type of what all men must
be, although all men but Him as yet have failed to be it.

    And yet again there was intense personality in Him
without a moment's bigotry. A special life, a life that
stands distinct and self-defined among all the lives of
men, and yet a life making the universal God all the
more universally manifest by its distinctness, appealing
to all lives just in proportion to the intensity of the
individuality that filled His own.   O, I think I need
only bid you look at Him, and you must see what it is to

which our feeble lights are struggling. There is the true
spiritual man who is the candle of the Lord, the light
that lighteth every man.

It is distinctly a new idea of life, new to the standards
of all our ordinary living, which this truth reveals. All
our ordinary appeals to men to be up and doing,
and make themselves shining lights, fade away and
become insignificant before this higher message which
comes in the words of Solomon and in the life of Jesus.
What does the higher message say ? "You are a part
of God ! You have no place or meaning in this world
but in relationship to Him. The full relationship can
only be realized by obedience. Be obedient to Him,
and you shall shine by His light, not your own. Then
you cannot be dark, for He shall kindle you. Then you
shall be as incapable of burning with false passion as
you shall be quick to answer with the true. Then the
devil may hold his torch to you, as he held it to the
heart of Jesus in the desert, and your heart shall be as
uninflammable as His. But as soon as God touches
you, you shall burn with a light so truly your own that
you shall reverence your own mysterious life, and yet
so truly His that pride shall be impossible." What a
philosophy of human life is that. "O, to be nothing,
nothing !" cries the mystic singer in his revival hymn,
desiring to lose himself in God. "Nay not that; O to
be something, something," remonstrates the unmystical
man, longing for work, ardent for personal life and character. Where is the meeting of the two ? How shall
self-surrender meet that high self-value without which
no man can justify his living and honor himself in his
humanity ? Where can they meet but in this truth ?

2

Man must be something that he may be nothing. The
something which he must be must consist in simple fitness to utter the divine life which is the only original
power in the universe. And then man must be nothing
that he may be something. He must submit himself in
obedience to God, that so God may use him, in some
way in which his special nature only could be used, to
illuminate and help the world. Tell me, do not the two
cries meet in that one aspiration of the Christian man
to find his life by losing it in God, to be himself by
being not his own but Christ's ?

In certain lands, for certain holy ceremonies, they
prepare the candles with most anxious care. The very
bees which distil the wax are sacred. They range in
gardens planted with sweet flowers for their use alone.
The wax is gathered by consecrated hands ; and then the
shaping of the candles is a holy task, performed in holy
places, to the sound of hymns, and in the atmosphere of
prayers. All this is done because the candles are to
burn in the most lofty ceremonies on most sacred days.
With what care must the man be made whose spirit is
to be the candle of the Lord ! It is his spirit which
God is to kindle with Himself. Therefore the spirit
must be the precious part of him. The body must be
valued only for the protection and the education which
the soul may gain by it. And the power by which his
spirit shall become a candle is obedience. Therefore
obedience must be the struggle and desire of his life ;
obedience, not hard and forced, but ready, loving, and
spontaneous ; the obedience of the child to the father,
of the candle to the flame ; the doing of duty not
merely that the duty may be done, but that the soul in

doing it may become capable of receiving and uttering God; the bearing of pain not merely because the pain must be borne, but that the bearing of it may make the soul able to burn with the divine fire which found it in the furnace; the repentance of sin and acceptance of forgiveness, not merely that the soul may be saved from the fire of hell, but that it may be touched with the fire of heaven, and shine with the love of God, as the stars, forever.

Above all the pictures of life, — of what it means, of what may be made out of it, — there stands out this picture of a human spirit burning with the light of the God whom it obeys, and showing Him to other men. O, my young friends, the old men will tell you that the lower pictures of life and its purposes turn out to be cheats and mistakes. But this picture can never cheat the soul that tries to realize it. The man whose life is a struggle after such obedience, when at last his earthly task is over, may look forward from the borders of this life into the other, and humbly say, as his history of the life that is ended, and his prayer for the life that is to come, the words that Jesus said — "I have glorified Thee on the earth; now, O Father, glorify Me with Thyself forever."

[When this sermon was preached in Westminster Abbey, on the evening of Sunday, the Fourth of July, 1880, the following sentences were added : —]

MY FRIENDS,—May I ask you to linger while I say to you a few words more, which shall not be unsuited to what I have been saying, and which shall, for just a moment, recall to you the sacredness which this day — the Fourth of July, the anniversary of American Independence — has in the hearts of us Americans. If I dare — generously permitted as I am to stand this evening in the venerable Abbey, so full of our history as well as yours — to claim that our festival shall have some sacredness for you as well as us, my claim rests on the simple truth that to all true men the birthday of a nation must always be a sacred thing. For in our modern thought the nation is the making-place of men. Not by the traditions of its history, nor by the splendor of its corporate achievements, nor by the abstract excellencies of its constitution, but by its fitness to make men, to beget and educate human character, to contribute to the complete humanity, the "perfect man" that is to be, — by this alone each nation must be judged to-day. The nations are the golden candlesticks which hold aloft the candles of the Lord. No candlestick can be so rich or venerable that men shall honor it if it holds no candle. "Show us your man," land cries to land.

In such days any nation, out of the midst of which God has led another nation as He led ours out of the midst of yours, must surely watch with anxiety and prayer the peculiar development of our common humanity of which that new nation is made the home, the special burning of the human candle in that new candlestick; and if she sees a hope and promise that God means to build in that new land some strong and free and characteristic manhood which shall help the world to its completeness, the mother-land will surely lose the thought and memory of whatever anguish accompanied the birth, for gratitude over the gain which humanity has made, "for joy that a man is born into the world."

It is not for me to glorify to-night the country which I love with all my heart and soul. I may not ask your praise for anything admirable which the United States has been or done. But on my country's birthday I may do something far more solemn and more worthy of the hour. I may ask you for your prayer in her behalf. That on the manifold and wondrous chance which God is giving her,—on her freedom (for she is free, since the old stain of slavery was washed out in blood); on her unconstrained religious life; on her passion for education, and her eager search for truth; on her jealous care for the poor man's rights and opportunities; on her countless quiet homes where the future generations of her men are growing; on her manufactures and her commerce; on her wide gates open to the east and to the west; on her strange meetings of the races out of which a new race is slowly being born; on her vast enterprise and her illimitable hopefulness,—on all these materials and machineries of manhood, on all that the life of my country must mean for humanity, I may ask you to pray that the blessing of God the Father of man, and Christ the Son of man, may rest forever.

Because you are Englishmen and I am an American; also because here, under this high and hospitable roof of God, we are all more than Englishmen and more than Americans; because we are all men, children of God, waiting for the full coming of our Father's kingdom, I ask you for that prayer.

II.

THE JOY OF SELF-SACRIFICE.

"And when the burnt offering began, the song of the Lord began also with the trumpets."—2 CHRON. xxix. 27.

IT had been a day of joy and triumph in Jerusalem. Hezekiah, the king, reviving the faith and worship of Jehovah, from which his fathers had departed, had opened the doors of the temple and cleared out all the rubbish of the long neglect, and gathered the priests and lighted the lamps and summoned the people, and to-day there had been a vast sacrifice to the Lord, in which the people had once more declared themselves His servants, and given up again their personal and national life to Him. The burnt offering declared their penitence and consecration. It was the nation's solemn sacrifice of itself to God. The verse which I have quoted tells us one thing about this sacrifice. It records the joy with which it was made — "When the burnt offering began, the song of the Lord began with the trumpets." Not in a gloomy silence, as if the people were doing a hard duty which they would not do if they could help it, did the smoke of their offering ascend to God; but with a burst of jubilant music and with a song of triumphant joy which rang down through the crowded courts, the host of the Jews claimed for themselves anew their place in the obedience of God. The act of sacrifice was done amid a chorus of delight.

The old sacrifices are past and done forever. There are no more smoking altars or bleeding beasts; but that which they represented still remains, and will remain so long as man and God are child and Father to each other. The giving up of the life of man away from himself to serve his true and rightful Master, the surrender of his life to another, self-sacrifice, which is what these burnt offerings picturesquely represented, is universally and perpetually necessary. As we study the old ceremony, that which it represented stands before us; and one question which comes up, the question which I want to make the subject of my sermon for this morning, is that which is suggested by the verse in the old book of Chronicles, in which the rejoicing of the people over their burnt offering is written. It is not beasts, but lives that we offer. Can the life, too, be offered now as the beast was offered of old, with song and trumpet? Can self-sacrifice be a thing of triumph and exhilaration? Can it be the conscious glorification of a life to give that life away in self-denial? The joy and glory of self-sacrifice shall be our subject.

You know how strangely such a subject must sound even to many very good and conscientious people. Multitudes of people there are all about us, who thoroughly accept it as the great law and necessity of human life that there must be self-sacrifice. It is not only that they have been taught it from their earliest youth; not merely that they find it written in what are recognized as the highest codes of human living; but their own experience and their own hearts have taught it to them.   They see that the world would be a dreadful· and intolerable place if every creature in it lived only for his own mere immediate indulgence.   They own that the higher nature and the higher purpose everywhere have a right to the submission of the lower, and they freely accept the conviction that the lower must submit.   The different forms of self-sacrifice stand around them with their demands.   There is the need that a man should sacrifice himself to himself, his lower self to his higher self, his passions to his principles. There is the need of sacrificing one's self for fellow-men. There is the highest need of all, the need of giving up our will to God's.   All of these needs a man will own and honor.   He will try to meet them all his life.   But when you come to talk of joy in meeting them, that is another matter.   Self-sacrifice seems to him something apart from the whole notion of enjoyment.   It is a disagreeable necessity of life.   It seems to be tied on to life by some strange fate, as if it were the result of some terrible mistake.   Perhaps the man is able to recognize that the necessity is made use of for some purposes of education, and so is not wholly unthankful that the necessity exists ; but to rejoice over it, to give up our own will, to sacrifice our pleasure and take up our task with a song, — that is something which most men, even those who work on most scrupulously at their duty cannot comprehend.   " I know it is my duty because I hate it so," somebody said to me once about some task. That is the look of duty to multitudes of men.   The highest dream of the poet is of a state of things in which we shall know that something is our duty because we love it so ; the condition in which "love is an unerring light and joy its own security." That condition, in whatever region of the universe the soul attained to it, would be heaven ; and yet it would be only the realization and completion of that which was set forth in the old ceremony of the book of Chronicles, in which the sacrifice was greeted with the blast of the trumpets and the songs of the people.

Heaven seems impossible, and yet there are promises and prophecies of heaven on every side of us. There are always glimpses of man's highest life which show us, like the first streaks of light before the dawn, what it would be if all the sky were filled with glory ; and so there are always exalted lives, and exalted moments in the lives, I hope, of all of us, in which we do catch sight of the joy and glory of self-sacrifice. Not many years ago, when the young men went to the war, was it not true that the fact of sacrifice intensified the joy ? It was a joy to save their country, to feel sure, as it is not often given to men vividly to feel, that they were doing a real and valuable part of her salvation. But tell me, what made the difference between their going and the patient plodding of the clerk up to the State House, or the quiet journey of the congressman to Washington to-day ? They too, if they are honest and faithful, are saving the country just as truly as the soldiers were. Why does the one trudge the streets unnoticed, while before the others trumpets blew, and around them the crowd shouted, and in their bosoms their hearts leaped for joy ? It is easy to say that it was the poetry, the romance, the enthusiasm. Those are mere words. The essence of it was that in their going the self-sacrifice was vivid and distinct. They were leaving home and friends and safety and comfort. Ah, you are very young, too young to remember the spirit of those days, if you do not know that that self-sacrifice was not a drawback on the joy of the truest men's enlistment; it was a part and parcel of that joy. No safe and easy task could ever have filled the heart with such a sober and deep delight.

Or think about a man who does something which you choose to call a piece of superfluous mercantile honesty, but something which, under the higher compulsions that press upon his loftier nature, he thinks that it is absolutely necessary for him to do. He has failed in business and he has settled with his creditors; and they are satisfied with what they have got from him, and give him a full discharge from all his obligations; and by and by the man succeeds again and then, as he begins to grow rich once more, he takes upon himself the payment, principal and interest, of his old debts. He lives like a poor man still. He will not let his life grow sumptuous till first it has grown honest. Do you say, "What a slavery! What a tyrant his conscience is to him!" But to him it is the most enthusiastic freedom. He goes his way with his heart making music to him all the day long, and following his conscience as no most devoted soldier ever followed his half-worshipped captain. Every time that another comfort is laid upon the altar of his honesty, the song of the Lord begins with the trumpets. There may be in it some mixture of unworthy pride; but, if there is, it is an alloy and not a refinement, a decrease and not an increase of the joy. It makes it nervous, restless, and impatient. But leave that out. Let the man simply want to be honest, and then the self-sacrifice, by which alone his honesty can be done, is a true element in his delight. He is happier in his slow payment of his self-recognized debt, in which each dollar that he pays means some distinct piece of self-sacrifice, than he could be if boundless wealth had suddenly tumbled upon him from the skies, of which he, without an effort, had easily handed over a little fragment to his creditors.

The words of our text then, however strangely they sound at first, are literally true as the history of many a man's life. Many and many a man has gone on year after year, with little or no zest in his existence, perfectly self-indulgent, seeing no need, hearing no call to be anything else than self-indulgent, until at last there came some change which seemed at first to be a terrible misfortune, something which threw the whole heavy weight of other people's lives upon the shoulders of this one life, so that it had to forget itself and live completely for these others. And then how can you tell the story of the difference which came into that burdened life ? What words can tell it more perfectly than these, "When the burnt offering began, the song of the Lord began also with the trumpets" ? From the moment that it began to live for other people, this nature, which had had no song in it before, became jubilant with music. The young self-indulgent man becomes the head of a family that taxes his thought by day and night. The merely selfish thinker, who has worked out his thoughts for the mere luxury of thinking, suddenly finds the world calling for him to plunge into the detail of some work of charity or education. Anything comes which makes a man take up his life as it were in his two hands and give it away to be thenceforth lived not for himself but for others, who, he has to acknowledge, have a better right to it, the right of an imperious need. At first there is reluctance, hesitation. The teeth are set. The hands are clenched. The eyes look back as if they were leaving all the happiness of life behind them. But ask the man a few years later; nay, look at him after he has thoroughly lost himself in his new work, and when you see what life has come to be to him, what spring there is in every movement, what sparkle in every thought, what eagerness, what interest, what hope; is it not clear that just that which has come to him, just the abandonment of selfishness and some strong impulsive giving of himself away to other people, was what was needed to fill all the accumulations of his life with joy, and to clothe all the qualities of his character with glory?

As one looks round upon the community to-day, how clear the problem of hundreds of unhappy lives appears. Do we not all know men for whom it is just as clear as daylight that that is what they need, the sacrifice of themselves for other people? Rich men who with all their wealth are weary and wretched; learned men whose learning only makes them querulous and jealous; believing men whose faith is always souring into bigotry and envy, — every man knows what these men need; just something which shall make them let themselves go out into the open ocean of a complete self-sacrifice. They are rubbing and fretting and chafing themselves against the wooden wharves of their own interests to which they are tied. Sometime or other a great, slow, quiet tide, or a great, strong, furious storm, must come and break every rope that binds them, and carry them clear out to sea; and then they will for the first time know the true, manly joy for which a man was made, as a ship for the first time knows the full joy for which a ship was made, when she trusts herself to the open sea and, with the wharf left far behind, feels the winds over her and the waters under her, and recognizes her true life. Only, the trust to the great ocean must be complete. No trial trip will do. No ship can tempt the sea and learn its glory, so long as she goes moored by any rope, however long, by which she means to be drawn back again if the sea grows too rough. The soul that trifles and toys with self-sacrifice never can get its true joy and power. Only the soul that with an overwhelming impulse and a perfect trust gives itself up forever to the life of other men, finds the delight and peace which such complete self-surrender has to give.

One would not seem to be so foolish as to say that self-sacrifice does not bring pain. Indeed it does. The life of Christ must be our teacher there. He carried the song and the trumpet always in his heart. That life, marking its way with drops of blood, on which the pity of the world has dwelt more tenderly than over any other life it knows, has yet always seemed to the world's best standards to be a true triumphal march, radiant with splendor all along the way, and closing in a true victory at last. Indeed I think that one of the brightest insights which we ever get into the human heart and its essential breadth and justice, and its power, when it is working at its best, to hold what seem contradictory ideas in their true spiritual harmony, is given to us when we see how men have been able to see together both sides of the life of Jesus, to pity His sorrow and to glory in His happiness, and yet to blend both of these two thoughts of Him into one single idea of one single self-consistent Christ. It is a sort of witness of how truly men, in that highest mood into which they are drawn when they try to study Christ, easily see the real truth with regard to human life, which is that in it joy and pain, so far from being inconsistent with and contradictory to one another, are, in some true sense, each others' complements, and neither alone, but both together, make the true sum of human life. There is a conceivable world where pure, unclouded joy can come, just as there are countries where the mountains are very lofty and all nature is on so grand a scale that it can bear a pure, unclouded sky, and in its unveiled splendor perfectly satisfy the eye. But there are other lands whose inferior grandeur needs for its perfect beauty the effects of mist and cloud that give its lower mountains the mystery and poetry which they could not have in themselves. So one may compare the Swiss and the Scotch landscapes. And something of the same sort is true about this world and marks its inferiority, proves that it is not yet the perfect state of being. It needs the pain of life to emphasize its joy. Its joy is not high or perfect enough to do without the emphasis of pain. And so, to come back to the point whence we digressed, it is not strange that that which is the necessary condition of joy in this human life — namely, self-sacrifice — should be also inevitably associated with suffering and pain.

There is another reason why it would seem to be absolutely necessary that man should have the power of
finding pleasure in his self-sacrifices, in the actual fulfilment of his compelled tasks, the actual doing of the
necessary duties of his life, and that is found in the
fact that joy or delight in what we are doing is not a
mere luxury; it is a means, a help for the more perfect
doing of our work. Indeed it may be truly said that
no man does any work perfectly who does not enjoy his
work. Joy in one's work is the consummate tool without which the work may be done indeed, but without
which the work will always be done slowly, clumsily,
and without its finest perfectness. Men who do their
work without enjoying it are like men carving statues
with hatchets. The statue gets carved perhaps, and is
a monument forever of the dogged perseverance of the
artist; but there is a perpetual waste of toil, and there
is no fine result in the end. A man who does his work
with thorough enjoyment of it is like an artist who
holds an exquisite tool which is almost as obedient to
him as his own hand, and seems to understand what he
is doing, and almost works intelligently with him. If
the only loss of a man who hates his work were the
mere loss of the luxury of enjoying it, that would be
bad; but if, in the loss of the enjoyment of his work,
he loses a large part of the power for the most effective
doing of his work, then it is a matter far more serious.
I passed, the other day, a pawn-broker's shop in an obscure street here in our city. Its windows showed the
usual shabby and wretched refuse which belongs to
such places, that sort of battered and broken driftwood
which the tide of human energy and hope and success

has left stranded on the beach when it has ebbed out to sea. But one window was a great deal sadder than the other. In the first window there were tawdry and faded trinkets, old jewelry and bits of cheap personal finery, which poverty had confiscated from their desperate or careless owners; but in the other window there were piles of workmen's tools — hammers and saws and planes and files and axes — the things with which men do their work and earn their living. That was the sadder window of the two. To lose a trinket is mortification and disappointment, but to lose a tool may be ruin. And so if joy in work were a mere polish and decoration of life, it would be sad that man should not have it; but if it is the means by which alone the work of life may be effectively and nobly done, then its loss may be the very loss of life itself.

I think we want to urge most strenuously upon young men the need, the absolute necessity, that in the appointed and demanded work of their life they should look for and should find the joy of their life. To do your work because you must; to do your work as a slavery; and then, having got it done as speedily and easily as possible, to look somewhere else for enjoyment, — that makes a very dreary life. No man who works so does the best work. No man who works so lingers lovingly over his work and asks himself if there is not something he can do to make it more perfect. "My meat is to do the will of Him that sent me, and to finish His work," said Jesus. No doubt it was the intrinsic nobleness of His special work that made it peculiarly abundant in the enjoyment which it furnished Him; and no doubt any young man who has the

choice of several occupations ought to choose that
which is intrinsically highest, that which is occupied
with the noblest things. This indeed is what makes
some professions more liberal than others, — the greater
power which they have to satisfy and cultivate the nature of the men who live in them; but our counsel
must not be confined to them. To any man engaged in
any honest, useful work, we want to say: Try just as
far as possible to find the pleasure of your life in the
work to which it has been settled that your life must
be given. Study its principles. Let your interest
dwell on its details. Make it delightful by the affections which cluster round it, by the help which you
are able through it to give to other people, by the education which your own faculties are getting out of it.
In all these ways make your business the centre and
fountain of your joy, and then life will be healthy and
strong. Then you will not be running everywhere to
find some outside pleasure which shall make up to you
for your self-sacrificing toil; but the scenes of your self-
sacrificing toil itself, your store or your office or your
work-bench, shall be bright with associations of delight,
and vocal with your thankfulness to the God who has
given you, in them, the most radiant revelations of
Himself. This is the only true transfiguration and success of labor and of life.

And now, what is to be done about all this? Men
say, "O, yes, it is easy to talk about finding your joy in
your self-sacrifice and work; but I have tried it, and
it cannot be done. Self-sacrifice is dreadful and unnatural. We know that we cannot escape it; but there is
no joy in it. The only thing to do is to get through

8

with it as doggedly and speedily as possible, and then
go off and in some self-indulgence find the real pleasure
of your life." But surely that is shallow, superficial
talk. To talk so is to take for granted that self-sacrifice
is one invariable thing, and not to see that it is infinitely
various according to the difference of the men who make
the sacrifice, and the difference of their relations to the
thing for which the sacrifice is made. Understand this
and then the difficulty disappears. Is the sacrifice
which the most scrupulous and faithful servant makes
for a child the same thing as the sacrifice which the
loving mother makes for him? Is the self-sacrifice of
the hired mercenary the same thing as the sacrifice of
the enthusiastic patriot? There is the key to the whole
truth. If you can change a man's relation to the thing
or the person for whom he makes his sacrifice, you may
change the whole character of the sacrifice itself; and
you may open in it fountains of delight which would
have seemed before to be impossible. Nothing less
deep than that will answer. You cannot go to men to
whom self-sacrifice is misery or drudgery, and exhort
them to be happy, and tell them and bid them believe
that self-sacrifice is joy. That is treating them like
children. That is merely beating a drum before them
at their work, and asking them to make believe that
work is play. Nor can you trust to mere animal spirits,
and that happy temperament which will let some people
find joy in life in spite of any sacrifices that they are
called to make. You must have something a great deal
realler, deeper, and more universal than either of these;
and that can be nothing short of such a relation of a
man to the object of his sacrifice, such an honor for it,

such a sense of its dignity, such a sight of its possibilities, as will make it a delight to give one's self up to
it, and will make every pain that is involved in such
surrender a welcome emphasis upon his value and
honor for it, and so an increase of his joy. Earlier in
this sermon I spoke of the three great classes into which
all the sacrifices which men are called upon to make
may really be divided. There are the sacrifices which
a man makes of himself to himself, of his lower nature
and needs to his higher nature and needs; there are the
sacrifices which he makes for his fellow-men; and there
are the sacrifices which he makes for God. In these
three services the world of conscientious men lives and
works. And very often these services are bondages.
Very often the world groans bitterly under these burdens which it will not cast away, and yet which press
very heavily upon its shoulders. Can anything relieve
all that? Suppose that some new power, some new
revelation or new fact, should come into the world, which
should change a man's relation to his own self, and to
his fellow-men, and to God. Then everything would
certainly be altered. Let some new light shine forth,
within whose radiance man should see his own spiritual
self in all its possibilities; and see his brethren with
their souls, and all that their souls might become, burning and glowing through their coarse, dull bodies; and
see God as the dear Father and glorious centre of the
world;—let all this come, and then the impossible may
surely become possible, and the self-sacrifice for things
so glorious, while it does not lose its pain, may find
within its pain a joy of which its pain shall be mysteriously a part. And, O my friends, the truth of these

days, the truth of this week, is that such a light has shone and is forever shining on the earth. "The time draws near the birth of Christ." This coming week is rich with Christmas glory. The thing that makes it glorious, the only thing that can give dignity to all this annual outbreak of thankfulness and joy, is that the Christmas days are full of the truth of Christ's redemption of the world. Christ's redemption of the world means, for each man who truly believes in it, just these three things: the revelation to the man of his own value, and of the value of his fellow-man, and of the dearness and greatness of God. The man who has despised himself and thought his life not worth the living, learns that this human nature of his is capable of being inhabited by divinity, and sees in the cross of the Son of God what God thinks is the preciousness of his human soul. Must not that man then stand in awe before himself, and rejoice if, by the sacrifice of his appetites, he can help this regal soul to its completeness? The man who has despised his fellow-men and asked himself, "Why should I give up my pleasure for their pleasure, or even for their good?" sees in the redemption how Christ values these lives, and is not so much shamed out of his contempt for them as drawn freely forward into the precious privilege of honoring them and working for them. The man whose God has been far off and cold sees God in Christ, and loves Him with a love which makes life seem worth the living, simply that it may be devoted to work for Him. This is the power of Christ's redemption. It transfigures to a man his own soul and his brethren and God; and, seeing them in the new light of Christ, the man lifts up his head, and his old tasks are altered. To work for such masters becomes the glory of his life. Not how he may do as little work as possible, and then escape to find his pleasure in some region of self-indulgence; but how he may do as much work as possible, because in work for such masters is the seat and fountain of his joy, becomes the problem of his life. To be shut out from any chance of signifying by self-sacrifice in their behalf his value and honor for these masters, would make his life seem very worthless. When a new chance to put his passions down that he may win character, or to give up some pleasure of his own out of the wish to honor his brother man and help him, or to sacrifice his own will to the will of God, — when such a chance is seen coming towards him in the distance, it is not, as it used to be, as if the culprit saw the executioner approaching him with the sword all drawn to take his life. Rather it is 'as if the born king, who had just discovered his royal lineage, saw the priest coming towards him with the crown which was to be put upon his head and make him thoroughly and manifestly king. He claims his self-sacrifice. It is the badge and means of his enthronement. And when he takes it; when he enters, for his own soul's good, or for the help of his fellow-men, or for the glory of his God, upon some path which men call very dark, or some work which men call very hard; it is with a leap of heart as if now at last the king had found his own. When his burnt offering begins, his song of the Lord begins also with the trumpets.

It is a wondrous change. The man who really lives in the world of Christ's redemption, claims his self-sacrifices. He goes up to his martyrdom with a song.

To live in this world, and do nothing for one's own spiritual self or for fellow-man or for God, is a terrible thing. I have a right to give the less as a burnt offering to the greater. There is no happy life except in such consecration. No one shall shut me out of that privilege of my redeemed humanity.

I wish that I could speak to the spirit of the most selfish creature here to-day. I wish I could show him what a vast region of pleasure and delight lies close at his side, on which he has never entered, of which he has never dreamed. The door that shuts him out of that great region of joy is his own contempt. If he will let Christ fill the world for him with the light of His redemption, contempt must fall to the ground, and the closed door must fly open, and then, " with the song of the Lord and with the trumpets," the selfish man must go out from his selfishness into the untasted and unguessed joy of self-sacrifice. He must " enter into the joy of his Lord," the joy of that Christ whose meat was to do His Father's will, who gave His life for His brethren, and whose throne was a cross.

III.

THE YOUNG AND OLD CHRISTIAN.

"The good will of Him that dwelt in the bush."—DEUT. XXXIII. 16.

MOSES had been young and now was old. These words are taken from his benediction, which he pronounced upon the children of Israel as he stood with them on the borders of the promised land. There is something very touching in the reminiscence. The long journey through the desert is over. He has done God's work nobly and successfully. Well may he be proud of this people that he has led up to the threshold of their inheritance. But now his mind is running backward. This crowning of his mission with clear success reminds him of the time when his mission started out in mystery and weakness. He sees again a bush which he once saw by a wayside. He is a young man again, a shepherd keeping his father-in-law's flock on the back side of the desert, by Mount Horeb. He sees once more the bush on fire. He draws near again with unshod feet, and once more in his aged ears he hears the voice out of the bush commissioning him for the great work of his life. With that impulse which I suppose we all have felt, that brings up at the close of any work the freshened memory of its beginning, this old man sees the burning bush again as he saw it years before, only with deeper understanding of its meaning,

and a completer sense of the love of God which it involved. He looks into the past, and all the mercy that
had come in between, — all the miraculous food, and
the wonderful victories, and the parted waters, and the
constant guidance, — he sees now were all certainly
involved in that first summons of God which he had
once obeyed so blindly ; and when he wants to give his
people the benediction that represents to him the most
complete and comprehensive love, it is touching to hear
the old man go back and invoke " The good will of Him
that dwelt in the bush."

Religion delights both in reminiscence and in anticipation. Being full of the sense of God, it finds
a unity in life which no atheistic thought can discover. The identity of God's eternal being stretches
under, and gives consistence to, our fragmentary lives.
God's eternity makes our time coherent. And so it
was God in the old bush that made it still visible
to Moses across the eventful interval. (He saw that
bush when all the other bushes of Egypt had faded
out of sight, because that bush was on fire with God.
And as Christianity is the most vivid of all religions,
with its personally manifested God, there is a more perfect unity in a Christian life than in any other. It
keeps all its parts, and from its consummations looks
back with gratitude and love to its beginnings. The
crown that it casts before the throne at last is the same
that it felt trembling on its brow in the first ecstatic
sense of Christ's forgiveness, and that has been steadily
glowing into greater clearness as perfecting love has
more and more completely cast out fear. The feet that
go up to God into the mountain, at the end, are the

same that first put off their shoes beside the burning
bush. This is why the Christian, more than other
men, not merely dares but loves to look back and remember.

But I wish to-day to call up this picture of Moses only
in order to suggest a certain topic. We have the beginning and the ripening of an experience brought close
together. Let us think of the young Christian and the
old Christian : the same man in his first apprehension,
and in his ripened knowledge, of Christ. | What is the
difference between the two ? What is the growth
which brings one into the other ? Everybody claims
that the Christian experience ripens and deepens.
What is there riper and deeper in the full existence
that there was not in the incipient life ? This is the
question which I want to study ; or, in other words, we
may call our subject, — The nature and method of the
growth of Christian · character. I know that every
Christian, old or young, will welcome such a study if
it can unfold to us any of the rich and mysterious laws
of the spiritual life.

·One general and obvious law of all true growth suggests itself at once, which we will just point out before
we go on to particulars. It is that every healthy
growth creates the conditions of new growth, makes
new growth possible. The illustrations are numberless
everywhere. Every ray of sunlight that gives some
ripeness to an apple makes the apple opener to more
sunlight, which shall ripen it still more. Or, think of a
nation ; every advance in liberty makes new advances
not merely possible but necessary. Or, think of man ;
the powers which develop either the physical or the men-

tal nature from fifteen years old to twenty open the
mind and body to new influences which are to feed it
from twenty to twenty-five. Every summer is also a
spring-time. Indeed we may make this a test of
growth. Every ray of sun which does not open the
ground to new sunlight, is not feeding it but baking it.
This is the true test of growing force. It opens the
beautiful reactions between itself and the growing thing,
and creates an openness for yet more of itself.

Now see how this is the method of all Christian
growth. A child becomes a Christian. He learns, that
is, to understand and claim the love of Christ. " I
know that Christ loves me, and wants to train me," the
glad young heart says. That consciousness makes the
child's soul purer and more Christlike. Into that soul,
become more Christly, a yet deeper sense of the love of
Christ can enter to work a yet greater change. Then,
to this still renewed soul, opens •some newer vision of
what Christ can do. This new work done unfolds
some new capacity of loving and receiving love. And
so, in this continual reaction between Christ and the
soul, — every new openness fed with a new love that
opens it still more, — the life-long, the eternal work
goes on. Heaven will be only the fuller, prompter,
more unhindered pulsing back and forth, between Christ
and the soul, of this sublime and sweet reaction. This
was the foundation of the certainty which Paul does for
his Philippians when he told them that he was " confident of this very thing, that He who had begun a
good work in them would perform it unto the day of
Jesus Christ." He foresaw for them what he had felt in
himself, — that love would mean receptivity, that every

new love would bring a fuller knowledge, and every knowledge lay the soul open to a completer love.

But, just suggesting this, let us go on and try to particularize some of the sorts of difference between the young and the maturer Christian, and so see what sorts of growth this law of growth, which we have pointed out, will produce.

And, for one thing, I should say that as every Christian becomes more and more a Christian, there must be a larger and larger absorption of truth or doctrine into life. We hear all around us now-a-days a great impatience with the prominence of dogma — that is, of truth abstractly and definitely stated — in Christianity. And most of those who are thus impatient really mean well. They feel that Christianity, being a thing of personal salvation, ought to show itself in characters and lives. There they are right. But to decry dogma in the interest of character, is like despising food as if it interfered with health. Food is not health. The human body is built just so as to turn food into health and strength. And truth is not holiness. The human soul is made to turn, by the subtle chemistry of its digestive experience, truth into goodness. And this, I think, is just what the Christian, as he goes on, finds himself doing under God's grace. Before the young Christian lie the doctrines of his faith, — God's being, God's care, Christ's incarnation, Christ's atonement, immortality. What has the old Christian, with his long experience, done with them? He holds them no longer crudely, as things to be believed merely. He has taken them home into his nature. He has transmuted them into forms of life. God's being appears now filling his life with reverence. God's care clothes every act and thought of his with gratitude. Christ's incarnation is the inspiration of his new, dear love of all humanity. The atonement is the power of his all pervading and deep-rooted faith. And immortality! He no longer thinks of that as a doctrine, which has become a great, constant flood of life, ever resting over and illuminating the far-off hill-tops — now grown so near, so real — of the eternal life. The young dogmatist boasts of his dogmas. The old saint lives his life. Both are natural in their places and times, as are the unripe and the ripened fruit. How soon you can tell the men whose soils have tugged at the roots of their doctrines and taken them in, and left them no longer lying on the surface, but made them germinate into life.

And in the second place, as a consequence of this feature of growth, there will come a growing variety in Christian character as Christians grow older. I think we should expect a uniformity and resemblance in younger Christians, and a diversity in older ones, because life is more various than doctrine. Each young Christian has his doctrine, crude and dogmatic still. The maturer Christians have not merely worked those doctrines into life, but each has worked them into his own sort of life. The truth is the same for all; the life it makes is infinite. The more deeply it has been digested, the more strongly the individuality comes out. The truth which God gives us is like the wheat that a bounteous country sends into the city. It is all the same wheat; but men go and buy it and eat it, and this same identical wheat is turned into different sorts of force in different men. It is turned into bartering force in one, and thinking force in another, and singing force in another, and governing force in another. It is made manifold as soon as it passes into men. So I think every minister finds that, as his disciples grow older, if he has really succeeded in getting the truth to be their truth, they grow into more various forms of Christian charity and usefulness. Each grows more evidently to be not merely a Christian, but the Christian that God intended him to be. They think more. They think differently. The pure white light breaks itself to each in different colors. Often the minister is alarmed. His confirmation classes, which took the truths he taught them out of the Bible all alike, and went out all to the same work, — see how they have scattered; see how different they are! What does it mean? Merely this: it is doctrine passing, growing, into life. Those twelve disciples must have seemed very much like one another, as they all followed Jesus on the road, or sat around Him in the temple, drinking in His words. But see, after His words had become their life, how clear, distinct, and individual they are — John, Peter, James, Matthew. The seed looks the same; the flowers are so different. Let us rejoice in the clear individuality of maturing Christian life. Its one principle is still identical; and so it already prophesies heaven, where we are sure we shall be all different illustrations of the one same grace, showing different characters, set to different works but all moved by one spirit, all illustrations of the one same grace still.

And as individuality is developed with the deepening spiritual life, so I am sure that the willingness to recognize and welcome individual differences of thought and feeling and action increases, too, as Christians grow riper. Seeing ourselves made more ourselves as our faith grows richer, we are glad to see other men made more themselves too. This is true charity. It is your undeveloped, crude, commonplace Christian who is uncharitable. He expects other Christians to be like himself. He has never felt that divine, deep movement of Christ in his own soul, telling him that from all eternity there has been one certain place for him to fill, one certain thing for him to be, and summoning him to come and fill his place and be himself; and so when some brother rises out of the crowd of undistinguishable believers, and goes out to stand upon his outpost, this other soul rebukes him, calls him arrogant, radical, wise beyond what is written, and foolish names like those. I can well understand that the seeds in a sower's basket might be very uncharitable to one brother-seed that had dropped out of the basket and taken root and grown to be a stalk of corn. It is too unlike them. It is too original and singular. But let them all fall together and take root, and then, with life in all of them, they will not compare their ears and tassels, each being so busy in growing to the best that its separate bit of earth can bring it to. (The true Christian charity is that which life teaches. It is the tried and cultured souls that understand each other's trials and cultures, though they be wholly different from their own. And no sight is more beautiful than to see this grace growing in a body of believers.

It helps us much, I think, if we can recognize the fitness of this progress. Narrowness of view and sympathy

is not unnatural in a new believer. It is very unnatural
in the maturer Christian life. In the one it is the
sourness of unripe fruit, showing only unripeness; in
the other it is the sourness of a ripe apple or of an apple
that ought to be ripe, and proves cramped and stunted
life. The figures which most naturally suggest themselves are these of vegetable life, when we are talking
of growth of any sort. I do not say that it is best for
the young Christian to be illiberal. Far better certainly
if he could leap at once to the full comprehension and
the wide charity which the older Christian gathers out
of the experience of life. But, as a fact, it is too apt to
be the case that only by experience does the Christian
reach this breadth of sympathy, which comes not from
indifference, but from the profoundest personal earnestness. It is something wholly different from the loose
toleration which some men praise, which is negative,
which cares nothing about what is absolutely true or
false. This is positive. It holds fast to its certain
truths, well proved, long tried. Just because those
truths have laid intense hold upon its deepest soul, and
become its truths in its own shapes, it expects and rejoices to see them, the same truths still, becoming other
men's in their own shapes. This is the only true Christian charity, the only charity that rejoiceth in the
truth.

And here comes in another noble characteristic of the
growing spiritual experience, its ever-increasing independence. This is the best personal result of charity.
There is an independence which is arrogant and defiant,
and there is a dependence that is weak and fawning.
Both come of narrowness. Both are the signs of imma-

ture and meagre life.   One man arms himself against his brethren because he holds them to be wholly wrong and himself wholly right.   Another man yields to his brethren because he fears that he is wrong and they are right.   There is a man of mellow strength who, deeply conscious of the work the Lord has done in him, made sure of it by long feeling the very pressures of God's hand kneading the truth into his nature, stands by that work; will let no man cavil it away from his tenacious consciousness; is so perfectly dependent upon Christ that he can hang upon no fellow-man ; respects himself by the same reverence for the individuality of the divine life that makes him also respect his brethren.

The analogies between a man's life and the world's life are so continually suggested that one often wonders whether there be not some analogy here; whether some such progress into charity by the very positiveness of faith, may not be possible, may not be coming as the final solution of all these problems which keep the world so full of jealousy and strife.   At present it seems to be assumed that narrowness is essential to positive belief, and that toleration can be reached only by general indifference.   Not long ago I read this sentence in what many hold to be our ablest and most thoughtful journal: "It is a law, which in the present condition of human nature holds good, that strength of conviction is always in the inverse ratio of the tolerant spirit."   If that is so, then the present condition of human nature is certainly very much depraved.   But if human nature ever can be rescued by a personal salvation, if mankind can ever become possessed by the Spirit of God, lifting the mass by filling the individuals

each with his own strong manifestation of its power,
then the world may still see some maturer type of
Christianity, in which new ages of positive faith may
still be filled with the broadest sympathy, and men
tolerate their brethren without enfeebling themselves.
Such ages may God hasten.

Let us pass on. I think another sign of the growth
of Christian character is to be found in what we may
call the growing transfiguration of duty. See what I
mean. To every young Christian the new service of
Christ comes largely with the look of a multitude of
commandments. They throng around his life, each one
demanding to be obeyed. He welcomes them joyously.
He takes up his tasks with glad hands still, because
they are his Master's tasks. But as he grows older in
grace, is there no difference? Tell me, you who have
long been the servants of our dear and gracious Lord, has
there come in your long Christian life no change in the
whole aspect of your service? Has not your more and
more intimate sympathy with Him let you in behind
many and many a duty which once seemed dark and
hard, and allowed you to see the light of His loving
intention burning there? Have you not grown into a
clearer and deeper understanding of what Jesus meant
by those sweet and wonderful words, "Henceforth I
call you not servants, for the servant knoweth not what
his Lord doeth; but I have called you friends, for all
things that I have heard of my Father I have made
known unto you"? In every opening Christian life
there is something Mosaic, something Hebrew. The
order of the Testaments is somewhat repeated in the
experience of every believer. At last, in the fulness of

4

time, the New Testament has perfectly come. The law
is given first, and then grace and truth come by Jesus
Christ. It is no sudden transformation. It cannot be,
because it cannot come otherwise than by the gradual
teaching of life. But when it has wholly come, then,
full of the complete consciousness of Christ, duty is done
not simply because Christ has commanded it and we
love Him, but because Christ has filled us with Himself,
transformed our standards, recreated our affections, and
we love the duty too, seeing its essential beauty as He
sees it, out of whose nature it proceeds. I am sure that
such a change does come both in our active and our
passive duties. The fight that we must fight, or the
sickness that we must bear, both change from tasks, to
be done because He commands them, into privileges
which we embrace because we love them. Do we not
all feel the change that had come between Paul crying
submissively "Lord, what wilt Thou have me to do?"
looking to an outside Christ for commandment, and the
same Paul crying "Not I live but Christ liveth in me!"
rejoicing in the inspiration of an inward Savior? This
was the perfect victory after which Paul was always
longing so intensely. It did not come perfectly to him
in this world. It cannot to any of us. Dependent as
it is upon the knowledge of Christ by the soul, it cannot be perfect till the soul's knowledge of Christ shall
be perfect in heaven. Here we must always see duty,
like God, "in a glass, darkly;" only there "face to face."
But as it begins to come here, duty already begins to be
transfigured before us. It puts on its divinity. Its
face shines as the sun. Its raiment, which seemed cold,
becomes white as the light. Already we see its beauty.

Already we see how we shall love it some day ; and we cry out like the apostles, " Lord, it is good for us to be here. Let us stay here where duty is seen to be nothing but the glorious atmosphere of Thy personal will."

But this brings us to what after all we must hold to be the profoundest and most reliable sign of the maturing spiritual life. All these of which we have been speaking are only secondary symptoms of the great privilege of the Christian, which is deepening personal intimacy with Him who is the Christian's life, the Lord Jesus Christ. All comes to that at last. Christianity begins with many motives. It all fastens itself at last upon one motive, which does not exclude, but is large enough to comprehend all that is good in all the rest, " That I may know Him." Those are Paul's words. How constantly we come back to his large, rounded life, as the picture of what the Christian is and becomes. If I could set before you the young man at Damascus and the old man at Rome, and bid you compare the two, this sermon I am preaching need not have been begun. " That I may know Him." We have all seen, I am sure, if it has been our privilege to watch true Christians growing old, the special and absorbing way with which the personal Christ, their knowledge of Him, and His knowledge of them, comes to be all their religion. You hear them talk of Him, and it seems already as if their lives had entered into that heaven, which, as we read the mystic description of it in the book of Revelations, seems to consist in His personality. He is its temple ; He is its sun ; His name is written on the foreheads of its happy saints. Indeed Christ, to the Christian growing older, seems to be what the sun is to the developing day, which it lightens from the morning to the evening.) When the sun is in the zenith in the broad noon-day, men do their various works by his light; but they do not so often look up to him. It is the sunlight that they glory in, flooding a thousand tasks with clearness, making a million things beautiful. But as the world rolls into the evening, it is the sun itself at sunset that men gather to look at and admire and love. So to the earlier and middle stages of a Christian life, Christ is the revealer of duty and truth; and duty and truth become clear and dear in His light. The young Christian glories in the way in which, under his Master's power, he can work for humanity, for truth, for his nation, for society, for his family. But as the Christian life ripens into evening, it is not these things, though they are not forgotten, that the soul dwells on most. It is the Lord Himself. It is that He is the soul's, and the soul is His. It is His wondrousness, His dearness, and His truth, that fill the life as it presses closer to where He stands, — as the setting earth rolls on towards the sun.

And this is philosophical. It is strictly in accordance with the whole nature of our religion that it should thus grow. It cannot be perfect all at once. For Christianity is knowing Christ, and personal knowledge can come only by experience; and experience takes time. A truth you may embrace, and embrace completely, so soon as you understand the terms of its statement and have learned its evidence. But you cannot bring a person, as you can a proposition, up to a man, and say "Here, know him!" as you say "Know this!" and be at once obeyed. "I cannot," he replies. "However thoroughly you vouch for him, I cannot know him till he shows himself to me. I thank you for bringing him to me. I thank you more than if I could know him all at once, for if he is really all you say, then there lies before me a long career of gradual knowledge that shall be all delight to me till I shall know him perfectly." This seems to me one difference of Christians. Make Christianity a doctrinal system, and when your new disciple has learned his catechism, he is all done; and pretty soon you will find him sitting with his hands in his lap, complaining that there is nothing more to learn, and either finding his well-learned faith dull and uninteresting, or supplementing it with dogmatic speculations of his own. Make Christianity a personal knowledge of Christ, and then, with ever new enticements, each little that he knows opening to him something more to know of the infinite personal life, obedience feeding love, and love stimulating obedience, he presses on in the never stale, never weary ambition of " knowing Christ."

Far be it from me to think or talk as if there were two religions, one for the young Christian and one for the older; as if the power of the personal Christ were not present to waken the first good desire of the new life, as it is at last to crown the victorious well-doer kneeling on the steps of the throne. I pointed out, in opening, that just this — the continuous presence of a manifested God — is what makes the unity of the Christian life. Do not misunderstand me then. I turn to the youngest child just beginning to try to do right, and I see the little hand clasped in the hand of a Savior who is holding it close, who is watching the feeble feet, who is bending over and listening to his prayers. But just because that child has already tasted the power of a present Christ, he is able to comprehend the beauty of the life you offer him when you tell him that it is all to be the development of that relationship in which he finds himself already, the deepening of that friendship between him and his Lord.

There is as yet no culture, no method of progress known to men, that is so rich and complete as that which is ministered by a truly great friendship.   No natural appetite, no artificial taste, no rivalry of competition, no contagion of social activity, calls out such a large, healthy, symmetrical working of a human nature, as the constant, half-unconscious power of a friend's presence whom we thoroughly respect and love.   In a true friendship there is emulation without its jealousy ; there is imitation without its servility.   When one friend teaches another by his present life, there is none of that divorce of truth from feeling, and of feeling from truth, which in so many of the world's teachings makes truth hard, and feeling weak ; but truth is taught, and feeling is inspired, by the same action of one nature on the other, and they keep each other true and warm. ⌈ Surely there is no more beautiful sight to see in all this world, — full as it is of beautiful adjustments and mutual ministrations, — than the growth of two friends' natures who, as they grow old together, are always fathoming, with newer needs, deeper depths of each other's life, and opening richer veins of one another's helpfulness. ⌈And this best culture of personal friendship is taken up and made, in its infinite completion, the gospel method of the progressive saving of the soul by Christ.

When we get this idea of Christianity, there is nothing strange in the halo of dearness which, to every Christian, hangs around the scenes with which the beginning of his new life is associated. The place where two friends first met is sacred to them all through their friendship — all the more sacred as their friendship deepens and grows old. It is the same sort of feeling which sent the heart of Moses back to the bush. And to how many a saint the day and place where he first heard God's voice will be earth's one sacred memory, even long after earth's life is over. Do you think that Moses will not speak of the bush, and Samuel of the little temple-chamber, and Peter and John of their boats on the still lake, and Paul of the Damascus road, and Matthew of his tax-table, and the poor woman of the wayside well, when they are met above? Only the last day shall tell how much of earth is hallowed ground. This is what makes the old churches holy with an accumulated sacredness which surpasses their first consecration. Who can tell how many this church of ours will find among the blessed to honor and treasure her forever, that she may not be forgotten when the birthplaces of souls are remembered? This has always been the feeling of the world about Palestine, the land where the world first knew Christ, — sometimes breaking out into a crusade for its recovery; sometimes cheering the weariness of pilgrims who were struggling on to see Jerusalem and the Mount of Olives before they died; sometimes showing itself in the mystical transfer of the names of Palestinian geography to the hills and valleys, the heights and depths of the spiritual life. A recent English scholar has pointed out how often St. Paul's religious thought looked back to the scene of Stephen's martyrdom, where, as he stood by and held the murderers' clothes, his own first earnest interest in Christianity was blindly stirred. Paul's speech at Antioch reminds us throughout of Stephen's defence before his judges. Paul's address at Athens uses some of Stephen's very words. Several of Paul's most difficult and deepest phrases in his Epistles seem to correspond with forms of thought which the martyr had uttered years before, and which had sunk into the mind of the thoughtful young Jew. It is indeed a goodly spirit that treasures its past miracles, that goes down the gracious avenues of life to find the bushes out of which it first heard God's voice.

But come back for a few moments to our thought about the personal presence of Christ becoming clearer to us as we grow riper in the Christian life. Let me point out, in a word or two, three or four of the effects that it must produce, which are the noble characteristics of the maturest Christians:

First, it must give us a more infinite view of life in general, or, in other words, must make us more unworldly. To be always living with One whose kingdom is not of this world; to be constantly conversant, as we hold intercourse with Him, with the thought that there are other worlds also over which He presides, and with which we have something to do through our union with Him, — how this breaks up and scatters the littleness of life, the bondage of the seen. How it lets us out, free to trace the course of every action, the career of every thought, as it seeks vast untold issues in other spheres. More and more terrible appears to me the crowding in of life, its inability to scale and grasp the things that it was made for. Even our religion busies itself with little temporal duties, with church machineries and observances. What is there that can lift it all, and enlarge it and let it free, except the constant known presence of One who is infinite and who lives in infinity — the God of eternity made known to us as our beloved Christ?

And, if we get this, then something else must come, namely, more hopefulness. St. Paul has a noble verse which says that "experience worketh hope." It must, if it is full of Christ. The soul that is getting deeper and deeper into the certain knowledge of Him must be learning that it has no right to fear; that however hopeless things look there can be nothing but success for every good cause in the hand of Christ. It is a noble process for a man's life that gradually changes the cold dogma that "truth is strong and must prevail" into a warm enthusiastic certainty that "my Christ must conquer." It is terrible to see a man calling himself a Christian who despairs more of the world the longer that he lives in it. It shows that he is letting the world's darkness come between him and his Lord's light. It shows that he is not near enough to Christ.

And with the growing hopefulness there comes a growing courage. How timid we are at first. I become a Christian, and it seems as if just to get this soul of mine saved were all that I could dare to try; but as the Savior's strength becomes more manifest to me, as I know Him more, I see that He is able to do much more than that. I begin to aspire to have a little part in the great conquest of the world in which He is engaged. And so the Soldier of the Cross at last is out in the very thick of the battle, striking at all his Master's enemies in the perfect assurance of his Master's strength.

And then, as the crown of all these, there comes to the maturing Christian, out of his constant companion-ship with Christ, that true and perfect poise of soul which I think grows more and more beautiful as we get tired, one after another, of the fantastic and one-sided types of character which the world admires, and which seem to us very attractive at first. Expectant without impatience; patient without stagnation; wait-ing, but always ready to advance; loving to advance, but always ready to wait; full of confidence, but never proud; full of certainty, but never arrogant; serene, but enthusiastic; rich as a great land is rich in the peace that comes to it from the government of a great, wise, trusty governor, — this is the life whose whole power is summed up in one word — Faith. "Here is the patience and faith of the saints." This is the life to which men come who, through long years, "follow the Lamb whithersoever He goeth."

"The good-will of Him that dwelt in the bush." I have tried to depict what comes between the Bush and the Mountain, what it is on which the aged follower of Christ looks back; what it is to which the young fol-lower of Christ looks forward. Some of you are stand-ing as Moses stood, — the desert crossed, the promised land almost entered, the work done lying back behind you. I know not where it was, — in some church-pew, in some closet's privacy, in some stillness or some crowd, — years ago the fire came; the common life about you burned with the sudden presence of Divinity;

God called you, and you gave yourself to God. I bid you look back and see the mercy that has led you ever since, and strengthen your hope and courage and charity and faith as you remember the long, long good-will of Him that dwelt in the bush. And some of you I hope, I know, are standing just by the bush-side still, the shoes off your feet, the voice of God in your ears, lifted up with the desire for the new life of Christ. You are determined to be His, for He has called you. Well, till the end, life here and hereafter will be only the unfolding of this personal love which seems to you so dear and so mysterious now. Christ will grow realler, nearer, more completely your Master and your Savior all your life. That is the whole of your religion. But as you go on you will find that that is enough, that it is more than eternity can exhaust. The mercy which takes you into its bosom at last in heaven, will be still the old familiar good-will of Him that dwelt in the bush.

IV.

THE PILLAR IN GOD'S TEMPLE.

"Him that overcometh will I make a pillar in the temple of my God,
and he shall go no more out; and I will write upon him the name of
my God, and the name of the city of my God, . . . and my new
name." — REV. iii. 12.

IT is very many years since these great words were
sent abroad into a world of struggle. We can hardly
read them without remembering on what countless souls
they have fallen in a shower of strength. Men and
women everywhere, wrestling with life, have heard the
promise to "him that overcometh;" and, though much of
the imagery in which the promise was conveyed was
blind to them, though they very vaguely identified
their conflict with the battle which these far-off people
in the Book of the Revelation were engaged in fighting,
still, the very sound of the words has brought them inspiration. Let us study the promise a little more carefully this morning. Perhaps it will always be worth
more to us if we do. A text which we have once studied
is like a star upon which we have once looked through
the telescope. We always see it afterwards, full of the
brightness and color which that look showed us. Even if
it grows dim behind a cloud, or other nearer stars seem
to outshine it, we never think it dull or small after we
have once looked deep into its depths.

"To him that overcometh," reads the promise; and

the first thing that we want to understand is what the struggle is in which the victory is to be won. It is the Savior Christ who speaks. His voice comes out of the mystery and glory of heaven to the church in Philadelphia, and this book, in which His words are written, stands last in the New Testament. The gospel story is all told. The work of incarnation and redemption is all done. Jesus has gone back to His Father, and now is speaking down to men and women on the earth, who are engaged there in the special struggle for which He has prepared the conditions, and to which it has been the purpose of His life and death to summon them. Let us remember that. It is a special struggle. It is not the mere human fight with pain and difficulty which every living mortal meets. It is not the wrestling for place, for knowledge, for esteem, for any of the prizes which men covet. Nay, it is not absolutely the struggle after righteousness; it is not the pure desire and determination to escape from sin, considered simply as the aspiration of a man's own nature and the determination of a man's own will. It is not to these that Christ looks down and sends His promise. He had called out a special struggle on the earth. He had bidden men struggle after goodness, out of love and gratitude and loyalty to Him.

If the motive, everywhere and always, is the greatest and most important part of every action, then there must always be a difference between men who are striving to do right and not to do wrong, according to the love which sets them striving. If it is love of themselves, their struggle will be one thing. If it is love of the abstract righteousness, it will be another. If it is love of

Christ, it will be still another. Jesus is talking to the
men and women there among the Asian mountains, and
to the hosts of men and women who were to come after
them upon the earth, who should be fighters against
sin, against their own sin, who should struggle to be pure
and brave and true and spiritual and unselfish, because
they loved Christ, because He had lived and died for
them, because they belonged to Him, because He would
be honored and pleased by their goodness, grieved and
dishonored by their wickedness; because by goodness
they would come into completer sympathy with Him,
and gain a fuller measure of His love. It is to men
and women in this struggle that Christ speaks, and
promises them the appropriate reward which belongs to
perseverance and success in just that obedience of loyalty and love.

For one of the discoveries that we make, as soon as
we grow thoughtful about life at all, is that the world is
not merely full of struggle, but full of many kinds of
struggle, which vary very much in value. We begin
by very broad and superficial classifications. Men are
happy or unhappy; men are wise or foolish; men are
generous or stingy. But by and by such broad divisions
will not satisfy us. The great regions into which we
have classified our fellow-men begin to break up and
divide. There are all kinds of happiness, all kinds of
wisdom, all kinds of generosity. It means little to us,
when we have once found this out, to be told that a
man is happy, wise, or generous, until we have learned
also the special quality of this quality as it appears in
him, how he came to possess it, and how he works it out
in life. And so in all the world-full of struggling men,

as we observe them we find by and by that there are differences. A great, broad mass of eager, dissatisfied, expectant faces it appears at first; a wild and restless tossing hither and thither, as if a great ship had broken asunder in mid-ocean, and her frightened people, with one common fear and dread of being drowned, were struggling indiscriminately in the waves. But at last all that changes, and we wonder how it ever could have looked so to us. Struggle comes to seem as various as life. The objects for which men struggle, and the strength by which men struggle, grow endlessly various. And then, among the mass that seemed one general and monotonous turmoil, there stand out these — there shine out these — whose struggle is against sin, for holiness, and by the love of Christ. Other men struggle against poverty, against neglect; for ease, for power, for fame; and by the love of self, the noble abstract love of righteousness; but, scattered through the whole mass thickly enough to give it character and add a new, controlling strain to the eternal music of aspiring discontent which rises from the swarm of human living, there are these strugglers against sin, by the love of Christ. They are by your side. They are in your houses. They meet you in the street. Your children are catching sight of that struggle, and its fascination and its power, in the times when they are silent and thoughtful, and seem to be passing out of your familiar understanding. Your friend, whose carelessness concerning the things about which you are eager seems so strange to you, is careless about them only because he is fighting a deeper fight. He is fighting against sin, by the love of Christ. Therefore, he does not dread the poverty and the unpopularity against which your selfishness makes you so eager to fear and fight.

This then is the peculiar struggle to the victory in which Christ, out of heaven, gives His promise. And now the promise can be understood if we understand the struggle. The two belong together. "Him that overcometh will I make a pillar in the temple of my God, and he shall go no more out." The ideas of the pillar in a building, in a temple, are these two: incorporation and permanence. The pillar is part of the structure; and when it is once set in its place it is to be there as long as the temple stands. How clear the picture stands before us. There is a great, bright, solemn temple, where men come to worship. Its doors are ever open; its windows tempt the sky. There are many and many things which have to do with such a temple. The winds come wandering through its high arches. Perhaps the birds stray in and build their nests, and stray away again when the short summer is done. The children roam across its threshold, and play for a few moments on its shining floor. Banners and draperies are hung upon its walls awhile, and then carried away. Poor men and women, with their burdens and distress, come in and say a moment's prayer, and hurry out. Stately processions pass from door to door, making a brief disturbance in its quiet air. Generation after generation comes and goes and is forgotten, each giving its place up to another; while still the temple stands, receiving and dismissing them in turn, and outliving them all. All these are transitory. All these come into the temple and then go out again. But a day comes when the great temple needs enlargement. The plan which it embodies must be made more perfect. It is to grow to a completer self. And then they bring up to the doors a column of cut stone, hewn in the quarry for this very place, fitted and fit for this place and no other; and, bringing it in with toil, they set it solidly down as part of the growing structure, part of the expanding plan. It blends with all the other stones. It loses while it keeps its individuality. It is useless, except there where it is; and yet there, where it is, it has a use which is peculiarly its own, and different from every other stone's. The walls are built around it. It shares the building's changes. The reverence that men do to the sacred place falls upon it. The lights of sacred festivals shine on its face. It glows in the morning sunlight, and grows dim and solemn as the dusk gathers through the great expanse. Generations pass before it in their worship. They come and go, and the new generations follow them, and still the pillar stands. The day when it was hewn and set there is forgotten; as children never think when an old patriarch, whom they see standing among them, was born. It is part of the temple where the men so long dead set it so long ago. From the day that they set it there, it "goes no more out."

Can we not see perfectly the meaning of the figure? There are men and women everywhere who have something to do with God. They cannot help touching and being touched by Him, and His vast purposes, and the treatment which He is giving to the world. They cross and recross the pavement of His providence. They come to Him for what they want, and He gives it to them, and they carry it away. They ask Him for bread, and then carry it off into the chambers of their own selfishness and eat it. They ask Him for power, and then go off to the battlefields or workshops of their own selfishness and use it. They are forever going in and out of the presence of God. They sweep through His temple like the wandering wind; or they come in like the chance worshipper, and bend a moment's knee before the altar. And then there are the other men who are struggling to escape from sin, by the love of Christ. How different they are. The end of everything for them is to get to Christ, and put themselves in Him, and stay there. They do not so much want to get to Christ that they may get away from sin, as they want to get away from sin that they may get to Christ. God is to them not merely a great helper of their plans; He is the sum of all their plans, the end of all their wishes, the Being to whom their souls say, not " Lord, help me do what I will ; " but, " Lord, show me Thy will that I may make it mine, and serve myself in serving Thee." When such a soul as that comes to Christ, it is like the day when the marble column from the quarry was dragged up and set into the temple aisle. Such a soul becomes part of the great purpose of God. It can go no more out. It has no purpose or meaning outside of God. Its life is hid there in the sacred aisles of God's life. If God's life grows dark, the dusk gathers around this pillar which is set in it. If God's life brightens, the pillar burns and glows. Men who behold this soul, think instantly of God. They cannot picture the pillar outside of the temple; they cannot picture the soul outside of the fear, the love, the communion, the obedience of God.

The New Testament abounds with this idea and the discrimination which we have been trying to make. When the Prodigal Son comes back to his Father, he cries out, " I am not worthy to be called Thy son;

make me as one of Thy hired servants;" but the Father answers, "This, My son, was dead, and is alive again;" and the pillar is set up in the temple. When Jesus looks into His disciples' faces at the last supper, He says: "Henceforth I call you not servants, for the servant knoweth not what his Lord doeth; but I have called you friends, for all things which I have heard of my Father I have made known unto you." The servant is the drapery hung upon the nails; the friend is the pillar built into the wall. Paul writes to the Romans: "Who shall separate us from the love of Christ? Shall tribulation, or distress, or persecution, or famine, or nakedness, or peril, or sword? I am persuaded that neither death, nor life, nor angels, nor principalities, nor powers, nor things present, nor things to come, nor height, nor depth, nor any other creature, shall be able to separate us from the love of God." It is the calm assurance of the pillar which feels the pressure of the wall around it, and defies any temptation to entice it, or any force to tear it away.

Nor is there anything unphilosophical, or unintelligible, or merely mystical in all this. The same thing essentially occurs everywhere. Two men both come to know another man, richer and larger than either of them. Something called friendship grows up between each of them and him. But the first of the two men who seek this greater man, comes and goes into and out of his great neighbor's life. He keeps the purposes of his own life distinct. He comes to his rich friend for knowledge, for strength, for inspiration, and then he carries them off and uses them for his own ends. The other friend gives up all ends in life which he has valued, and makes this new man's, this greater man's purposes, his. He wants what this great man wants, because this great man wants it. Naturally and easily we say that he "lives in" this other man. By and by you cannot conceive of him as separate from this greater life. The reward of his loving devotion is that he is made a pillar in the temple of his friend, and goes no more out.

Two men both love their country. One loves her because of the advantage that he gets from her, the help that she gives to his peculiar interests. The other loves her for herself, for her embodiment of the ideas which he believes are truest and divinest and most human. One uses the country. The other asks the country to use him. One goes into the country's service and gathers up money or knowledge or strength, and then, as it were, goes out and carries them with him to help the tasks which he has to do in his own private life. The other takes all his private interests, and sacrifices them to the country's good. And what is the reward of this supreme devotion, which there will always be some little group of supremely patriotic men ready to make in every healthy state? Will they not belong to the state, and will it not belong continually to them? They will never be lost out of its history. They will become its pillars and share its glory, as they helped to support its life.

The same is true about the church. There are the multitudes who go in and out, who count the church as theirs, who gather from her thought, knowledge, the comfort of good company, the sense of safety; and then there are others who think they truly, as the light phrase

so deeply means, "belong to the church." They are given
to it, and no compulsion could separate them from it.
They are part of its structure. They are its pillars.
Here and hereafter they can never go out of it. Life
would mean nothing to them outside the church of
Christ.

And, to give just one more example, so it is with
truth. The men who seek truth for what she has to
give them, who want to be scholars for the emoluments,
the honors, the associations, which scholarship will bring,
these are the men who will turn away from truth so
soon as she has given them her gifts, and leave herself
dishonored, — who will turn away from any truth which
has no gifts to give. But, always, there are a few seekers
who want truth's self, and not her gifts. Once scholars,
they are scholars always. They really put their lives
into the structure of the world's advancing knowledge.
There those lives always remain, like solid stones for the
scholarship of the years to come to build upon. There
is no world conceivable to which their souls can go,
where they will not turn to seek what it is possible there
for souls like theirs to know.

Thus everywhere, in every interest of human life, there
is a deeper entrance and a more permanent abiding which
is reserved for those who have come into the profoundest
sympathy with its principles, and the most thorough unselfish consecration to its work. Come back, then, from
these illustrations, to the Christian life, and see there the
larger exhibition of the same law which they illustrate.
God is the Governor of all the world. The purpose of
His government, the one design on which it all proceeds, is that the whole world, through obedience to

Him, should be wrought into His likeness, and made the utterance of His character. Let that thought dwell before your mind, and feel, as you must feel, what a sublime and glorious picture it involves. Then remember that God does not treat the world in one great, vague generality. He sees the world all made up of free souls, of men and women. The world can become like Him by obedience, only as the souls of men and women become like Him by obedience. Each soul, your soul and mine, must enter into that consummation, must realize the idea of that picture by itself, by its own free submission; helped, no doubt, by the movement of souls all about it, and by the great promise of the world's salvation, but yet acting for itself, by its own personal resolve. To each soul, then, to yours and mine, God brings all the material of this terrestrial struggle, — all the temptations, all the disappointments, all the successes, all the doubts and perplexities, all the jarring of interests, all the chances of hinderance and chances of help which come flocking about every new-born life. The struggle begins, begins with every living creature, is beginning to-day with these boys and girls about you, just as you can remember that years and years ago it began with you. What is it to succeed in that struggle? What success shall you set before them to excite their hope and energy? On what success shall you congratulate yourself? Is it success in the struggle of life simply to get through with decency and die without disgrace or shame? Is it success in the struggle of life just to have so laid hold on God's mercy, to have so made our peace with Him, that we know we shall not be punished for our sins? Is it success in the struggle of life even to have so lived in His presence that every day has been bright with the sense that He was taking care of us? These things are very good; but if the purpose of God's government of the world and of us is what I said, then the real victory in the struggle can be nothing less than the accomplishment in us of that which it is the object of all His government to accomplish in the world. When, truly obedient, we have been made like Him whom we obey, then, only then, we have overcome in the struggle of life. And then we must be pillars in His temple. With wills harmonized with His will; with souls that love and hate in truest unison of sympathy with His; with no purposes left in us but His purposes, — then we have come to what He wants the world to come to. We have taken our places in the slowly rising temple of His will. To whatever worlds He carries our souls when they shall pass out of these imprisoning bodies, in those worlds these souls of ours shall find themselves part of the same great temple; for it belongs not to this earth alone. There can be no end of the universe where God is, to which that growing temple does not reach, the temple of a creation to be wrought at last into a perfect utterance of God by a perfect obedience to God.

O my dear friends, that is the victory that is awaiting you. Slowly, through all the universe, that temple of God is being built. Wherever, in any world, a soul, by free-willed obedience, catches the fire of God's likeness, it is set into the growing walls, a living stone. When, in your hard fight, in your tiresome drudgery, or in your terrible temptation, you catch the purpose of your being, and give yourself to God, and so give Him the chance to

give Himself to you, your life, a living stone, is taken
up and set into that growing wall. And the other living,
burning stones claim and welcome and embrace it.
They bind it in with themselves. They make it sure
with their assurance, and they gather sureness out of
it. The great wall of divine likeness through human
obedience grows and grows, as one tried and purified and
ripened life after another is laid into it; and down at
the base, the corner-stone of all, there lies the life of
Him who, though He was a son, yet learned obedience
by the things which He suffered, and, being made perfect,
became the author of eternal salvation unto all them that
obey Him.

In what strange quarries and stone-yards the stones
for that celestial wall are being hewn ! Out of the hillsides of humiliated pride ; deep in the darkness of crushed
despair; in the fretting and dusty atmosphere of little
cares ; in the hard, cruel contacts that man has with man ;
wherever souls are being tried and ripened, in whatever commonplace and homely ways ; — there God is
hewing out the pillars for His temple. O, if the stone
can only have some vision of the temple of which it is
to lie a part forever, what patience must fill it as it
feels the blows of the hammer, and knows that success
for it is simply to let itself be wrought into what shape
the Master wills.

Upon the pillar thus wrought into the temple of
God's loving kingdom there are three inscriptions. I
can only in one word ask you to remember what they
are : "I will write upon him the name of my God, and
the name of the city of my God, and my new name."

The soul that in obedience to God is growing into His likeness, is dedicated to the divine love, to the hope of the perfect society, and to the ever new knowledge of redemption and the great Redeemer. Those are its hopes; and, reaching out forever and ever, all through eternity, those hopes it never can exhaust. Those writings on the pillar shall burn with purer and brighter fire the longer that the pillar stands in the temple of Him whom Jesus calls " My God."

May all this great promise ennoble and illumine the struggle of our life; keep us from ever thinking that it is mean and little; lift us above its details while it keeps us forever faithful to them; and give us victory at last through Him who has already overcome.

V.

THE EYE OF THE SOUL.

"The light of the body is the eye: if, therefore, thine eye be single, thy whole body shall be full of light."—MATT. vi. 22.

IT sometimes seems to me as if, in our Christian earnestness and eagerness to establish the authority of the words of Jesus, and to enforce their application, we were in danger of neglecting to seek their deepest meaning and full interpretation. These three questions every thoughtful and conscientious disciple must ask about his Master: first, Why should I believe His teachings? third, What ought my belief in His teachings to make me do? but certainly also, second, What do His teachings mean? Without the serious asking and careful answering of this second question, the answering of the first question must be well-nigh useless, and the correct and full answering of the third question must be, in great degree, impossible.

All this is true of every word of Jesus; but it is specially true with regard to certain great words of His, in which it seems as if He summed up the principles of His teaching, and gave a comprehensive statement of His work. Such words there are; words which rise like mountains in the midst of His discourse, and seem to draw up, into conclusive points, the whole expanse of His great teaching. They are not deliberate and formal.

He does not turn aside from His work of saving the world, to deliver lectures on theology. These comprehensive words of His grow naturally out of the ordinary circumstances and conversations into which He fell; but in them there meet the currents of His thought, and the great final truths of man and God lie open to the mind that reverently tries to understand them. Surely such words tempt and deserve our most reverent and loving study.

It is one of these words of Jesus that I have chosen for my text this morning. I choose it because it seems to me to have something to say very directly to some of the questions about the possibility of knowing about God, and the way of knowing about God, which one hears asked with most astonishing frequency and most impressive earnestness in these days and places. In this utterance Jesus, I think, makes it wonderfully clear how man must hope to know those spiritual things, without some knowledge of which the heart of man is not and cannot be content; after which man is forever struggling; and the despair of which makes the great gloom which in these days seems, to some prophets, to be settling down upon the human soul.

Jesus builds all His teaching upon an illustrative figure which every one could then, and can always, understand. "The light of the body is the eye," He said. Try to get the picture back before your mind. These words are part of the Sermon on the Mount. On a bright, fresh morning, Jesus is sitting half-way up a hillside in Galilee, with a group of attentive hearers clustered at his side. All around Him is the radiant landscape. Almost at the mountain's foot the lake of

Galilee is flashing in the morning sun. The soft rounded hills roll away like waves on every side, the quiet valleys nestling in between them. Here and there the little white villages give life and movement to the scene. The birds fly through the air; the cattle are plodding at their tasks; all the earth seems bright and fresh and clear, full of vitality and beauty. And then here, close around Him, are these men with all their sensitiveness, all their human power to enjoy and understand this world, — these men whose understanding and enjoyment of it seem to give worthiness and dignity to all this outward nature. They are the other half of the picture in the mind of Jesus. Nature and man, these two, make up the world for Him. The hills and rocks and trees and beasts and villages, and the sun shining on them all, — that on one side; and on the other, — man, with his power of knowing what all these things mean, of loving them, of thinking about them, of using them. The world of nature radiant with light; the soul of man rich in intelligence, — these two facing and claiming each other on that bright morning in Syria, as they have faced and claimed each other every day since God said, "Let us make man," and Adam began to live in Eden. And now, as Jesus looks at all this, He begins to praise the human eye. "The light of the body is the eye," He says. What does He mean by that? Is it not that He is rejoicing in the one appointed channel through which these two halves of the world may come into connection? Nature and man must stand apart, not two halves of one world, but two separate worlds, were it not for that marvellous and precious avenue of sight which brings the two together, and lets the man, with his inner power of knowledge, know the outer world. Through it, the Lake of Galilee and beautiful Mount Tabor in the distance, — aye, and the dear, sweet face of the Lord himself, — flow in upon the soul of John, and become a part of him. Without the eye the world might still be real; but it must be forever unknowable to this man, able to know it, but sitting in the prison of his sightlessness where all the glory cannot reach him. He opens the window of his eye and it all comes pouring in; runs through his frame and finds out his intelligence; says to his brain: "Here I am, know me!" Says to his heart: "Here I am, love me!" To the man sitting in darkness, the whole bright world has sprung to life; and the window of the prison, the gateway of the entering glory, the light of the body is the eye.

So Jesus spoke; and we can well imagine that His words awoke some new grateful delight in their own blessed power of vision among those thoughtful men who heard Him. But it was not for that purpose that he had spoken. He was not lecturing on optics. The visible world, and its entrance to the human intelligence through the eye, was but an illustration. His thought was aimed through the illustration at that which it was the purpose of His life to teach mankind. He was thinking of the world of unseen, invisible, spiritual life; and what He meant to say by His suggestive picture must have been that that world, too, must and could testify itself, report itself to the human intelligence through its appropriate channel of communication, just exactly as the world of visible nature manifests and reports itself through the organ of the eye. Now it is just the existence of that spiritual world, and the possibility of man's being in communication with it, intelligently knowing it, intelligently loving it, — that it is about which man's profoundest hopes and fears have always clustered, about which they are clustering to-day, perhaps more anxiously than ever yet. It is a world certainly that is conceivable. The invisible may at least be imagined, whether it can be believed or not. All man's mental history bears witness that he can picture to himself a world in which the true existences are souls instead of bodies ; where the forces are not those which any physics can measure, but the temptations and aspirations which only the spiritual life can feel ; where the issues are not those of physical growth or catastrophe, but of the culture or decay of character ; and whose central sun, the source and fountain of whose life, is not a burning globe hung in the heavens, but a personal God who feeds all the souls of His children with His love, and guides them by His wisdom, and blesses or punishes them by His judgment. Those are the components of that spiritual world, the human soul and God. No man has ever seen either of them. They cannot report themselves through the eye. But Jesus says that the world of which they are the constituents is a real world ; and that though the eye cannot give them admission to the intelligence to which all worlds must report themselves before they can become part of the life of man, there is an organ which is to this world of spiritual life what the eye of the body is to a world of trees and lakes.

And what then is that organ ? The name by which it is best known is Conscience ; and, though we may have to remind ourselves before we finish that some of

the ordinary uses of that word make it too small and
meagre, yet we may freely use the name of Conscience
to represent that organ which stands between the intelligence of man and the spiritual world, just as the eye
stands between the intelligence of man and the world of
physical nature, and brings the two together. This is
Christ's doctrine in many places. He that uses his
conscience, he that means to do what is right out of
obedience to God, shall come to the knowledge of
God and of his own soul. That is the plain, unfigura-
tive statement of the doctrine which He is constantly
reïterating.

And we can see how His doctrine has its root in the
nature of things. Conscience is the faculty by which
we judge of acts as right or wrong. It follows then, of
necessity, that all knowledge of the deeper natures of
things by which they become possibly the instruments
of righteousness or wickedness, and all knowledge of
those deeper and higher parts of the universe which are
capable of being known only in their moral characters,
must of necessity come in through some such organ or
faculty as this, which each man knows that he possesses, and by which he says of characters, "This is
good or bad," just as by his eye he says of the branch
of a tree, "This is straight or crooked." Is not that
clear? A tree is growing outside your window. You,
who inside the window are sitting with your face
toward the tree, are blind. Some miracle touches you
and you get your sight. Instantly that tree leaps into
being for you, and by the channel of your opened eye-
sight pours the recognition of itself through all your
intelligence. Just so God, — a Being whose essence is

morality, a Being who is good and who loves or hates all things in the world according as they are good or bad, — God is here before you; and you have no open conscience. You do not care whether things are right or wrong. You have no perception of the essential difference between right and wrong. You do not feel the dreadfulness of being bad, the beauty of being good. You are not trying to do right. You are not trying to keep from doing wrong. By and by, suddenly or gradually, all that changes. Your shut conscience opens. I will not ask now what makes it open. I will not speak now of the power which the world of God beyond the conscience may have to tempt the conscience into activity. Let us simply watch the fact. You do begin to feel the difference of right and wrong. You begin to try to do right. And then it is, in the pursuance of that effort, that there become gradually impressed upon your intelligence certain things which had found no recognition there before. The spiritual nature of the world; that all this mass of things and events is fitted for and naturally struggles towards the education of character; — the spiritual nature of man; the truth that man is fully satisfied only with what satisfies his soul, only with character, and with an endless chance for that character to grow; — and God; the existence, behind all standards and laws, of righteousness, of a perfectly righteous One, from Whom they all proceed and by Whom those who try to follow them are both judged and helped; — these are the before unseen realities which come pressing into your intelligence, tempting, demanding your recognition when your conscience is once open, when you have once begun to live in the desire and struggle to do right.

Do you not see then what I mean when I say that the conscience stands between man's power of knowledge and the spiritual world, just as the eye stands between man's power of knowledge and the world of visible nature? It is the opened or unopened window through which flows the glorious knowledge of God and heaven; or outside of which that knowledge waits, as the sun with its glory or the flower with its beauty waits outside the closed eye of a blind or sleeping man.

In both the cases, — in the sight through the eye and the sight through the conscience,—the intelligence which waits within, and does not yet see for itself, is not, of course, shut out from testimony. If a man is thoroughly blind and never sees the sun himself, other men who do see it with their open eyes may, no doubt, come and tell him of it; and in his darkened soul, if he believes them, there grows up some dim, distorted image of the sun which he has never seen. Nay, other senses have some stray messages to tell him of the world, whose full revelation can come only through the opened eye. He feels the sun in its warmth; he smells the rose in its sweetness; he tastes the flavor of the peach. Through these chinks there steal in some tidings of the wondrous world, even while the window through which it can report itself entirely is shut and shuttered. I am impressed by seeing how exactly all this has its correspondent in man's knowledge of the universe of spiritual things. There too, through testimony and through sideway and accidental intimations, as it were, some

6

knowledge comes even when conscience is shut and no struggle to do right is urging it open to its work. Some man who knows that there is a God, and that the soul is precious and immortal, comes and tells me so. The Bible speaks it with such power that I cannot disbelieve. Nay, the things that are spiritual bring their own sidelong testimonies of themselves. They touch my sense of beauty. They make me feel how good it would be for the world if they were true. I hear their movement in the depths of history. In all these ways they do not leave themselves unwitnessed. These are the ways in which, while I am most unconscientious and least anxious to do right, I may still know that God and spirit are the basis and the issue of the world. Yet still, in spite of all this, there stands the separate glory of the revelation of that day when to me, at last beginning to try to do right, the God whose faint reports have come to me pours in upon my opened soul the glorious conviction of His righteousness and love; and my soul, in which I have half believed, becomes the centre of my life ; *becomes* my life, that for which all the other parts of me are made. Then, in the knowledge which pours through my opened conscience, then I know with an assurance which makes all the knowledge that I had before seem but a guess and dim suspicion.

And there is yet another point of resemblance in this comparison of the eye and the conscience, which is striking. When one declares thus, that through the conscience man arrives at the knowledge of unseen things, and conceptions of God and spiritual force and immortality reveal themselves to the intelligence, at once the suggestion comes from some one who is listening, " Can we be sure of the reality of what thus seems to be made known ? How can we be sure that what the conscience sends in to the understanding are not mere creations of its own ; things which it thinks exist because it seems to need them ; mere forms in which it has been led to clothe with outward and substantial life its own emotions ? " Everybody knows such questions. They are thrown up, on every side, to the man who, trying to do right, thinks that through his effort he has found God. They come to him not merely from other men ; but his own heart, suspecting its own faiths and hopes, suggests them. But now think how exactly they are the same questions which have always haunted man's whole thought about his vision of the world of nature. How often we are told that none of us can prove that all these things which our eyes see have any real existence outside our sense of sight ; that all that we are sure of is certain sensations and impressions in our own brains. Are not then the questions which haunt the conscience the same as those which haunt the eye ? And as the eye deals with its questions, so will the conscience always deal with its. A conviction of the reality of what it sees, which is a part of its consciousness that no suspicion can disturb ; a use of its knowledge, which brings ever a more and more complete assurance of its trustworthiness, — these are the practical issue of every such question with regard to what the brain sees through the eye ; and the same will be the practical issue of every question with regard to what the soul sees through the conscience. At least we may say this, that it would be a very deep confidence indeed if the soul felt as sure of God as the mind feels of nature. This we feel very deeply in these days, when to so many minds the certainty of nature seems to stand in strong contrast with the uncertainty of God. It is much if we can see that the doubts which are suggested as to the sight of the soul, are but the same with the doubts which we easily overcome when we are dealing with the sight of the body.

Before the parallel, which Christ's illustration suggests, is quite completely apprehended, there is one thing more which we ought to observe; and the observation of it may perhaps touch a difficulty which, I dare say, has suggested itself to some minds while I have been speaking. We have talked as if all that was necessary, in order that the eye of man should see the world of nature, was that the eye should be open; but we know very well that something else is needed. The world of nature may be there in all its beauty, but the openest eye will not see it, if it be not turned that way. The eye, wide open, turned to the blank wall, will not see the mountain and the meadow. "Open your eyes and look here," we say to a child into whose intelligence we want the wonder of nature to be poured. And now, is there anything that corresponds to this second necessity in the case of conscience and its perception of spiritual truth? Surely there is. There is an openness of conscience, a desire and struggle to do right, which is distinctly turned away from God and the world of spiritual things, so that, even if they were there, it would not see them. On the other hand, there is an openness of conscience, a desire and struggle to do right, which is turned towards God and the supernatural,

which is expectant of spiritual revelation; and to that
conscience the spiritual revelation comes. This does
not amount to saying that the conscience sees what it
wants to see. It is very different from that. Many
things the conscience, like the eye, wants to see, and
does not see them because they do not exist. But those
things which do exist,— though they be the plainest of
realities,—no conscience can see which, with the greatest
scrupulousness and faithfulness, is turned the other way
and expecting revelation from another quarter. Does
this explain nothing? If we can recall a time when
we did our duty just as faithfully as we knew how, and
found all our duty a drudgery and toil, — a time when
conscience was intensely, almost morbidly scrupulous,
and would not rest; and yet, when, for a purpose of
duty, we never looked, or tried to look, beyond ourselves
and the world in which we lived; when we tried to be
good because we were ashamed of wickedness, or because
wickedness we knew would bring us pain; and if,
remembering that all our struggle after goodness in
those days brought us no sight of God, we ask ourselves
what such a failure of the truly open conscience meant,
is there no suggestion of an answer here? It was the
open eye looking down and not up, looking away
from God and not to Him. Of course it did not see
Him. When the desire to do right began to turn itself
and to look up; when it began to desire to obey and
please, and depend upon, whatever highest being in the
universe might have anything to do with that soul and
its struggles, then the soul knew God. The man who
is not trying to do right at all may stand with his blind
conscience in the very blaze of God's presence and not

see Him. The man who is trying to do right in selfishness and self-dependence may toil on unenlightened and unaided. The man who is trying to do right Godward, who in all his scrupulousness is devoutly humble and hopeful of things higher than himself, to him, through the openness of his faithful conscience, the vision comes, and he sees God.

My friends, may we not pause a moment here in the midst of our definitions, and let ourselves see what a great truth this is that we have reached? Is it then true that every man carries about with him such a capacity as this? This impulse, the necessity of doing right, of struggling with temptation, which has so often seemed to make life a hard slavery,— see what it really is! It is the opening of the organ through which the whole world of unseen spiritual light and life, all the being and power and love of God, all our own untold future in the regions of immortal growth, may flow in on us and become real and influential in our life. That boy keeping himself true when other boys are tempting him to be false, keeping himself lofty when other boys are tempting him to be base, he is no toiler in a treadmill which he would be well out of if he dared but leave it. He is a climber of the delectable mountains from whose height he shall see heaven and God. And, as he climbs, the promise of the vision is already making his dull eyes strong and fine, so that when the vision comes he shall be able to look right into its deep and glorious heart. "Blessed are the pure in heart, for they shall see God." We praise the hand, the ear, the eye, the brain, for all the knowledge they so wonderfully bring to man. Is there among them all any organ which a man should honor and glorify and enshrine in such reverent obedience as this, the Conscience; if indeed, through it, God and the unseen world of God may come to him, and his poor humanity grow rich in knowing them ?

And so we are led quietly onward to that which Jesus teaches in the text which has given us our starting point for all this long discussion, — "If thine eye be single thy whole body shall be full of light;" the critical importance of a pure, true conscience, of a steady, self-sacrificing struggle to do right Godward. So only can the channel be kept open, through which the knowledge of God and of the spiritual things which belong to Him, can enter into our souls. O, my dear friends, has there been nothing in our experience which has taught us to understand that and to believe it ? Is there one of us who cannot remember how, in the hours when he tried to do what was right, the possibility of God, perhaps the certainty of God, grew clear to him, and it seemed to him as if the world opened, and spiritual things bore direct testimony of themselves ? And is there one of us who has not the other recollection also, of hours when, in the tumult of indulged passion, or in times when we let ourselves be mean, or when we cared only for ourselves, the whole world of spiritual being, God, heaven, immortality, the power of divine love, the vast, infinite hopes, aye, even the spiritual quality of our own soul itself, — all seemed to fade away from us as the landscape fades away out of the sight of the eye when blindness drops upon it ? Still, out of the darkened landscape may come mysterious sounds which fill the soul with fear; and still, out of the hidden world of spiritual life may come to the sinful and unbelieving soul whispers of dread which make him tremble at the unseen presence of the awful verities which he does not believe in. But all true, healthy, inspiring faith, — all knowledge that can live by love and open into action, grows dim to the soul, dimmer and ever dimmer as it gives itself up to sin.

All this seems to me to throw so much light upon the nature and purpose of Christ's incarnation. Men say: "He came to show us God." Other men say, "No, but He came to save us from our sins." Are not the two really one? It would be easy to ask whether He who showed men God must not save them from their sins. But — what is to our purpose now to ask — must not He who saved men from their sins show men God? The work of Jesus was to make men do right Godward; to make men do right not merely that the world might be more quiet and peaceable and decent, but in order that into souls thus open through their consecrated consciences, the knowledge of that God might enter in whose knowledge is eternal life.

Remember how Jesus always found, in His own obedience to His Father, the secret of His Father's perpetual revelation of Himself to Him. "The Father hath not left me alone, for I do always those things that please Him," He said. Those words are the key to it all. He did right Godward. He did always those things that pleased God. In Him was neither the abstract meditation and study of divine things which thinks that the knowledge of them is like the knowledge of the rocks or the stars, something quite independent of moral conditions in the knower; nor, on the other hand, was there in Him that mere slavery to duty on its lower grounds of economy and prudence, which often paralyzes the conscience and shuts it up as a channel for the higher knowledge. He did right Godward. And if in the wilderness, when the devil was tempting Him, He came for any instant near to faltering, a large part of His strength of resistance must have been in the certainty that if He yielded and sinned, the door would close through which the perpetual knowledge of His Father was forever flowing into Him and filling Him with rich joy and peace.

And what His own life was, Jesus is always trying to make the lives of His disciples be. He is always trying to lead men to do right with hopes and expectations Godward. Men debate again whether Jesus is a human example and teacher, or a divine Power and Redeemer. Surely He is both, and between the two there is no conflict. They are most congruous. Both are parts of that completeness of life by which He would draw the conscience of man upward and make it clear and pure, so that through it the knowledge of God should descend. He taught men holiness by His example and His words; and He declared, in all He was and did, the love of God; and the result of all of it, to John and Mary and Nicodemus and the Magdalen and countless other unnamed disciples, was that they saw God through consciences made scrupulous and holy, and turned to God by the attraction of His manifested love.

I turn to the consummate act of His life, the act in which His life was all summed up, and I see all this in its completeness. I look at Jesus on the cross. I see Him there convicting sin by the sight of its terrific consequence. I see Him also drawing men's souls up, away from the earth and from themselves, up to God, by that amazing sign of how God loved them. And when I turn from looking at the sufferer and look into the faces of those men and women to whom His suffering has brought its power, I see how, in the struggle against sin under the power of the love of God, to which the cross has summoned them, they are knowing God; how, in St. Paul's great words, "the God of our Lord Jesus Christ, the Father of Glory, is giving unto them the spirit of wisdom and revelation in the knowledge of Him, the eyes of their understanding being enlightened." I see all that in the group around the cross on Calvary; and all that also in the host of Christian souls who have been filled with the knowledge of God, through the sacrifice of Christ, in all the ages since.

I should be more glad than I can say if I could know that I had opened up to any one of you to-day a hope that you might know the things of the spiritual life, the things of God, of which many men are telling you now that they are unknowable by man. That you must not believe. So long as man is able to do right Godward, to keep his conscience pure and true and reverent, set upon doing the best things on the highest grounds, he carries with him an eye through which the everlasting light may, and assuredly will, shine in upon his soul. Such faithfulness and consecration and hope may God give to all, that we may know Him more and more.

VI.

THE MAN OF MACEDONIA.

"And a vision appeared unto Paul in the night. There stood a man of Macedonia, and prayed him, saying: Come over into Macedonia and help us."—Acts xvi. 9.

IT was the moment when a new work was opening before the great apostle; nothing less than the carrying of the gospel into Europe. He had passed through Asia and was sleeping at Troas, with the Mediterranean waters sounding in his ears; and, visible across them, the islands which were the broken fringes of another continent. We cannot think that this was the first time that it had come into Paul's mind to think of christianizing Europe. We can well believe that on the past day he had stood and looked westward, and thought of the souls of men as hardly any man since him has known how to think of them, and longed to win for his Master the unknown world that lay beyond the waters. But now, in his sleep, a vision comes, and that completes whatever preparation may have been begun before, and in the morning he is ready to start.

And so it is that before every well-done work the vision comes. We dream before we accomplish. We start with the glorified image of what we are to do shining before our eyes, and it is its splendor that encourages and entices us through all the drudgery of the labor that we meet. The captain dreams out his battle

sleeping in his tent. The quick and subtle-brained in-
ventor has visions of his new wonder of machinery
before the first toothed wheel is fitted to its place. You
merchants see the great enterprise that is to make your
fortune break out of vacancy and develop all its richness
to you, as if it were a very inspiration from above.
Nay, what is all our boyhood, that comes before our
life, and thinks and pictures to itself what life shall be,
that fancies and resolves and is impatient, — what is it
but just the vision before the work, the dream of
Europe coming to many a young life, as it sleeps at
Troas, on the margin of the sea? The visions before the
work; it is their strength which conquers the difficulties,
and lifts men up out of the failures, and redeems the
tawdriness or squalidness of the labor that succeeds.

And such preparatory visions, the best of them, take
the form and tone of importunate demands. The man
hears the world crying out for just this thing which he
is going to start to do to-morrow morning. This battle
is to save the cause. This new invention is to turn the
tide of wealth. This mighty bargain is to make trade
another thing. The world must have it. And the long
vision of boyhood is in the same strain too. There is
something in him, this new boy says, which other men
have never had. His new life has its own distinctive
difference. He will fill some little unfilled necessary
place. He will touch some little untouched spring.
The world needs him. It may prove afterwards that
the vision was not wholly true. It may seem as if,
after all, only another duplicate life was added to a million others, which the world might very well have done
without; but still the power of the vision is not soon

exhausted, the mortifying confession is not made at once, and before it wholly fades away the vision gives a power and momentum to the life which the life never wholly loses.

And indeed we well may doubt whether the vision was a false one, even when the man himself, in his colder and less hopeful years, comes to think and say that it was. We well may doubt whether, with the infinite difference of personal life and character which God sends into the world, every true and earnest man has not some work that he alone can do, some place that he alone can fill; whether there is not somewhere a demand that he alone can satisfy; whether the world does not need him, is not calling to him, "Come and help us," as he used to hear it in the vision that was shown to him upon the sea-shore.

So much we say of preparatory visions in general. I want to look with you at this vision of Paul's, and see how far we can understand its meaning, and how much we can learn from it. A Macedonian comes before the apostle of Christ, and asks him for the gospel. The messenger is the representative, not of Macedonia only, but of all Europe. Macedonia is only the nearest country into which the traveller from Asia must cross first. There he stands in his strange dress, with his strange western look, with his strange gestures, before the waking or the sleeping Paul, begging in a strange language, which only the pentecostal power of spiritual appreciative sympathy can understand, — "Come over and help us." But what was this Macedonia and this Europe which he represented? Did it want the gospel? Had it sent him out because it was restless and craving and uneasy, and could not be satisfied until it heard the truth about Jesus Christ, which Paul of Tarsus had to tell? Nothing of that kind whatsoever. Europe was going on perfectly contented in its heathenism. Its millions knew of nothing that was wanting to their happiness. They were full of their business and their pleasures, scheming for little self-advancements, taking care of their families, living in their tastes or their passions; a few questioning with themselves deep problems of perplexed philosophy, a few hanging votive wreaths on the cold altars of marble gods and goddesses, some looking upward and some downward and some inward for their life; but none looking eastward to where the apostle was sleeping, or, farther east, beyond him, to where the new sun of the new religion was making the dark sky bright with promise on that silent night. So far as we can know there was not one man in Macedonia who wanted Paul. When he went over there the next day, he found what?—a few bigoted Jews, some crazy soothsayers and witches, multitudes of indifferent heathen, a few open-hearted men and women who heard and believed what he had to tell them, but not one who had believed before, or wanted to believe, — not one who met him at the ship and said, "Come, we have waited for you; we sent for you; we want your help." But what then means the man from Macedonia? If he was not the messenger of the Macedonians, who was he? Who sent him? Ah! there is just the key to it. God sent him. Not the Macedonians themselves. They did not want the gospel. God sent him, because He saw that they needed the gospel. The mysterious man was an utterance not of the conscious want but of the unconscious need of those poor people. A heart and being of them, deeper and more essential than they knew themselves, took shape in some strange method by the power of God, and came and stood before the sleeping minister and said, "Come over and help us." The "man of Macedonia" was the very heart and essence of Macedonia, the profoundest capacities of truth and goodness and faith and salvation which Macedonia itself knew nothing of, but which were its real self. These were what took form and pleaded for satisfaction. It is not easy to state it; but look at Europe as it has been since, see the new life which has come forth, the profound spirituality, the earnest faith, the thoughtful devotion, the active unselfishness which has been the Europe of succeeding days; and then we may say that this, and more than this, all that is yet to come, was what God saw lying hidden and hampered, and set free to go and beg for help and release, from the disciple who held the key which has unlocked the fetters.

And is not this a very noble and a very true idea? It is the unsatisfied soul, the deep need, all the more needy because the outside life, perfectly satisfied with itself, does not know that it is needy all the time, — it is this that God hears pleading. This soul is the true Macedonia. And so this, as the representative Macedonian, the man of Macedonia, brings the appeal. How noble and touching is the picture which this gives us of God. The unconscious needs of the world are all appeals and cries to Him. He does not wait to hear the voice of conscious want. The mere vacancy is a begging after fulness; the mere poverty is a supplication for wealth; the mere darkness cries for light. Think

then a moment of God's infinite view of the capacities
of His universe, and consider what a great cry must be
forever going up into His ears to which His soul longs
and endeavors to respond. Wherever any man is
capable of being better or wiser or purer than he is,
God hears the soul of that man crying out after the
purity and wisdom and goodness which is its right, and
of which it is being defrauded by the angry passions or
the stubborn will. When you shut out any light or
truth from your inner self, by the shutters of avarice
or indolence which your outer, superficial, worldly self
so easily slips up, — that inner self, robbed, starved,
darkened, not conscious of its want, hidden away there
under the hard surface of your worldliness, has yet a
voice which God can hear, accusing before Him your
own cruelty to yourself. What a strong piteous wail of
dissatisfaction must He hear from this world which
seems so satisfied with itself. Wherever a nation is
sunk in slavery or barbarism it cannot be so perfectly
contented with its chains but that He hears the soul of
it crying out after liberty and civilization. Wherever a
man or a body of men is given to bigotry and prejudice,
the love of darkness cannot be so complete but that He
hears the human heart begging for the light that it was
made for. Wherever lust is ruling, He hears the appeal
of a hidden, outraged purity somewhere under the foul
outside, and sends to it His help. Alas for us if God
helped us only when we knew we needed Him and went
to Him with full self-conscious wants! Alas for us if
every need which we know not, had not a voice for
Him and did not call Him to us! Did the world want
the Savior? Was it not into a blindness so dark that

it did not know that it was blind, into a wickedness so wicked that it was not looking for a Savior, that the Savior came? And when we look back can we say that we wanted the Lord who has taken us into His service and made us His children? Tell me, O Christian, was it a conscious want, — was it not the cry of a silent need, that brought the Master to your side at first and so drew you to His? "He first loved us!" Our hope is in the ear which God has for simple need; so that mere emptiness cries out to Him for filling, mere poverty for wealth.

I cannot help turning aside a moment here just to bid you think what the world would be if men were like God in this respect. Suppose that we, all of us, heard every kind of need crying to us with an appeal which we could not resist. Out of every suffering and constraint and wrong, suppose there came to us, as out of Macedonia there came to Paul, a ghost, a vision, presenting at once to us the fact of need and the possibility of what the needy man might be if the need were satisfied and the chain broken. Suppose such visions came and stood around us crying out "Help us." You go through some wretched street and not a beggar touches your robe or looks up in your face, but the bare, dreadful presence of poverty cries out of every tumbling shanty and every ragged pretence of dress. You go among the ignorant, and out from under their contented ignorance their hidden power of knowledge utters itself and says "O teach us." It is not enough for you that the oppressed are satisfied with their oppression. That only makes you the more eager to feed into consciousness and strength that hunger after liberty which they

7

are too degraded to feel.   You see a sick man contented with dogged acquiescence and submission, and you want to show him the possibility and to lead him to the realization, of a resignation and delight in suffering which he never dreams of now.   Mere pain is itself a cry for sympathy ; mere darkness an appeal for light.

"Ah," do you say, "that must be a most uncomfortable way of living.   The world forever clamoring for help !   Those things are not my mission, not my work. If the world does not know its needs I will not tell it.   Let it rest content.   That is best for it"?   But there have been, and, thank God, there are, men of a better stuff than you ; men who cannot know of a need in all the world, from the need of a child fallen in the street, whose tears are to be wiped away, to the need of a nation lying in sin, whose wickedness must be rebuked to its face at the cost of the rebuker's life ; there are men who cannot know of a need in all the world without its taking the shape of a personal appeal to them.   They must go and do this thing.   There are such men who seem to have a sort of magnetic attraction for all wrongs and pains.   All grievances and woes fly to them to be righted and consoled.   They attract need.   They who cannot sleep at Troas but the soul of Macedonia finds them out and comes across and begs them " Come and help us."   We all must be thankful to know that there are such men among us, however little we may feel that we are such men ourselves ; nay, however little we may want to be such men.

But let us come a little nearer to the truth that we are studying. It seems to me that all which we have said about the man of Macedonia includes the real state of the case with reference to the essential need of the human soul for the Gospel. We often hear of the great cry of human nature for the truth of Christ, man craving the Savior. What does it mean? The world moves on and every face looks satisfied. Eating and drinking and working and studying, loving and hating, struggling and enjoying, — those things seem to be sufficient for men's wants. There is no discontent that men will tell you of. They are not conscious of a need. I stop you, the most careless hearer in the church to-night, as you go out, and say "Are you satisfied?" and honestly you answer "Yes! My business and my family, they are enough for me"; "Do you feel any need of Christ?" and honestly you answer "No! Sometimes I fear that it will go ill with me by and by, if I do not seek Him, but at present I do not want Him; I do not see how I should be happier if I had Him here." That is about the honest answer which your heart would make. But what then? Just as below the actual Macedonia which did not care for Paul nor want him, there was another possible, ideal Macedonia which God saw and called forth and sent in a visionary form to beg the help it could not do without, so to that civil flippant answerer of my question at the church door I could say: "Below this outer self of yours which is satisfied with family and business, there is another self which you know nothing of but which God sees, which He values as your truest and deepest self, which to His sight is a real person pleading so piteously for help that

He has not been able to resist its pleading, but has sent His ministers, has sent His Bible, — nay, has come Himself to satisfy it with that spiritual aid it cannot do without." I can imagine a look of perplexity and wonder, a turning back, an inward search for this inner self, a strange, bewildered doubt whether it exists at all.

And yet, this coming forth of inner selves with their demands, is it not the one method of all progress? What does it mean when a slave, long satisfied with being fed and housed and clothed, some day comes to the knowledge that he was meant to be free, and can rest satisfied as a slave no longer? What is it when the savage's inner nature is touched by the ambition of knowledge, and he cannot rest until he grows to be a scholar? What is it when a hard, selfish man's crust is broken, and a sensitive, tender soul uncovered, which makes life a wretched thing to him from that moment, unless he has somebody besides himself to love and help and cherish? These men would not believe an hour before that such appetites and faculties were in them; but God knew them, and heard them all the time; and long before the men dreamed of it themselves, the slave was crying out to Him for freedom, and the savage for culture, and the tyrant for love. Now is it strange that, also unknown to you, there should be other appetites and faculties in you which need a satisfaction? The Bible says there are. Experience says there are. Let us see if we can find some of them.

1. The first need is a God to love and worship. Anybody who looks wisely back into history sees, I think, regarding man's need of a God to love and worship, just what I have stated to be true. Not that man was

always seeking God, or always miserable, when he did not find Him. One sees multitudes of men, and sometimes whole periods, or whole countries, that seem to have no sense of want whatever, to have settled down into the purest materialism and the most utter self-content. But he sees also indications everywhere that the need was present, even where the want was not felt. He sees the idea of God keeping a sort of persistent foothold in the human heart, which proves to him that it belongs there; that, whether the heart wants it or not, it and the heart are mates, made for one another, and so tending towards each other by a certain essential gravitation, whatever accidental causes may have tried to produce an estrangement between them. Take one such indication only, a very striking one, I think. There is in man a certain power of veneration, of awe, of adoration. This has always showed itself. In all sorts of men, in all sorts of places, it has broken out; and men have tried to adapt it to all sorts of objects, to satisfy it with all sorts of food. The idolater has offered to his faculty of reverence his wooden idol, and said "There, worship that;" the philosopher has offered it his abstract truth, and said "Venerate that;" the philanthropist has offered it his ideal humanity, and said "Worship that;" and one result has always followed. Everywhere where nothing higher than the idol, the theory, or the humanity was offered for the reverence to fasten on, everywhere where it was offered no one supreme causal God, not merely the object of reverence has ceased to be reverenced, but the very power of reverence itself has been dissipated and lost; and idolatry, philosophy, philanthropy alike have grown irreverent, and man has lost and often come to despise that faculty of venerating and submissive awe, the awe of love, for which he found no use. If this be true, that there is a faculty in man which dies out on any other food, and thrives only on the personal Deity, then have we not exactly what I tried to describe, a need of which one may be utterly unconscious, and yet which is no less a need, crying, though the man does not hear it, for supply?

This is precisely the ground which I would take with any thoughtful man who told me seriously and without flippancy that he felt no want of God, that he felt no lack in the absence of relations between his life and that of a supreme infinite Father. "Yes," I would say, "but there is in you a power of loving awe which needs infinite perfection and mercy to call it out and satisfy it. There is an affection which you cannot exercise towards any imperfect being. It is that mixture of admiration and reverence and fear and love, which we call worship. Now ask yourself, Are you not losing the power of worship? Is it not dying for want of an object? Are you not conscious that a power of the soul, which other men use, which you used once perhaps, is going from you? Are you not substituting critical, carefully limited, philosophical, partial approbations of imperfect men and things, for that absolute, unhindered, whole-souled outpouring of worship which nothing but the perfect can demand or justify? If this power is not utterly to die within you, do you not need God? If you are not to lose that highest reach of love and fear where, uniting, they make worship, must you not have God? Lo! before this expiring faculty the personal

God comes and stands, and it lifts up its dying hands to reach after Him; it opens its dying eyes to look upon Him; as when a man is perishing of starvation, the sight of bread summons him back to life. He need not die, but live, for here is his own life-food come to him."

Woe to the man who loses the faculty of worship, the faculty of honoring and loving and fearing not merely something better than himself, but something which is the absolute best, the perfect good, — his God! The life is gone out of his life when this is gone. There is a cloud upon his thought, a palsy on his action, a chill upon his love. Because you must worship, therefore you must have God.

2. But more than this. Every man needs not merely a God to worship, but also, taking the fact which meets us everywhere of an estrangement by sin between mankind and God, every man needs some power to turn him and bring him back; some reconciliation, some Reconciler, some Savior for his soul. Again I say he may not know his need, but none the less the need is there. But, if a man has reached the first want and really is desiring God, then I think he generally does know, or in some vague way suspect, this second want, and does desire reconciliation. It is so natural! Two of you, who have been friends, have quarrelled. Your very quarrel, it may be, has brought out to each of you how much you need each other. You never knew your friend was so necessary to your comfort and your happiness. You cannot do without him. Then at once, "How shall I get to him?" becomes your question. O the awkwardness and difficulty, the stumbling and shuffling and blundering of such efforts at return. Men are afraid

and ashamed to try. They do not know how they will be received. They cannot give up their old pride. Rebellious tempers and bad habits block the way. I doubt not, so frequent are they, that there are people here to-night who are stumbling about in some such bog of unsettled quarrel, longing to get back to some friend whom they value more in their disagreement than even in the old days of unbroken peace. Their whole soul is hungering for reconciliation. The misery of their separation is that each at heart desires what neither has the frankness and the courage to attain.

Now under all outward rebellion and wickedness, there is in every man who ought to be a friend of God, and that means every man whom God has made, a need of reconciliation. To get back to God, that is the struggle. The soul is Godlike and seeks its own. It wants its Father. There is an orphanage, a home-sickness of the heart which has gone up into the ear of God, and called the Savior, the Reconciler, to meet it by His wondrous life and death. I, for my part, love to see in every restlessness of man's moral life everywhere, whatever forms it takes, the struggles of this imprisoned desire. The reason may be rebellious, and vehemently cast aside the whole story of the New Testament, but the soul is never wholly at its rest away from God. Does this not put it most impressively before us? Is it not something at least to startle us and make us think, if we come to know that the very God of heaven saw a want, a struggle, a longing of our souls after Himself, which was too deep, too obscure, too clouded over with other interests for even us to see ourselves, and came to meet that want with the wonderful mani-

festation of the incarnation, the atonement? We hear
of the marvellous power of the Gospel, and we come to
doubt it when we see the multitudes of unsaved men.
But it is true. The Gospel is powerful, omnipotent. A
truth like this, thoroughly believed, and taken in, must
melt the hardest heart and break down the most stubborn will. It does not save men, simply because it is
not taken in, not believed. The Gospel is powerless,
just as the medicine that you keep corked in its vial on
the shelf is powerless. If you will not take it, what
matters it what marvellous drugs have lent their subtle
virtues to it? Believe and thou art saved. Understand
and know, and thoroughly take home into your affection and your will, the certain truth that Christ saw
your need of Him when you did not know it yourself,
and came to help you at a cost past all calculation, —
really believe this and you must be a new man and be
saved.

3. I should like to point out another of the needs
of man which God has heard appealing to Him and has
satisfied completely. I know that I must speak about it
very briefly. It is the need of spiritual guidance ; and it
is a need whose utterance not God's ear alone can hear.
Every man hears it in the race at large, and hears it
in his brethren, however deaf he may be to it in himself.
I think there never was a materialist so complete that
he did not realize that the great mass of men were not
materialists, but believed in spiritual forces and longed
for spiritual companies. He might think the spiritual
tendency the wildest of delusions, but he could not
doubt its prevalence. How could he? Here is the
whole earth full of it. Language is all shaped upon it.

Thought is all saturated with it. In the most imposing and the most vulgar methods, by solemn oracles and rocking tables, men have been always trying to put themselves into communication with the spiritual world and to get counsel and help from within the vail. And if we hear the cry from one another, how much more God hears it. Do you think, poor stumbler, that God did not know it when you found no man to tell you what you ought to do in a perplexity which, as it rose around you, seemed, as it was, unlike any bewilderment that had ever puzzled any man before? Do you think, poor sufferer, that God did not hear it when in your sickness and pain men came about you with their kindness, fed you with delicacies, and spread soft cushions under the tortured body, and all the time the mind diseased, feeling so bitterly that these tender cares for the body's comfort did not begin to touch its spiritual pain, lay moaning and wailing out its hopeless woe? Do you think now, my brother, when you have got a hard duty to do, a hard temptation to resist; when you have felt all about you for strength, called in prudence and custom and respectability and interest to keep you straight, and found them all fail because, by their very nature, they have no spiritual strength to give; when now you stand just ready to give way and fall, ready to go to-morrow morning and do the wrong thing that you have struggled against so long, — do you think that God does not know it all, and does not hear the poor frightened soul's cry for help against the outrage that is threatening her, and has not prepared a way of aid? The power of the Holy Spirit!—an everlasting spiritual presence among men. What but that is the thing we want? That is what the old oracles were dreaming of, what the modern spiritualists to-night are fumbling after. The power of the Holy Ghost by which every man who is in doubt may know what is right, every man whose soul is sick may be made spiritually whole, every weak man may be made a strong man, — that is God's one sufficient answer to the endless appeal of man's spiritual life; that is God's one great response to the unconscious need of spiritual guidance, which he hears crying out of the deep heart of every man.

I hope that I have made clear to you what I mean. I would that we might understand ourselves, see what we might be; nay, see what we are. While you are living a worldly and a wicked life, letting all sacred things go, caring for no duty, serving no God, there is another self, your possibility, the thing that you might be, the thing that God gave you a chance to be; and that self, wronged and trampled on by your recklessness, escapes and flies to God with its appeal: — "O, come and help me. I am dying. I am dying. Give me Thyself for Father. Give me Thy Son for Savior. Give me Thy Spirit for my guide." So your soul pleads before God; pleads with a pathos all the more piteous in his ears, because you do not hear the plea yourself; pleads with such sacred prevalence that the great merciful Heart yields and gives all that the dumb appeal has asked.

What does it mean? Here is the Gospel in its fulness. Here is God for you to worship. Here is Christ to save you. Here is the Comforter. Have you asked for them, my poor careless brother, that here they stand with such profusion of blessing, waiting to help you? "Ah, no," you say, "I never asked." Suppose, when Paul landed in Macedonia, he had turned to the careless group who watched him as he stepped ashore, and said, "Here am I; you sent for me. Here am I with the truth, the Christ you need," — what must their answer have been? "O, no, you are mistaken; we never sent; we do not know you; we do not want you!" Yet they had sent. Their needs had stood and begged him to come over, out of the lips of that mysterious man of Macedonia. And when they came to know this, they must have found all the more precious the preciousness of a gospel which had come to them in answer to a need they did not know themselves.

And so your needs have stood, they are standing now before God. They have moved Him to deep pity and care for you. And He has sent the supply for them before you knew you wanted it. And here it is, — a God to worship, a Savior to believe in, a Comforter to rest upon. O, if you ever do come, as I would to God that you might come to-night, to take this mercy, and let your thirsty soul drink of this water of life! then you will feel most deeply the goodness which provided for you before you even knew that you needed any such provision; then you will understand those words of Paul: "God commendeth His love toward us, in that while we were yet sinners Christ died for us."

Till that time comes, what can God do but stand and call you and warn you and beg you to know yourself. "Because thou sayest, I am rich and increased with goods, and have need of nothing, and knowest not that thou art wretched and miserable and. poor and blind and naked, I counsel thee to buy of Me gold tried in the fire, that thou mayest be rich. Behold, I stand at the door and knock. If any man hear My voice, and open the door, I will come in and sup with him, and he with Me."

VII.

THE SYMMETRY OF LIFE.

"The Length and the Breadth and the Height of it are equal." —
REV. xxi. 16.

ST. JOHN in his great vision sees the mystic city,
"the holy Jerusalem," descending out of heaven from
God. It is the picture of glorified humanity, of humanity as it shall be when it is brought to its completeness
by being thoroughly filled with God. And one of the
glories of the city which he saw was its symmetry.
Our cities, our developments and presentations of
human life, are partial and one-sided. This city out of
heaven was symmetrical. In all its three dimensions it
was complete. Neither was sacrificed to the other.
"The length and the breadth and the height of it are
equal."

No man can say what mysteries of the yet unopened
future are hidden in the picture of the mystic city;
but if that city represents, as I have said, the glorified
humanity, then there is much of it that we can understand already. It declares that the perfect life of man
will be perfect on every side. One token of its perfectness will be its symmetry. In each of its three dimensions it will be complete.

So much of the noblest life which the world has seen
dissatisfies us with its partialness; so many of the

greatest men we see are great only upon certain sides, and have their other sides all shrunken, flat, and small, that it may be well for us to dwell upon the picture, which these words suggest, of a humanity rich and full and strong all round, complete on every side, the perfect cube of human life which comes down out of heaven from God.

As I speak I should like to keep before my mind and before yours, that picture which I think is the most interesting that the world has to show, the picture of a young man, brave and strong and generous, just starting out into life, and meaning with all his might to be the very best and most perfect man he can ; meaning to make life the fullest and most genuine success. Let us see him before us as I speak. We shall see how natural his dangers and temptations are ; we shall see how his very strength tends to partialness ; we shall see how every power that is in him will grow doubly strong if he can buttress and steady it with strength upon the other sides, if in his growing character he can attain the symmetry and completeness of the new Jerusalem.

There are, then, three directions or dimensions of human life to which we may fitly give these three names, Length and Breadth and Height. The Length of a life, in this meaning of it, is, of course, not its duration. It is rather the reaching on and out of a man, in the line of activity and thought and self-development, which is indicated and prophesied by the character which is natural within him, by the special ambitions which spring up out of his special powers. It is the push of a life forward to its own personal ends and ambitions. The Breadth of a life, on the other hand, is

its outreach laterally, if we may say so. It is the
constantly diffusive tendency which is always drawing
a man outward into sympathy with other men. And
the Height of a life is its reach upward towards God ; its
sense of childhood ; its consciousness of the Divine Life .
over it with which it tries to live in love, communion,
and obedience. These are the three dimensions of a
life, — its length and breadth and height, — without the
due development of all of which no life becomes
complete.

Think first about the Length of life in this understanding of the word. Here is a man who, as he comes to
self-consciousness, recognizes in himself a certain nature.
He cannot be mistaken. Other men have their special
powers and dispositions. As this young man studies
himself he finds that he has his. That nature which he
has discovered in himself decides for him his career.
He says to himself " Whatever I am to do in the world
must be done in this direction." It is a fascinating
discovery. It is an ever-memorable time for a man
when he first makes it. It is almost as if a star woke
to some subtle knowledge of itself, and felt within its
shining frame the forces which decided what its orbit
was to be. Because it is the star it is, that track
through space must be its track. Out on that track
it looks ; along that line which sweeps through the
great host of stars it sends out all its hopes ; and
all the rest of space is merely the field through which
that track is flung ; all the great host of stars is but the
audience which wait to hear it as it goes singing on its
way. So starts the young life which has come to self-
discovery and found out what it is to do by finding out

what it is. It starts to do that destined thing; to run out that appointed course. Nay, the man when he arrives at this self-discovery finds that his nature has not waited for him to recognize himself. What he is, even before he knows it, has decided what he does. It may be late in life before he learns to say of himself "This is what I am." But then he looks back and discerns that, even without his knowing himself enough to have found it out, his life has run out in a line which had the promise and potency of its direction in the nature which his birth and education gave him. But if he does know it, the course is yet more definite and clear. Every act that he does is a new section of that line which runs between his nature and his appointed work. Just in proportion to the definiteness with which he has measured and understood himself, is the sharpness of that line which every thought and act and word is projecting a little farther, through the host of human lives, towards the purpose of his living, towards the thing which he believes that he is set into the world to do.

Your own experience will tell you what I mean. Have you known any young man who early found-out what his nature was; found out, for instance, that he had a legal mind and character? He said to himself "I am made to be a lawyer." Instantly with that discovery it was as if two points stood out clearly to him; he with his legal nature here; the full, completed lawyer's work and fame afar off there. Two unconnected points they seemed at first, which simply beckoned to each other across the great distance, and knew that, however unconnected they might be, they had to do with one another and must ultimately meet. Then

8

that man's life became one long extension of his nature
and his powers and his will along a line which should
at last attain that distant goal. All his self-culture
strove that way. He read no book, he sought no
friend, he gave himself no recreation, which was not
somehow going to help him to his end and make him a
better lawyer. Through the confusion and whirl of
human lives, his life ran in one sharp, narrow line,
almost as straight and clear as the railroad track across
a continent, from what he knew he was, to what he
meant to be and do. As the railroad track sweeps
through the towns which string themselves along it,
climbs mountains and plunges into valleys, hides itself
in forests and flashes out again into broad plains and
along the sunny sides of happy lakes, and evidently
cares nothing for them all except as they just give it
ground on which to roll out its length towards its end
by the shore of the Pacific, — so this man's life pierces
right on through all the tempting and perplexing complications of our human living, and will not rest until
it has attained the mastery of legal power. That clear,
straight line of its unswerving intention, that struggle
and push right onward to the end, — that is the length
of this man's life.

And if you recognize this, as of course you do, then
you know also how necessary an element or dimension
of any useful and successful life this is. To have an
end and seek it eagerly, no man does anything in the
world without that. If we let our thoughts leap at once
to the summit of human living, and think of Jesus, we
see it in perfection. The onward reach, the struggle to
an apprehended purpose, the straight clear line right

from His own self-knowledge to His work, was perfect in the Lord. " For this cause was I born," He cried. His life pierced like an arrow through the cloud of aimless lives, never for a moment losing its direction, hurrying on with a haste and assurance which were divine. And this which He illustrates perfectly is, in our own fashion, one of the favorite thoughts of our own time. No man finds less tolerance to-day than the aimless man, the man whose life lies and swings like a pool, instead of flowing straight onward like a river. We revel in the making of specialists. Often it seems as if the more narrow and straight we could make the line which runs between the nature and its work, the more beautiful we thought it. We make our boys choose their electives when they go to college, decide at once on what they mean to do, and pour all the stream of knowledge down the sluiceway which leads to that one wheel. Perhaps we overdo it, but no thinking man dreams of saying that the thing itself is wrong. This movement of a man's whole life along some clearly apprehended line of self-development and self-accomplishment, this reaching of a life out forward to its own best attainment, no man can live as a man ought to live without it. The men who have no purpose, the men in whose life this first dimension of length is wanting or is very weak, are good for nothing. They lie in the world like mere pulpy masses, giving it no strength or interest or character.

Set yourself earnestly to see what you were made to do, and then set yourself earnestly to do it. That is the first thing that we want to say to our young man in the building of whose life we feel an interest. As we say it we feel almost a hesitation, it may be, because the exhortation sounds so selfish. Self-study and self-culture, surely that makes a very selfish life. Indeed it does. But he has thought very little who has not discovered two things concerning selfishness. First, that there is a lofty selfishness, a high care for our own culture, which is a duty, and not a fault. And secondly, that he who in this highest way cares for himself and seeks for himself his own best good, must, whether he thinks of doing it or not, help other men's development as well as his own. It is only the line which is seeking something that is low, that can pierce through the live mass of men's lives and interests and be as wholly independent of them all as I pictured just now. Even the railroad track, hurrying to the Pacific, must leave something of civilizing influence on the prairies which it crosses. In the highest and purest sense of the word there certainly was selfishness in Jesus. No man might tempt or force Him from the resolute determination to unfold His appointed life and be His perfect self. The world is right when it follows its blind instinct and stands, with some kind of gratitude though not a gratitude of the most loving sort, beside the grave of some man who in life has been loftily possessed with the passion for self-culture, and has never thought of benefiting the world ; for if his passion for self-culture has really been of the most lofty kind, the world must be the better for it.

Therefore we may freely say to any young man, Find your purpose and fling your life out to it ; and the loftier your purpose is, the more sure you will be to make the world richer with every enrichment of yourself. And

this, you see, comes to the same thing as saying that
this first dimension of life, which we call Length, the
more loftily it is sought, has always a tendency to produce the second dimension of life, which we called
Breadth. Of that second dimension let us go on now to
speak. I have ventured to call this quality of breadth
in a man's life its outreach laterally. When that tendency of which I have just been talking, the tendency
of a man's career, the more loftily it is pursued, to bring
him into sympathy and relationship with other men,
— when that tendency, I say, is consciously and deliberately acknowledged, and a man comes to value his
own personal career because of the way in which it re-
lates him to his brethren and the help which it permits
him to offer them, then his life has distinctly begun to
open in this new direction, and to its length it has added
breadth. There are men enough with whom no such
opening seems to take place. You know them well;
men eager, earnest, and intense, reaching forward toward
their prize, living straight onward in their clearly apprehended line of life; but to all appearance, so far as you
and I can see, living exactly as they would live if they
were the only living beings on the surface of the earth,
or as if all the other beings with whom they came
in contact were only like the wooden rounds upon the
ladder by which they climbed to their own personal
ambition. Such men you have all known; men who
could not conceive of any other life as valuable, happy,
or respectable, except their own; men " wrapped up in
themselves," as we say,— an envelope as thick as leather,
through which no pressure of any other life or character
could reach them. And the one feeling that you have

about such perfect specialists is the wonder that so great intelligence can be compressed into such narrowness. They are as bright and sharp as needles, and as hard and narrow.

But when a man has length and breadth of life together, we feel at once how the two help each other. Length without breadth is hard and narrow. Breadth without length,—sympathy with others in a man who has no intense and clear direction for himself, — is soft and weak. You see this in the instinctive and strong dislike which all men have for the professional reformer and philanthropist. The world dislikes a man who, with no definite occupation of his own, not trying to be anything particular himself, devotes himself to telling other people what they ought to be. It may allow his good intentions, but it will not feel his influence. The man whom the world delights to feel is the man who has evidently conceived some strong and distinct purpose for himself, from which he will allow nothing to turn his feet aside, who means to be something with all his soul; and yet who finds, in his own earnest effort to fill out his own career, the interpretation of the careers of other men; and also finds, in sympathy with other men, the transfiguration and sustainment of his own appointed struggle.

Indeed these are the two ways in which the relation between the length and breadth of a man's life, between his energy in his own career and his sympathy with the careers of other men, comes out and shows itself. First, the man's own career becomes to him the interpretation of the careers of other men; and secondly, by his sympathy with other men, his own life displays to him its best capacity. The first of these is very beautiful to watch. Imagine the reformer, whom I spoke of, suddenly called to forget the work of helping other men, and to plunge into some work of his own. With what surprise at his own increase of wisdom he would come back, by and by, to the help of his brethren! What far wiser and more reverent hands he would lay upon their lives; with what tones of deepened understanding he would speak to their needs and sins and temptations, after he had himself tried to live a true life of his own! This is the reason, I suppose, why, in the Bible, the ministry of angels to mankind, while it is clearly intimated, is made so little of. It is because, however real it is, it could not be brought very close to the intelligence and gratitude of men, so long as the personal lives of the angels are hidden in mystery. Only he who lives a life of his own can help the lives of other men. Surely there is here one of the simplest and strongest views which a man possibly can take of his own life. "Let me live," he may say, "as fully as I can, in order that in this life of mine I may learn what life really is, and so be fit to understand and help the lives of men about me. Let me make my own career as vivid and successful as possible, that in it I may get at the secret of life, which, when I have once found it, will surely be the key to other lives besides my own." He who should talk and think so of his own career would evidently have gone far towards solving the problem of the apparent incompatibility between intense devotion to one's own pursuit and cordial sympathy with other men. He would find, in the very heart of his own work, the clew to the works of other men. He

would be no mere specialist, and yet he would toil
hardest of all men in the special task in which he was
engaged.   But his task would be always glorified and
kept from narrowness by his perpetual demand upon it,
that it should give him such a broad understanding of
human life in general as should make him fit to read
and touch and help all other kinds of life.

And if thus the special life does much to make the
sympathy with other lives intelligent and strong, the
debt is yet not wholly on one side.   There is a wonderful power in sympathy to open and display the hidden
richness of a man's own seemingly narrow life.   You
think that God has been training you in one sort of discipline, but when you let yourself go out in sympathy
with other men whose disciplines have been completely
different from your own, you find that in your discipline
the power of theirs was hidden.   This is the power
which sympathy has to multiply life and make out of
one experience the substance and value of a hundred.
The well man sympathizes with the sick man, and
thereby exchanges, as it were, some of the superfluous
riches of his health into the other coin of sickness, gets
something of the culture which would have come to him
if he had himself been sick.   The sick man, in return,
gets something, even in all his pain and weakness, of
the discipline of health and strength.   The same is true
about the sympathy of the rich with the poor, of the
believer with the doubter, of the hopeful with the de-
spondent, of the liberal with the bigoted; aye, even of
the saint with the sinner.   The holiest soul, pitying the
brother-soul which has fallen into vilest vice, gains,
while it keeps its own purity unsoiled, something of the

sight of that other side of God, the side where justice and forgiveness blend in the opal mystery of grace, which it would seem as if only the soul that looked up out of the depths of guilt could see. All this is perfect in the vicariousness of Christ; and what was perfect there, is echoed imperfectly in the way in which every man's special life becomes enlarged and multiplied as he looks abroad from it in sympathy with other men.

So much I say about the length and breadth of life. One other dimension still remains. The length and breadth and height of it are equal. The Height of life is its reach upward toward something distinctly greater than humanity. Evidently all that I have yet described, all the length and breadth of life, might exist, and yet man be a creature wholly of the earth. He might move on straight forward in his own career. He might even enter into living sympathy with his brother-men; and yet never look up, never seem to have anything to do with anything above this flat and level plain of human life. A world without a sky! How near any one man's life here and there may come to that, I dare not undertake to say. Some men will earnestly insist that that is just their life; that there is no divine appetite, no reaching Godward in them anywhere. But to a man who thoroughly believes in God, I think that it will always seem that such a life, however any man may think that he is living it, must always be impossible for every man. There cannot be a God and yet any one of His creatures live exactly and entirely as if there was no God.

The reaching of mankind towards God! Evidently, in order that that may become a true dimension of a man's life, it must not be a special action. It must be something which pervades all that he is and does. It must not be a solitary column set on one holy spot of the nature. It must be a movement of the whole nature upward. Here has been one of the great hinderances of the power of religion in the world. Religion has been treated as if it were a special exercise of a special power, not as if it were the possible loftiness of everything that a man could think or be or do. The result has been that certain men and certain parts of men have stood forth as distinctively religious, and that the possible religiousness of all life has been but very imperfectly felt and acknowledged. This has made religion weak. Man's strongest powers, man's intensest passions, have been involved in the working out of his career, and in the development of his relations with his fellow-men. What has been left over for religion has been the weakest part of him, his sentiments and fears; and so religion, very often, has come to seem a thing of mystic moods and frightened superstitions. This picture from the city of the Revelation seems to me to make the matter very clear. The height of life, its reach toward God, must be coextensive with, must be part of the one same symmetrical whole with, the length of life or its reach towards its personal ambition, and the breadth of life or its reach towards the sympathy of brother-lives. It is when a man begins to know the ambition of his life not simply as the choice of his own will but as the wise assignment of God's love; and to know his relations to his brethren not simply as the result of his own impulsive affections but as the seeking of his soul for these souls because they all belong to the great Father-soul; it is then that life for that man begins to lift itself all over and to grow towards completion upward through all its length and breadth. That is a noble time, a bewildering and exalting time in any of our lives, when into everything that we are doing enters the spirit of God, and thenceforth moving ever up toward the God to whom it belongs, that Spirit, dwelling in our life, carries our life up with it; not separating our life from the earth, but making every part of it while it still keeps its hold on earth, soar up and have to do with heaven; so completing life in its height, by making it divine.

To any man in whom that uplifting of life has genuinely begun, all life without it must seem very flat and poor. My dear friends, this is Advent Sunday. Once more wrought into all our service, pressed into all our hearts, has come to-day the rich, wonderful truth that God once came into our world. And that one coming of God we know gets its great value from being the type and promise of the truth that God is always coming. And for God to come into the world means for Him to come into our lives. On Advent Sunday, then, let us get close hold of this truth. These lives of ours, hurrying on in their ambitions, spreading out in their loves, they are capable of being filled with God, possessed by His love, eager after His communion; and, if they can be, if they are, then, without losing their eager pursuit of their appointed task, without losing their cordial reaching after the lives around them, they shall be quietly, steadily, nobly lifted into something of the peace and dignity of the God whom they aspire to. The fret and restlessness shall fade out of their ambitions; the jealousy shall disappear out of their loves. Love for themselves and love for their brethren, robed and enfolded into the love for God, shall be purified and cleared of all meanness, shall be filled with a strength as calm as it is strong. O, my dear friends, there is room for that new dimension over the lives that all of you are living. Above the head of the most earthly of you heaven is open. You may aspire into it and complete yourself upward if you will. All that you are now imperfectly, as an energetic, sympathetic man, you may be perfectly as the child of God, knowing your Father and living in consecrated obedience to Him.

These are the three dimensions then of a full human life, its length, its breadth, its height. The life which has only length, only intensity of ambition, is narrow. The life that has length and breadth, intense ambition and broad humanity, is thin. It is like a great, flat plain, of which one wearies, and which sooner or later wearies of itself. The life which to its length and breadth adds height, which to its personal ambition and sympathy with man, adds the love and obedience of God, completes itself into the cube of the eternal city and is the life complete.

Think for a moment of the life of the great apostle, the manly, many-sided Paul. "I press toward the mark for the prize of my high calling;" he writes to the Philippians. That is the length of life for him. "I will gladly spend and be spent for you;" he writes to the Corinthians. There is the breadth of life for him. "God hath raised us up and made us sit together in heavenly places in Christ Jesus;" he writes

to the Ephesians. There is the height of life for him.
You can add nothing to these three dimensions when
you try to account to yourself for the impression of
completeness which comes to you out of his simple,
lofty story.

We need not stop with him. Look at the Lord
of Paul. See how in Christ the same symmetrical
manhood shines yet more complete. See what intense
ambition to complete His work, what tender sympathy
with every struggling brother by His side, and at the
same time what a perpetual dependence on His Father
is in Him. "For this cause came I into the world."
"For their sakes I sanctify myself." "Now, O Father,
glorify Thou me." Leave either of those out and you
have not the perfect Christ, not the entire symmetry of
manhood.

If we try to gather into shape some picture of what
the perfect man of heaven is to be, still we must keep
the symmetry of these his three dimensions. It must
be that forever before each glorified spirit in the other
life there shall be set one goal of peculiar ambition, his
goal, after which he is peculiarly to strive, the struggle
after which is to make his eternal life to be forever
different from every other among all the hosts of
heaven. And yet it must be that as each soul strives
towards his own attainment he shall be knit forever
into closer and closer union with all the other countless
souls which are striving after theirs. And the inspiring
power of it all, the source of all the energy and all the
love, must then be clear beyond all doubt; the ceaseless
flood of light forever pouring forth from the self-living
God to fill and feed the open lives of His redeemed who

live by Him. There is the symmetry of manhood perfect. There, in redeemed and glorified human nature, is the true heavenly Jerusalem.

I hope that we are all striving and praying now that we may come to some such symmetrical completeness. This is the glory of a young man's life. Do not dare to live without some clear intention toward which your living shall be bent. Mean to be something with all your might. Do not add act to act and day to day in perfect thoughtlessness, never asking yourself whither the growing line is leading. But at the same time do not dare to be so absorbed in your own life, so wrapped up in listening to the sound of your own hurrying wheels, that all this vast pathetic music, made up of the mingled joy and sorrow of your fellow-men, shall not find out your heart and claim it and make you rejoice to give yourself for them. And yet, all the while, keep the upward windows open. Do not dare to think that a child of God can worthily work out his career or worthily serve God's other children unless he does both in the love and fear of God their Father. Be sure that ambition and charity will both grow mean unless they are both inspired and exalted by religion. Energy, love, and faith, those make the perfect man. And Christ, who is the perfectness of all of them, gives them all three to any young man who, at the very outset of his life, gives up himself to Him. If this morning there is any young man here who generously wants to live a whole life, wants to complete himself on every side, to him Christ, the Lord, stands ready to give these three, energy, love, and faith, and to train them in him all together, till they make in him the perfect man.

VIII.

HOW MANY LOAVES HAVE YE?

"And Jesus said unto them, How many loaves have ye?"—
MATT. xv. 34.

It was one of the miracles of Jesus in which His
nature was seen most interestingly. A multitude of
people had followed him into the country, anxious to
hear Him preach, some of them also needing and
expecting that He would cure their sicknesses. They
had lingered with Him for three days, not finding it in
their hearts to leave Him and return, until their food
was all exhausted and they were in wretched plight.
Then Jesus declared His pity for them and consulted
with His disciples. "I have compassion on the multitude," He said, "because they continue with Me now
three days and have nothing to eat, and I will not send
them away fasting lest they faint in the way." And
His disciples reminded Him how impossible it was to
buy any food off in the desert where they were; and
then Jesus, intending to relieve the people's wants by
extraordinary power, turned to His disciples and asked
them how many loaves of bread they had. They told
Him seven, and a few little fishes. And He took the
little which they had and blessed it, and it became under
His blessing abundant for the supply of all the crowd.

Such is the story. The need of the great, hungry

host before Him touches the Lord and makes Him use
His power to relieve them. But what is striking in the
narrative is this, that when Jesus is moved by their
suffering, He is moved in all His nature. Every part
of Him is stirred. Not merely His emotions and His
impulses, so that He is eager to relieve at once the
wretchedness which looks up to Him out of their famished
eyes, but His wisdom is stirred. All the principles of
His life' start into action together, all His care and
pity. His care and pity for the soul as well as for the
body move at once. It is this completeness of His
nature, the way in which it is all one, and works
and lives as one, that makes Him often so very different from us. Our lives are disjointed. One part of us
works at a time. It is hard for us to be brave and
prudent together ; hard for us to be liberal and just at
the same time. Our sympathy is excited, and we help
a man often in a way that does more harm than good,
because we help with only one hand, with only half
our nature ; with our pity but not with our wisdom ;
with care for his hunger but with no care for his self-
respect and manliness. But when Christ helps a man
His whole nature in complete balance moves upon that
other life. He feels all its claims and needs in their
just proportion. So He meets Nicodemus in the midnight chamber, and the young man who comes to Him
in the temple, and Thomas after the resurrection.

Now in this miracle of Jesus which I have recalled
to you there is a meeting of generosity and frugality
which is striking and suggestive. These two things
do meet indeed with us. We try to be generous and
frugal at the same time, but the result in us is mean.

We try to give and yet to save. We try to satisfy the instinct which makes us want to aid our brethren, and at the same time not to disappoint the instinct which makes us want to save and spare the things we have. But the result in us is mean. When Christ unites generosity and frugality the result in Him is noble. We feel His pity and care for the poor people a great deal more when we see Him take the wretched little stock of food which they possessed into His hands and make that the basis of His bounty, than if with an easy sweep of His hand He had bid the skies open and rain manna and quails once more upon the hungry host. His generosity is emphasized for us by its frugal methods, and His frugality is dignified by its generous purpose.

But surely the act is a very striking one. Here was He who could do everything. What hindered Him from sweeping the loaves they had aside and, by a superb exercise of power, bidding the very desert where they stood burst into a wilderness of fruits, break its hard ground with orchard trees all grown and laden, with streams of sweet water running down between them. But no ! He brings out the poor remnant which was so little and so miserable that they had thought nothing of it. He has to ask for it. They do not offer it. He says "How many loaves have ye ?" and they seem to answer "Here is this, but what is this good for ?" Then He takes that and multiplies it into all they need. It seems as if there were two principles here, so fundamental that the divine power of Jesus worked by them almost of necessity, so important that they must be made prominent even in all His impetuous eagerness to help those starving men. The first is the

9

principle of continuity, that what is to be must come
out of what has been, that new things must come to be
by an enlargement, a development, a change and growth
of old things; and the second is the principle of economy, that nothing however little or poor is to be wasted.
They are two simple principles. I want to trace with
you to-day the way in which they run through many
departments of life. But notice, first, how clearly they
stand out here in the miracle.

There are two ideas which belong to the notion of
vast power in our crude conceptions of it. One is
spasmodicalness and the other is waste. It is strange
how both of these ideas appear in all men's first conceptions of the supernatural and of omnipotence. The
first notions of a Deity are of One who is above all law
and order and economy. Let the poor be niggardly, a
slave to rules, counting over his little stock, squeezing
every penny that he pays; but let the All-Powerful be
open-handed, counting as nothing what other beings
must save, originating life whenever life is needed, full
of an easy spontaneity, flinging the miracles of creation
everywhere. But it is striking to see how as men go
on and learn more of God, these ideas which were at
first cast almost indignantly out of their conception of
Him, gradually come back and are set in the place of
highest honor. It is God's highest glory that He is a
God of law. Continuousness is the crown of His government. That He brings every future out of some
past is the charm of all His government. That He
lets nothing go to waste is the highest perfection of
His boundless resource. This is the highest knowledge
of God. Continuity and economy are His solemn foot-

prints by which we trace His presence in our world. The need of evolution, the necessity that everything which is to be should come out of something which has been before, and the abhorrence of waste, — continuity and economy, — these are the proof-marks of Divinity.

Let us remember, first, how these two principles are stamped on all the operations of nature. We are all learning more and more, to some people's dismay, to other people's joy and inspiration, how nature loves to develop, how rare the acts of real creation are. The farmer goes and stands among rich western fields, and they cry out to him, "Give us seed and we will give you back a harvest that shall bewilder you with its immensity. There is no end to what we can do if you give us seed, but without seed we can do nothing." You go to Nature and say, "Feed me or I shall starve;" and her question comes back to you, "How many loaves have you? Give me something to begin with, however little it may be." Drop the old remnants of a past life into the ever fruitful soil, and all the possibilities of new life open. The spring-time finds last summer's roots still remaining in the ground, and quickens them to life again, and multiplies them into a richer summer still. Ingenious Nature finds a germ wherever it is dropped; but without the germ she will do nothing. Mere spontaneity she disowns and disproves more and more. Think what a place the world would be to live in if this were not so, if nature were a wizard, fitful and whimsical, doing her wonders in no sequel or connection with each other, with her pets and favorites, instead of being, as she is, a mother with her great, wise, reasonable laws of the house which press alike on all her

children, which no one of the children thinks of seeing
changed or violated.   That is what makes the world
such a good home for man to dwell in, his school-
room and his home at once.   If anywhere in all the
world it were on certain record, past all doubt, that just
one solitary field, hidden away in some remote valley,
had burst into a harvest of corn without a seed of corn
having been sown in it by design or accident, that one
freak of spontaneousness must work great harm among
mankind.   Men enough there are who would make that
fact their one fact in natural science, and, disregarding
the million fields which gave no harvest except in answer
to seed, would go looking for the second field that was
to give its crop for nothing; as when one man has found
a pot of gold, a hundred more forget that gold, by the
world's great general law, is earned, not found, and so
go digging where they have buried nothing, seeking a
prize that is not there.   It is the continuity of life, the
continuity of nature, that is our salvation.   " Nothing
from nothing " is the first law of her household, and her
dullest children must learn it, for it is written on the
walls that shelter them, on the ground they tread, on
the table from which they eat, and on the tools with
which they work.

And her law of economy is just as clear.   Profusion,
but no waste ; this is the lesson that nature reads us
everywhere.   The dead leaves of this autumn are worked
into next year's soil.   The little stream that has watered
the greenness of many meadows goes afterwards to do
duty in the great sea.   The vast surrounding atmosphere
is made efficient over and over again for the breath of
living men.   Everywhere profusion, but no waste.   For

men who need to be trained to reasonableness and care,
God has built just the home they needed for their training, and sent us to live in this star which shines among
His other stars steadily and soberly with its double
light of continuity and economy.

The same truth appears in the use which God makes
of men in the world. One of the most interesting
studies of history is to see how unspasmodic is the appearance of great men. They are not accidents. Their
lives are not isolated unaccountable meteors. However
little it may be seen at the time of their lives, those who
live after them, and look back over the ranges of history,
can sée that the heroes and great men are the culmina-
tion and reşult of processes. The times in which they
live, the smaller men who have gone before them, are
necessary to make them what they come to be. If it
were not so, such lives might be expected to start forth
indiscriminately everywhere, in all ages alike, in all
stages and kinds of civilization. But barbarism is a flat
level of monotony ; and certain artificial periods of culture are barren of all greatness. The personal element
in the hero must be recognized. No age or circumstances can make a great man of a little one. But still
all history bears witness that when God means to make
a great man, He puts the circumstances of the world and
the lives of lesser men under tribute. He does not fling
His hero like an aërolite out of the sky. He bids him
grow like an oak out of the earth. All earnest, pure,
unselfish, faithful men who have lived their obscure
lives well, have helped to make him. God has let none
of them be wasted. A thousand unrecorded patriots
helped to make Washington ; a thousand lovers of

liberty contributed to Lincoln.   It is the continuity and
economy of human life.   The great feast grows out of
the few loaves and fishes.   And any man who in his
small degree is living like the child of God, has a right
to all the comfort of knowing that God will not let his
life be lost, but will use it in the making of some great
child of God, as he used centuries of Jewish lives,
prophets, priests, patriots, kings, peasants, women, children, to make the human life of His Incarnate Son.

The same is true of truths, as well as of men.   All the
history of the progress of men's thought bears witness
that when God wants to give men knowledge which
they have not had before, He always opens it to them
out of something which they have already known.
There is no such thing as the dropping of a great truth
any more than of a great man, suddenly, ready-made,
out of the sky.   " How is it with Revelation ?   How is
it with Christianity ? " you say.   There, more than anywhere, it certainly is true that God works continuously
and economically.   What does Judaism mean ?   When
God wanted to give the world the truth of Christ, He
took that Hebrew nation which had some truth, truth
of the right sort, though it was very meagre and in-
sufficient, and mixed up with other things which were
not true ; He took that truth and brought Christianity
out of that.   And so when He has wanted to bring His
Christianity, His highest truth, into any new region, He
has always made it appear as the fulfilment, the completion, of what the people of that region knew already.
Paul stands upon Mars' Hill at Athens, and wants to
show those people Christ.   How does he begin ?   He
takes what he finds there.   He points to their altar to

the unknown god, and says, " Him whom ye ignorantly
worship I declare to you." He opens the books of their
own writers and finds there his text, " As certain of
your own poets have said." Out of their bit of truth he
opens the rich completeness of the truth he has to tell.
Is it not just exactly the miracle of Christ ? Paul comes
and says to Athens, " How many loaves have you ?"
and they say, " Seven, and a few little fishes. We
believe in God ; we believe in responsibility ; we believe
in man's childhood to God ; we believe in worship."
And there, upon the Areopagus, Paul did what His
Master did long before, by the Sea of Galilee; " He took
the seven loaves and the fishes, and gave thanks, and
brake them and gave to the multitude ; and they did all
eat and were filled."

And so it always is. There is a doctrine which we
hear from time to time, that it is not the amount of truth
which a man knows, but his earnestness in holding
what he does know; not his opinions, but his sincerity
in holding his opinions, which is of value. That seems
to me after all to be probably only a clumsy way of
getting hold of this idea, that God always brings new
truth out of old truth, and so that whoever has any bit
of truth and really holds it fast is within the possibility
of all the truth that God can give to man. There is no
spontaneous generation of truth. " To him that hath
shall be given." It seems to me that there is a great
deal of light here of just the sort which a great many
people need now. Men look around them and they say
that old systems of religious thought are changing.
Certainly they are. They always have been changing.
There never was a time when they stood still. There

is no delusion about history more complete than to
suppose that there has ever been a time when, from year
to year and over a large body of mankind, religious
ideas have been fixed and permanent and unanimously
held. No man can put his finger upon such a period.
They have always been changing as they are to-day.
But this has been always true, that the new idea has
always been born of the old, that when men have advanced to higher truth it has been from the basis of the
truth which they have held already. It has been not
by flinging their net out into the heavens in hopes to
catch a star, but by digging deeper into the substance
of the earth on which they stood, and finding there a
root. And that is what we have to look for in the
future. You and I cling to the old historic statements
of our faith. We hold fast by the old historic church
as it appears to-day. What is our feeling as we hold
fast there ? Is it that the church to-day knows all the
truth which man will ever know ? Is it that the religious conceptions which prevail to-day will never change?
A man must be deaf to the voices of the history behind
him, blind to the signs of times around him, before he
can think that. We stand expecting change and progress, new truth, new light. But we stand here in the
historic church, in the historic truth, because we believe
that the new truth must come out of this old truth, the
perfect truth out of this partial truth, some day. We
keep close to the seven loaves because we believe that
when the multitude is fed it will be with an abundance
blessed by God out of this, which, however meagre, is
still real.

I would that men might understand that invitation

from the Christian Church to-day. It is not as the present possessor of all truth that she invites men to her household. She must not claim that. Men will discover that her claim is false if she does. But it is as the possessor of truth out of which God will call, nay is forever calling new truth, that she summons men not merely to a present which she offers, but to a future in which she believes. The church is progressive by her very essence. The church is man occupied by Christ. And since Christ cannot at once occupy man completely, and cannot be satisfied until He has occupied man completely, the church must make progress. If she ceases to advance she dies. Only in all her progress she believes in the continuity and economy of God. She looks for the truth which she is to know to come out of the truth which she knows already ; and she is sure that no duty done or light attained in any most obscure corner of her life is wasted, but helps to the perfect duty and the perfect light that are to be. That is why in her is the true home for the man who most hopes and prays for the progress of mankind.

To every man who has advanced or who hopes that he may advance to higher, fuller, truer views of Christian truth, I think that this lesson of the loaves has something very plain to say. I see a man who thinks differently to-day from the way in which he thought ten years ago. He knows more truth. He is sure that God has given him new knowledge. How shall that man look back to what he used to know, to his old creed ? Surely he may, with all rejoicing for the fuller light to which he has been brought, own the half-light in which he used to walk, and honor it. He may remember with

reverence how through some most imperfect conception
of truth, which he could not possibly hold now, he came
into the larger knowledge where he now finds his joy.
Out of the notions which are dead now, he has drawn
the life by which he lives. I think it is always a shame
for a man to abuse any creed out of which he has passed
into what he holds to be a truer creed. When he held
that old creed he was either sincere or insincere. If he
was insincere, let him abuse himself and not the creed
which, whatever was its power or its weakness, could do
nothing for a man like him. If he was sincere, let him
know that much of the good faith with which he holds
his new dear truth comes from the training of that old
devotion.' No, if God has led you to see truth which
once you did not see, and to reject as error what once
you thought was true, do not try to signalize your new
allegiance by defaming your old master. The man who
thinks to make much of the fuller truth to which he has
come, by upbraiding the partial truth through which he
came to it, is a poor creature. If I met a Mohammedan
who had turned Christian, I would not like to hear him
revile Mohammedanism. If I talk with a man from some
other communion who has come into our church, I think
the less and not the more of his churchmanship if he is
always ready to defame the mother that bore him. If
you are a more liberal believer than you used to be, the
best proof that you can give of it will be in gratefully
honoring the narrower creed in which you lived and by
whose power you grew up and passed on.

Such is the message of our story to the man who has
already advanced to larger truth than he once held.
And when he turns from looking back and still looks

forward, when he hopes still to advance, then it has
something else to say to him. It bids him hold fast all
the truth that he has learned, to hold it all the faster
because he knows it is not final. The preciousness of
every particle of truth ! That is the lesson. If one
gives me a diamond to carry across the sea, I may
estimate its value and know just how much poorer I
shall be and the world will be if I let it drop into the
water and it sinks to the bottom. But if one gives me
a seed of some new fruit to bring to this new land,
I look at it with awe. It is mysteriously valuable. I
cannot tell what preciousness is in it. Harvests on
harvests, food for whole generations, are shut up in its
little bulk. There always must be a difference as to the
essential value set on truth, between him who thinks
that truth is final and him who thinks that truth is
germinal, between him who thinks it a diamond and him
who thinks it a seed. It is a great mistake to think
that a man will value a truth more if you teach him
that it is the end of truth, than if you teach him that
it is only the beginning. Nathanael clings all the more
closely to the certainty that Jesus saw him under the
fig-tree, because of the promise that he shall " see greater
things than these." In the name of all you hope to
know, cling close to what you know already. Make
much of it, live up to it, count it very precious, hold it
fast in the bosom of a loving life. Bring what you have
and put it reverently into the Master's hands that He
may make it more. It is not good for any man to let
the vastness of unknown truth make him disparage the
little that he knows. It is good for him to count his
little precious because it is of the same kind with,

and may introduce him to, the greater after which he aspires.

I must not linger longer upon the application of our story to the matter of belief and truth. More interesting still are the ways in which it applies to character, and especially to the religious life. In all training of character the law of continuity and economy must be supreme. We often do not think so. We are ready to fancy that character can be spasmodic, a thing of constant new creations, of abrupt and sudden changes. I think that is the idea with which almost all people start in life. By and by, as life goes on, and they find that character does not change but perpetuates itself, they are very apt to turn to the other extreme and to believe that character once fixed is fixed forever, and so to settle into hopelessness. Hosts of young men are reckless because they believe that by and by they can be what they will. Hosts of old men are hopeless because it seems impossible that they can ever be anything but what they are. But both are wrong. Not lawlessness, and not slavish subjection to law, is the system under which we live. Progress and growth; but growth from old conditions, progress from the basis of the old life; this is our law. A man comes to you and says, " I have always been a bad man, and I never can be anything else." You answer him, if you are a true servant of Christ, " Poor soul, you little know the hope for all of us which is in Him who can make all things new." Another man comes and says, " I have been a bad man, but I am going to break with all my past, to live as if it all had never been, to be throughout another man." Again you must reply, " Poor soul, that too is

impossible. Be as different as you will, you must be
the same man still. Your future must come out of your
past. Your old failures, your old hopes, your old resolu-
tions, your old shames, these cannot all be wasted. They
can be wonderfully transformed, but they cannot be
thrown away." The good man stands at last, the true
man, fed with truth and glorifying God in daily action.
But he learns more and more that he is the same with
the old man whose memory he hates. He has been
made anew, but it is the old humanity out of which the
new life has been evoked. Is not this what many a
poor creature needs to know? You understand that you
are wicked. You understand what it is to be good.
But the gulf between is dreadful and impassable. What
is there in you that can grow into that? Nothing,
nothing, that can grow into that of its own strength.
You must go on forever, and be forever what you are,
unless some higher power touches you. But none the
less is it true that when that higher power touches you
it must make what you are to be out of what you are
already. The development out of the old still needs
the mightier force. Evolution is not atheism. God
must do what must be done, but God will do it.
God will make you good, by sending His light and love
into this past of yours and giving all that there is good
in it its true development and consecration.

How natural this method is. How necessarily any
one who tries to do the work of God falls into God's
ways of doing it. Never are you so near to God as
when you try to help some miserable sinner to a better
life. And how instinctively you take God's method then.
Here is a poor outcast with a wretched, wicked, it may

be a hideous life.   How will you go to work to lift that
wretchedness ?   Will you not try to find something in
all that life that you can speak to, something that you
can cultivate and make to grow ?   You find perhaps
some one affection.   The mother's love is left when
everything else seems to have gone in brutishness.   The
power to feel a kindness is still there when the power
to feel a blow has long since died.   The sensitiveness
to the cry of need is still alive when the ear can no
longer hear the calls and threats of duty.   Shame lingers
where ambition has departed.   To these you speak.
Over the life of each poor outcast you let your hands
wander till, in the midst of all the death, they find one
spot which, however feebly, trembles with life.   You
can do nothing till you have found that.   When you
have found that, everything is possible.   O my dear
friends, if you have not learned it, this is the lesson you
must learn.   If you are moved with a vague desire to
help men be better men, you must know that you can
do it not by belaboring the evil but by training the good
that there is in them.   If you could kill all a man's sins
you would only make him a less bad man.   You would
not make him a better man.   That you could make him
only by developing his goodness.   So imitate your Lord.
When you stand face to face with a hungry-eyed creature whom you want to feed with better life, be sure
that you imitate your Lord.   Be sure that you begin by
asking him " How many loaves have you, my poor
friend ?   What can you give me to begin with ?   What
has God done for you already ?   Show me your best,
and we will pray to God together that as you put it into
His hands He will bless it and multiply it, till your

whole life is fed with the grace which is all His but which He has made yours by bidding it work upon the substance of what He had given you already."

The unreality of conversion! The inability of a man to realize that he can be the subject of such a change, can enter upon such a new life as he hears other men describe! Surely you recognize that unreality. Where does it come from? Is it not largely from the fact that men do not understand this truth of the continuity and economy of grace. This is the fundamental truth about conversion. Not to sweep the old manhood off and make a new one in its place; but to make a new manhood out of the old one, that is what God's Spirit is always trying to do. If I could picture God's Spirit coming for the first time to a soul; if I could forget that all our descriptions of the Spirit coming to the soul of man are figures, because God's Spirit has been with every soul from its first moment; if I could picture God's Spirit coming for the first time to your soul, I can imagine only one beginning of His work. "How many loaves have you?" "What is there for me to go to work on here?" An honorable love of truth, an unswerving business faithfulness, a keen, quick sensitiveness to the rights of others, a tender pity which leaps up at the sight of suffering. The Spirit finds these there. These, and what are they? They are not religion. O, no! surely they are not. More and more clear, I think, it grows that they are not. More and more distinctly over our human life, with all its best affections, hangs the serene heaven of the divine life, the heaven of the love of God into which our human affections must enter before they become religious,

into which they cannot enter till they have been born
again. No! These which the Spirit finds in you are
not religion. Never let yourself think that they are, and
so depreciate and disregard the work which the Spirit has
to do in you. They are not religion; but they are the
material of the religious life. They are the part of your
nature in which you may become religious. They are
the stone in your nature out of which the temple may
be built. When the temple is built out of that native
stone, no less wonderful, indispensable, and gracious
will appear the skill of the Architect, without whom it
never could have been; yet still the temple, standing
there with its divine strength and beauty of tower and
pinnacle, will be real to you, will be your temple while
it is God's, because of the nativeness of the stone from
which God made it. The love of truth, touched by God,
has been lifted into a sublime aspiration after Him.
The business faithfulness has been transfigured into the
patient doing of His will. The regard for the rights of
others has been exalted into a passionate desire that
every man should have the chance to do, and be his
best. And pity for men's sorrows has been changed
into a lofty honor for man's value as the son of God in
Christ. How shall we tell what has come to pass? Let
us take St.. Peter's great words, "Until the day dawn
and the day-star arise in your hearts." The coming of
God's Spirit is the rising of the sun. The world is a
new world when the sun has arisen. Light and life
filling it everywhere proclaim how new it is. But the
sunrise needs a world already there to shine upon, and
it is out of the same old mountains and valleys which
have been dreary in the darkness that it makes its
miracles of light.

That is conversion. Would that men might learn it, so that it need not seem so unnatural to them, so that it need not seem so impossible for them. And the same is true about every progress of the Christian soul to the higher and higher, even to the highest Christian life. Continuity and economy; these are the laws of Him who is leading us, the Captain of our salvation. He always binds the future to the past, and He wastes nothing. O, there are some here who want to get away from all their past; who, if they could, would fain begin all over again. Their life with Christ seems one long failure. But you must learn, you must let God teach you, that the only way to get rid of your past is to get a future out of it. God will waste nothing. There is something in your past, something, even if it only be the sin of which you have repented, which, if you can put into the Savior's hands, will be a new life for you. Doubt that; doubt that God in all these years has given you something through which He may give you vastly more if you will let Him, and what reasonable conception have you left of God ? I think it is a dreadful thing to hear a man or woman say, "I have been a Christian, I have tried to serve God for such and such a number of years, and it has been all a mistake." O, how little they know God, to think it could have been a mistake ! It is as much a wrong to the honor of God to disown what He has done for us, as to disown what He has done for any other man; and yet we very often call it humility.

We want to honor our own present as the material for a possible future. In order that we may honor it we must know how Christ honors it. He honors it for what it can produce in His hands. He honors it as a

10

seed. I think sometimes of how, if the Lord had preached to men who were mostly farmers instead of shepherds, He would have made them another parable. Instead of the lost sheep on the mountains, He would have told of the lost seed on the barn floor. Instead of the love that sought the wanderer and brought it to the fold, He would have wonderfully pictured the love that found the trampled grain, with all its power of life, and buried it in the rich ground.

"How many loaves have you ? " It is the Lord's first question ; and the hands of those who really want His help, search their robes to see what they have hidden there. One brings his joy ; another brings his pain ; another brings his helpless desire ; another brings his poor resolution ; another has nothing to bring except just his sorrow that he has nothing. It is a poor collection ; only seven loaves, and a few little fishes ; but it is enough. His blessing falls upon them, and they come back to the souls which gave them up to Him, multiplied into the means of healthy, holy, happy life.

May God help us all, every day of our lives, to come to Christ just as we are, that He may make us more and more just what we ought to be.

IX.

THE NEED OF SELF-RESPECT.

A THANKSGIVING SERMON.

"And He said unto me : Son of Man, stand upon thy feet, and I will
speak unto thee." — EZEK. ii. 1.

THERE are many passages in the Bible which describe
the servants of God, as their Lord's messages came to
them, falling upon their faces on the earth, and in that
attitude of most profound humiliation listening to what
God had to say. Moses, Joshua, David, Daniel, they
are all seen at one time or another prostrate, and signifying their readiness to receive what God should tell
them by the complete disowning of anything like worth
or dignity in themselves. There is a great truth set
forth in all such pictures. It is that only to human
humility can God speak intelligibly. Only when a
man is humble can he hear and understand the words of
God. But in the passage which I have taken for my
text this morning, there is another picture with another
truth. When God was going to give a message to
Ezekiel, He said to him, "Son of man, stand upon thy
feet and I will speak unto thee." Not on his face but
on his feet; not in the attitude of humiliation but in the
attitude of self-respect; not stripped of all strength, and
lying like a dead man waiting for life to be given him,
but strong in the intelligent consciousness of privilege,

and standing alive, ready to co-operate with the living God who spoke to him ; so the man now is to receive the word of God. I hope that we shall be able to comprehend this idea largely and truly enough to see that it is not contradictory to the other, but certainly it is different from it. When God raised Ezekiel and set him on his feet before He spoke to him, was it not a declaration of the truth that man might lose the words of God because of a low and grovelling estimate of himself, as well as because of a conceited one ? The best understanding of God could come to man only when man was upright and self-reverent in his privilege as the child of God.

If this be true, is it not a great truth ? Is it not a truth well worthy of being set out in one of these graphic Bible-pictures, and one that needs continually to be preached ? The other truth is often urged upon us ; that if we are proud we shall be ignorant ; if we do not listen humbly we shall listen in vain to hear the Divine voice of which the world is full. We are pointed continually to men on every side who have evidently no wisdom but their own, because they have never deeply felt that they needed any other, and who, therefore, are filling the land with their foolishness. But this other truth is not so often preached, nor, I think, so generally felt ; unless you honor your life you cannot get God's best and fullest wisdom ; unless you stand upon your feet you will not hear God speak to you.

There is much to-day of thoughtless and foolish depre- ciation of man and his condition. I want upon Thanks- giving Day, in the light of the Thanksgiving truth, to enter a quiet, earnest and profoundly sincere protest against it. I want to claim that it is blind to facts. I want to assert that it is not truly humble. I want to denounce it as the very spirit of ignorance, shutting men's ears hopelessly against the hearing of all the highest truth. The question comes to us most pressingly to-day. Shall we, can we, thank God for His mercies, standing upon our feet and rejoicing that we are men, thoroughly grateful for the real joy of life? Back of all the special causes for thanksgiving which our hearts recognize, is there a thankfulness for that on which they all rest and in which they are sewn like jewels in a cloth of gold; for the mere fact of human life, for the mere privilege and honor of being men and women? If there is not this, no gratitude is possible; or only such a gratitude as the poor wretch in his dungeon, for whom life has been robbed of every charm, feels to his jailor who thrusts through the window to him the crust of bread and jug of water which are to prolong his miserable life. It may seem like an awful and unreasonable question; but indeed it is not so. The latest, and in many quarters the favorite, philosophy of the day, — that which boasts itself as being the supreme achievement of the nineteenth century, the perfect flower of the wisdom of mankind, — is that which under its fantastic name of Pessimism, declares deliberately that human life is a woe and a curse, and that the " will to live " is the fiend which persecutes humanity, which must be utterly destroyed before man can be happy. So speaks philosophy; and when we talk with unphilosophical men who have no theory, I think we are astonished to see how their view of life is essentially what

this philosophy would give them. Either in the soft
way or the hard way, either in sentimental whimper-
ings or in dogged, rude defiance, men are saying that
life is miserable. Either in large or little view, either
looking at the great course of history or at the petty
course of their own lives, men say the world is growing
worse from day to day. The calm pessimism of the
schools becomes the querulous discontent of the street
philosopher, or the bitter cynicism of the newspaper
satirist, or, what is far more significant than either, the
silent distress and bewilderment of the man who sees
no bright hope for himself or fellow-man. I am sure
you know whereof I speak. In large circles of life (and
they are just those circles in which a great many of us
live) there is an habitual disparagement of human life,
its joys and its prospects. Man is on his face. It
seems to me that he must hear God's voice calling him
to another attitude, or he is hopeless. "Son of man,
stand upon thy feet and I will speak unto thee."

What shall we say then of this prevalent depression
as to the character and hopes of our human life, which
is, I think, one of the symptoms of our time? Sometimes it is very sweeping and talks despairingly of man
in general. Sometimes it is special and merely believes
that our own age or our own land is given up to moral
corruption and decay. As to its general character, I
think it may be said that it comes from an inspection
of human life which is neither the shallowest nor the
deepest. It has got below the surface facts and first
appearances of things, but it has not got down to their
essential and central truth. The surface of the earth is
warm with the direct rays of the sun. The centre of

the earth, perhaps, is warm with its own essential and quenchless fire. But between the two, after you get below the warm surface, and before you approach the warm heart of the globe, it is all cold and damp and dark and dreary. And so there is the surface sight of life, which is bright and enthusiastic. There is the sight of life which is deeper than this, which is sad and puzzled. There is the deepest sight of all, which is bright again with a truer light, and enthusiastic again with a soberer but a more genuine happiness. The character of the first sight, the most simple and superficial, very few people will be inclined to dispute. There are not many misanthropes who will deny that the first aspect of things which meets the eye of man is tempting and exhilarating. The external world is too manifestly beautiful; the sun is too bright, the fields too green, the sea too blue, the breeze too fresh, the luxuries of taste and sound and smell too manifold and sweet; the human frame is strung too thickly with the faculties of pleasure; the first and universal relationships of men, friendship and childhood and fatherhood, are too spontaneous sources of delight for any reasonable man to say that the first and simplest aspect of human life is not a happy thing. The charm may be only apparent, but at least there is an apparent charm. These men may be very foolish to find such joy in life, but certainly the men whom we see do find joy in it. To the child it is all joyous. Sometimes the light foot breaks through the thin crust for a moment, but the spring of the young walker sets him the next instant on the crust again, with only sufficient sense of danger to exhilarate, not to depress. And many men who never cease to be children keep the first sight of life all through, and never see below its bright surface nor hear another sound behind the music of its most palpable delights. So that the first aspect of life makes the bright optimist which every live and healthy boy ought to be and is. But this is only on the surface, as most men soon find out. It is real but superficial. By and by the exceptions and the contradictions and the limitations begin to show themselves. This first happiness of life is spotted with unhappiness; and it is not enough, even if it were unspotted, to satisfy the man who tries to find his satisfaction in it. Then comes the danger of misanthropy. There, just below the surface, lie the abject or defiant misanthropes; the men who count the sick people till they say there is no health, who count the dull days till they say there is no sunshine, who count the failures till they say there is no success, who count the frauds till they declare there is no honesty, and the fools till they laugh at the idea of wisdom. You see they have crawled down out of the sunlight. They have left the surface and its simple presumptions to burrow just under them among the exceptions and contradictions. They keep the same idea of what the purpose of life is and what sort of happiness it ought to have; only, while the boy in his optimism cried, as he saw the bird flash up in the sunlight, "Here it is," the middle-aged pessimist creeps with the mole underground and says, "It is not anywhere." Now what comes deeper still? What is there more profound than the lamentations over the sin and misery of life, which have succeeded to the first enthusiastic praise of everything, which came first of all? What is the next step if a

man can take it? I answer, certainly a new idea of
what life is for, of what happiness a man really needs;
that is what must come. The notion of education and
of character as the end of life, of something which a man
is to be made, and by the power to make which all of
life's experiences are to be judged, that opens to a man;
and as he passes into that he finds the heat beginning·
to glow once more around him. He is coming in to
the warm centre of the world. There come forth adap-
tations for the higher work in things which have seemed
wholly unfitted to produce the lower. Things which
never could have made a man happy, develop a power
to make him strong. Strength and not happiness, or
rather only that happiness which comes by strength, is
recognized as the end of human living. And with that
test and standard the lost order and beauty reappear.
The world is man's servant and friend; and man, full of
the deeper self-respect, is ready to·hear deeper and
diviner messages of God.

This is the order. This is the way in which we pass
to deeper knowledge, which is always tending to the
happiest knowledge of our own life. First, life is a
success because the skies are bright and the whole world
is beautiful. Then life is a failure because every joy is
in danger of disappointment, and every confidence may
prove untrue. Then life is a success again because
through disappointment and deceit it still has power to
make a man pure and strong. He who has delighted in
the outside pleasures and then bowed down in misery
because they disappeared, rises up at last and stands
upon his feet when he discovers that God has a far
deeper purpose about him than to keep him gay and

cheerful, and that is to make him good; and with that
deepest intention no accidents can interfere; with that
discovery all his despair disappears, and a self-respect,
which is full of hope and ready for intelligence, comes
in its place.

This is the way in which a man's despair or contempt
about himself is thoroughly undermined, by his getting a truer view of what the world and all its treatments of man's life are for.   But now, I think, another
fact comes in.   Many men own the possibility of good
which is open to them, while still they are despairing
or cynical about the world itself, about the course of
human life in general.   There are many good people, I
believe, who devoutly recognize the chance of character,
of spiritual culture, which is offered to them by living
in the midst of a world of sin and sorrow; but the
sinful and sorrowful world itself seems to them desperate.   They may be purified, but the fire that purifies
them is the burning up of a miserable world.   This is
the strange hopelessness about the world, joined to a
strong hope for themselves, which we see in many good
religious people.   It is what really lies at the heart of
all the exclusive and seemingly selfish systems of religion, what makes it possible for good men to believe
in election.   In their own hearts they recognize indu-
bitably that God is saving them, while the aspect of the
world around them seems to show them that the world
is going to perdition.   That is a common enough condition of mind; but I think it may be surely said that
it is not a good, nor can it be a permanent, condition.
God has mercifully made us so that no man can constantly and purely believe in any great privilege for

himself unless he believes in at least the possibility of the same privilege for other men. A man's hold on his own privilege either disappears or grows impure the moment that he gives the rest of the world up in despair. Under this principle, no man who believes that the world at large is growing hopelessly worse, can keep a lively and effectual hope that he himself is growing better. Indeed this is the danger of that current habit of depreciating man, and especially of depreciating our own times and surroundings, which is very common among us. It is not merely a speculative opinion. It is an influence which must reach a man's character. A man can have no high respect for himself unless he has a high respect for his human kind. He can have no strong hope for himself unless he has a strong hope for his human kind. And so, whatever be his pure tastes and lofty principles, one trembles for any man whom he hears hopelessly decrying human life in general, or the special condition of his own time.

It is time, perhaps, that we looked a little more closely at this, which is no doubt a notable and alarming characteristic of our time; the number of intelligent men who think and talk despairingly of human nature and of human life. You meet them everywhere. Their books are on your tables. Their talk is in your ears at every corner of the streets. Where has this fact, then, come from if it is, as we believe, the growingly prominent characteristic of our generation? It is not hard to point out some of its sources. Sometimes, with some men, it is a deliberate philosophy. Some of our brightest men have, as I said, really reasoned about the world, and have come to the conclusion that it is bad and not good, and that it is growing worse and not better. It is the issue of all the fatalistic philosophies, and we all know how the strong interest of men in the working of second causes, and in the uniformity of law, has aroused a tendency to fatalism in almost all departments of thinking. Make all life a machine, and the individual is lost; with individual life, goes responsibility; with responsibility, go hope and chance. This is the way in which the philosophical pessimism of our time is made. It begins by the denial of the individual and his free will; and then, with the only power capable of moral goodness taken out, the universe is left unmoral, and an unmoral universe becomes immoral. Its salt is gone and its corruption comes.

But the number of speculative pessimists is small; the number of believers in the badness of the world is large. Where do the rest of them come from? In large part, I believe, from another characteristic of our time, from the strong feeling of interest in, and responsibility for, the world's condition, which comes from the increased activity of mind and conscience, and which begets often narrowness of view about the world's condition. A thousand men to-day care whether the state is pure, for one who cared in the last century. A thousand eyes are anxiously watching the church, for one that looked to see whether she did her work a hundred years ago. A thousand hearts sink at a catastrophe in the purity of social life, where once only one felt the disgrace. Out of all this watchfulness has come a sensitiveness and a narrowness. Because our own age has its vices which distress us, we forget the vices of other times, and we let ourselves judge the world by that bit of the world which is just under our own eyes. When one thing is being done here in New England, just the opposite thing may be coming to pass on the Ganges or the Nile. Almost every day you hear men assuming that, because America happens to have grown from a very poor country to a very rich one within the last century, and has developed, of course, the vices that belong to wealth, therefore the world is worse to-day than it was a century ago. It is vastly unreasonable, but it is very natural for a conscientious American to think so. Only when he lifts up his eyes and finds it simply impossible to let them fall on any century in all the world's history which was better than this; any century when government was purer, thought or action freer, society sweeter, the word of man more sacred than it is to-day, only then does he come back and recognize how he has been allowing the nearness and pressingness of his own circumstances to delude him.

But yet, again, this time of ours, these men of ours, are marked by a singular depth of personal experience. The personal emotions, the anxieties with regard to personal conditions, are very intense. It is a time of much morbidness, and so I think that the danger under which men always labor, of letting the universe take the color of the windows of their own life through which they look at it, was never so dangerous as to-day. More men to-day think the world is wretched because they are sad and bewildered, than would have transferred their own conditions to the outside universe in less introspective and self-conscious times. The simplest men in the simplest ages, when they were in sorrow, opened their windows inward to let the world's sunlight in. The elaborate and subtle men in the elaborate and subtle ages, in their sorrow, open their windows outward and darken the bright world with their darkness. And among such men, in such an age, we live.

And one point more. When all these causes, in a time like ours, have set a few earnest, serious, sad men to the hard task of depreciating human life, then it becomes the fashion, and all the light, flippant tongues catch up their cry and repeat it. A few strong men go wrapt in melancholy because they so intensely feel the evil of the world, and straightway every weakling who wants to be thought wise must twist his cloak about his head too, and go stalking tragically among his fellow-men, — blind in his mock misery, stumbling over them and making them stumble over him. This was the Byronism of the generation of our fathers, and this is a large part of the pessimism of ours. Sometimes it scowls and frowns and scolds; sometimes it smiles and bows as it declares that religion and politics and social life and personal character are hurrying to ruin; but it is an affectation and a fashion, and is to be discriminated carefully, and set aside in contempt, when we are trying to estimate what there is really respectable and significant in the present defamation of humanity.

Such is a statement of some of the reasons, the principal ones I think, why men have come to talk of their race and its hopes as we very often hear them talk to-day. They are connected, as you see, with much that is noblest in our age. All together they produce this condition of distrust and fear and wonder about what is coming, with a certain preference for believing that something very bad is coming, with which we are all of us familiar. Men are off their feet, as it were. They are demoralized. There is less readiness to assert the essential nobleness and lofty destiny of man. A state of things like this seems to me to be significant as to where we stand in the world's moral history. We have passed out of the first light-heartedness of youth. We are preparing, by disappointment and bewilderment, for the more serious and earnest satisfactions of middle life. If you recall what I said about the degrees or stages in men's conception of the world's character and prospects, you can apply it now to what I have just been saying. The light and airy optimism which believed that everything was right because the sun shone in the sky, is past for thoughtful mortals. You cannot persuade men to-day that the world is good because there are many pleasant things in it. They probably never will believe that in the old easy way again. Once having come to see that a pleasant world which is all full of sin and pain, is all the more dreadful because of its outside pleasantness, there is no return to the first easy satisfaction. The only two things that are still open to man are these : a blank despair, which gives itself up to inevitable deterioration; or a new thought of the world as a place of moral training where happiness or unhappiness are accidents, but where, by both happiness and unhappiness, men and nations must be made and can be made just and pure and good.

Which of these two are we bound for ? Surely the second, not the first. But to that second we can come only as we keep, in all our bewilderment over the world's misery and sin, the sense, the certainty of God. There is the point of all. If a man dwells upon the

misery of human life and does not believe in God, he is
dragged down among the brutes. If a man believes in
the misery of human life and does believe in God, he is
carried up to higher notions of God's government, which
have loftier purposes than mere happiness or pain. The
one great question about all the kind of temper of which
I have spoken is whether it still believes in God. If it
does, it must come out in light through whatever darkness it may have first to pass. If it does not, however
wise it grows, it certainly must end in folly and despair.
Whether our philosophy is theistic or atheistic ; whether
you, as you look at the snarl of life with all its misery
and sin, know for a surety that God is within it all;
these are the questions, the answer to which decides
whether our philosophy and our observation of life are
on their face or on their feet, are full of the curse of
despair or full of the blessing of hope.

For all belief in God is, must be, belief in ultimate
good. No view of the universe can be despairing which
keeps Him still in sight. "Ah," but you say, "do we
not all believe in God ? Is there one of us that denies
His existence ?" Probably not ; only remember that
there is an atheism which still repeats the creed. There
is a belief in God which does not bring Him, nay, rather
say which does not let Him come, into close contact with
our daily life. The very reverence with which we honor
God may make us shut Him out from the hard tasks and
puzzling problems with which we have to do. Many of
us who call ourselves theists are like the savages who,
in the desire to honor the wonderful sun-dial which had
been given them, built a roof over it. Break down the
roof; let God in on your life. And then, however your

first light optimism may be broken up, and the evil of the world may be made known to you, you never can be crushed by it. You will stand strong on your feet and hear God when He comes to teach you the lessons of the higher, soberer, spiritual optimism to which they come who are able to believe that all things work together for good to the man or the people that serve Him.

That was the optimism of Jesus. There was no blindness in His eyes, no foolish indiscriminate praise of humanity upon His lips. He saw the sin of that first century and of Jerusalem a thousand times more keenly than you see the sins of this nineteenth century and of America. But He believed in God. Therefore He saw beyond the sin, salvation. He never upbraided the sin except to save men from it. He never beat the chains except to set the captive free; never, as our cynics do, for the mere pleasure of their clanking. "Not to condemn the world, but to save the world," was His story of His mission. And at His cross the shame and hope of humankind joined hands.

O that the truth of our Thanksgiving Day might be His truth; the truth that all the sin we see, all the woe that is around us, are pledges dark and dreadful, but still certain pledges, of man's possible higher life. May I not beg you now to think whether you have been doing wholly right about the matter of which I have spoken to you to-day? If you have been dwelling solely on the evil that is in man, or on the special evil which you think is in your church, your nation, or your age, see whether that habit has not blinded your intelligence and weakened your strength. It has cast you down upon

11

your face.   Stand up, on this Thanksgiving Day, stand up upon your feet!   Believe in man!   Soberly and with clear eyes believe in your own time and place.   There is not, and there has never been, a better time or a better place to live in.   Only with this belief can you believe in hope and believe in work.   Only to a self-respect which stands erect in conscious privilege, erect for expected duty, can God speak His great and blessed messages and be completely understood.

X.

THE HEROISM OF FOREIGN MISSIONS.

"As they ministered to the Lord and fasted, the Holy Ghost said, Separate me Barnabas and Saul for the work whereunto I have called them. And when they had fasted and prayed and laid their hands on them, they sent them away."—ACTS xiii. 2, 3.

THE work was foreign missions. The disciples in Judea were sending out two of their number to preach the gospel in other parts of Asia and, by and by, in Europe. And therefore these words belong to us to-day, upon this one Sunday in the year when we give our especial thoughts to the foreign missionary work. This Sunday always comes back to us with the same feeling and color. It enters in among our common Sundays with a larger power than belongs to them. It seems as if the arms of Christ were stretched out a little more widely. As sometimes when our Lord was preaching in the temple, those who stood nearest to Him and caught His words the freshest from His lips, those to whom His words had been long familiar, must have seen Him lift up His eyes and look across their heads to the multitude beyond who stood upon the outskirts of the crowd; and as, while they watched Him finding out and speaking to those strangers, their own thoughts of Him must have enlarged; as, perhaps at first surprised and jealous, they must have come to understand Him more and love Him better for this new sight of

His love for all men, — so it is with us to-day. Indeed there is no feeling which the Jew had when he found that what had been his religion was going to become the possession of the world, which does not repeat itself now in men's minds when they hear their gospel demanding of them to send it to the heathen. It must have been a surprise and bewilderment at first to find that they were not the final objects of God's care, but only the medium through which the light was to shine that it might reach other men. I can conceive that Joseph and Mary may have wondered why those Gentiles should have come out of the East to worship their Messiah. But very soon the enlargement of their faith to be the world's heritage proved its power by making their faith a far holier thing for them than it could have been if it had remained wholly their own. Christ was more thoroughly theirs when through them He had been manifested to the Gentiles. And so always the enlargement of the faith brings the endearment of the faith, and to give the Savior to others makes Him more thoroughly our own.

With this thought let me speak to you to-day. Let me plead for the foreign missionary idea as the necessary completion of the Christian life. It is the apex to which all the lines of the pyramid lead up. The Christian life without it is a mangled and imperfect thing. The glory and the heroism of Christianity lies in its missionary life. This is the subject of which I wish to speak to you this morning.

The event which is recorded in the text, the departure of the disciples on their first missionary journey, was a distinct epoch in the history of Christianity. There had been some anticipations of it. The gospel had been preached to the Samaritans. Philip had baptized the Ethiopian. Peter had carried his message to the Roman centurion. But now for the first time a distinct, deliberate, irrevocable step was taken, and two disciples turned their back upon the home of Judaism, which had been thus far the home of Christianity, and went forth with the world before them. They went indeed in the first place to the Jews who lived in foreign lands; but when they went away from Judea they started on a work from which there was no turning back and which could not be limited. Before they had been many weeks upon their journey, it had become distinctly a mission to the Gentiles. And now, from the time when Paul and Barnabas went out upon this mission, the body of the disciples divides itself into two parts. There are the disciples who stay at home and manage affairs in Jerusalem, and there are the disciples who go abroad to tell the story of the cross. Peter and James are in Jerusalem. Paul and Barnabas and Luke go wandering to Ephesus and Athens and Corinth. And, as we read our Bibles, gradually the history detaches itself from the Holy City. The interest of Christianity does not linger with the wise and faithful souls who stay at home. Peter and James pass out of our thought. It is Paul, with his fiery zeal and eager tongue, restless to find some new ears into which to pour the story of his Master; it is he in whom the interest of Christianity is concentrated. He evidently represents its spirit. Its glory and its heroism are in him. The other disciples seem to feel this. They recognize that it is coming. They are almost like John the Baptist when he beheld

Jesus. As they come down to the ship to see their companions embark, as they fast and pray and lay their hands on them and send them away, there is a solemnity about it all which is like the giving up of the most precious privilege of their work, its flower and crown, to these its missionaries; and they turn back to their administrative work at home as to a humbler and less heroic task.

The relation of the disciples who stayed at home to the disciples who went abroad to preach is the perpetual relation of the home pastor to the foreign missionary. The work of the two is not essentially different. It is essentially the same. Both have the same gospel to proclaim. But the color of their lives is different. Paul is heroic. James is unheroic, or is far less heroic. I think as we go on we shall see that those words have very clear meanings. They are not vague. But even before we have defined them carefully they express a feeling with which the missionary and the pastor impress us. Heroism is in the very thought of missions. Patient devotedness, but nothing heroic, is associated with the ministry of him who works for the building up of Christian lives where Christianity already is the established faith.

I am sure that I speak for a very great many of my brethren in the home ministry when I say that we feel this continually. "Sent to tell men of Christ," — that is our commission. And men certainly need to be told of Christ over and over again. Those who have known Him longest need to hear His name again and again in their temptations, their troubles, their joys. We need to tell men of Him all their lives, until we whisper His familiar name into their ears just growing dull in death.   I rejoice to tell you of Him always, those of you who have heard of Him most and longest; but you can imagine, I am sure, how, standing here in your presence, and letting my thought wander off to a foreign land where some missionary is standing face to face with people who never heard of Christ before, I feel that that man is "telling men of Christ" in a realler, directer way than I am.   He is coming nearer to the heart, the true idea and meaning of the work we both are doing, than I am.   We are like soldiers holding the fortress.   He is the soldier who makes the sally and really does the fighting.   I know the answer.   I know what some of you are saying in your hearts whenever we talk together about foreign missions.   "There are heathen here in Boston," you declare; "heathen enough here in America.   Let us convert them first, before we go to China." That plea we all know, and I think it sounds more cheap and more shameful every year.   What can be more shameful than to make the imperfection of our Christianity at home an excuse for not doing our work abroad?   It is as shameless as it is shameful.   It pleads for exemption and indulgence on the ground of its own neglect and sin.   It is like a murderer of his father asking the judge to have pity on his orphanhood.   Even the men who make such a plea feel, I think, how unheroic it is.   The minister who does what they bid him do feels his task of preaching to such men perhaps all the more necessary but certainly all the less heroic, as he sees how utterly they have failed to feel the very nature of the gospel which he preaches to them.

But I must come closer to our subject.   "The heroism of Christianity lies in its missionary life."   And let us

start with this.   Every great interest and work of men
has its higher and its lower, its heroic and its unheroic
phases.   Take public life for instance.   Two servants of
the people work together in the same office, and both
alike are faithful, both are honest.   Both try to do their
duty.   But one thinks of the state and of that interest of
the state for which he labors, as serving him.   The other
thinks of himself as serving the state.   There is the difference.   To one the currents of life flow inward towards
the centre, which is his person.   To the other the currents of life flow outward towards the interests for which
he lives.   So it is with every man's profession.   Of two
men who are practising law, one dwells upon the idea
of the law and gives himself to its development.   The
other dwells upon the idea of himself and considers that
the law is given to him for his support.   Of two doctors,
one makes medicine his servant to build up his fame or
fortune; the other makes himself the servant of medicine, to give what strength there is in him to her development and application. - In every one of your professions
there are both kinds of workers.   There are the men
who are given to their work, and the men who consider
that their work is given to them.   Their methods may
be just alike.   They may study in the same school, read
the same books, work in the same office; but anybody
who comes near them feels the difference.   There is the
heroic element in one, and the heroic element is absent
in the other.

And what is true about a special occupation is true
about life as a whole.   The fundamental difference lies
between the men who think that life is for them, that
this great world of living things is the reservoir out of

which they are to draw pleasure and good ; and the other
men who think that they are for life, that in this universe of living things there is a divine idea and purpose
to which they, coming in their appointed time in the
long ages, are to minister with what power of service
they possess. Everywhere there runs this difference.
It appears in men's thought about God. To one man
God is a vast means, working for his comfort. To another man God is a vast end, to which his powers strive
to make their contribution. Everywhere there runs this
difference. And it is just this larger conception of life
everywhere to which the name heroic properly belongs.
This largeness involves unselfishness. The heroic public man or lawyer or doctor or liver of human life is
he who gives himself to his interest instead of asking
his interest to give itself to him. The heroic moments
in all of our most unheroic lives have been those in
which we have been able to give ourselves to our art or
occupation, counting our lives contributions to its idea,
instead of demanding that it should give itself to us
and contribute to our wealth or welfare.

It is clear then, first of all, that heroism is not merely
a thing of circumstances. There are two ideas which men
are apt vulgarly to associate with their idea of a hero.
One of them is prominence, and the other is suffering.
The ordinary notion of a hero is either of a prominent
and famous man, or of a man who has borne suffering
manfully. Now it may be that an unselfish and devoted
life in such a world as this in which we live has such a
tendency to bring a man into hard conflict with the hard
things about him, that pain will come to be a very
frequent accompaniment of heroism. But evidently, if

what I have said is true, there is no necessary company between them. There may be pain without heroism, pain inspired by selfishness, and making the man who suffers all the smaller and more self-involved. On the other hand there may be heroism without pain, self-devotion with all the circumstances of happiness. And so with regard to prominence. The essence of heroic life is the apprehension by any man of the idea of a cause, and the abandonment of his life to that idea. Such an abandonment, such a filling of his life with such an idea, will make him naturally the type-man of his cause, will set him in its fore-front and will bring him into conflict with all men who oppose his cause ; but these are accidents. In obscurity and luxury it may be that a man still is a hero. Even there he may fasten upon the idea of a cause and give himself up to it and effectively live for it, and if he does that he is a hero. In heaven all life will be heroic. Every being there will live for the divine ideas of things. No man will think that the golden streets and the hosts that fill them, and the unspeakable Majesty which sits in the centre of all upon the throne, are for him. Every soul will delight to count its eternity a contribution to them. But there will be no unhappiness, no pain in heaven. The accidents will have been changed, and will show that they were never more than accidents, but the essence of heroism will be the same forever.

I put then as the first element of heroism this quality of Ideality ; the power, that is, of getting hold of the idea of any cause or occupation or of life in general, so that the cause, the occupation, or life becomes a living thing to which a man may give himself with all his powers.

That quality of ideality is the essential thing in heroism. There can be no hero without that. It is just what makes the difference between the "dumb, driven cattle" and the "heroes in the strife." Look through the ranks of your profession. Are there not both cattle and heroes there? Are there not times in your work when you are of the cattle sort, when the idea fades out of what you are doing, and nothing but the clatter of its machinery remains? Alas for you if such times are in the preponderance, if they are not lost in the general presence of the idea of your labor, making it an inspiration and making you heroic in your dedication to it.

Along with this primary quality of all heroism there go two others, closely related to it. They are Magnanimity and Bravery. The true hero is generous and brave. Whence comes his generosity? Is it not of the very essence of his ideality. Let me be a scholar, for instance. The first question will be whether I have got hold of the idea of scholarship and have given myself to it. Am I studying for my own sake, to make myself famous or accomplished; or am I studying for scholarship's sake, to make my branch of study more complete, to glorify and multiply the cause of knowledge in the world? If the first, I have no real ground of sympathy with other scholars. I do not take a cordial interest in their success. I am not tempted to help them. I am tempted again and again to hinder them. I am open to all kinds of jealousy and spite and little-mindedness. If the latter, I am anxious for every other worker's success, as well as for my own. I am as glad of another man's discovery as if I had made it. I cannot be jealous of the light which some new hand flings on that subject

which it is the object of my life to glorify.   I will help
every brother student as eagerly as I will help myself.
Here is magnanimity.   You see how closely it is bound
up with ideality.   The magnanimous public man is he
who so lives for the ideas of his country that he is not
jealous but glad when he sees other men doing more
for the development of these ideas than he can do.   The
magnanimous churchman is he who cares so much for
the church that he will help any other man's work for
her as devotedly as if it were his own.   The magnanimous man is he who has so conceived the idea of manhood, to whom humanity is so sublime a thing, that he
will help another man to complete himself, to be as good
and as great as he can be, with as much earnestness as
he will expend in his own culture.   Here is generosity.
You see that it is not mere good-nature.   It is most
intelligent and has its reasons.   And this is the second
element of heroism.

And the third element is Bravery.   We can see how
heroic bravery too belongs with the quality which discovers and fastens upon ideas.   There are two kinds of
bravery; one which comes from the recollection of self,
the other which comes from the forgetfulness of self.
An Indian is brave when out of sheer pride he lets men
drive their burning fagots into his flesh and utters no
cry.   A fireman is brave when for his duty he rushes
into a burning house and, all scorched and bleeding,
brings out the ransomed child.   The first is brave by
self-recollection.   The second is brave by self-forgetfulness.   The first has gathered up all his self-possession
and said, " Now I will not flinch or fear because it is
unworthy of me."   The second has cast all recollection

of himself aside and said, " That child will die if I stay here." We need not ask which of these two braveries is heroic. There is a courage that comes of fear. A man learns that on the whole it is safer in the world not to dodge and shirk, and so he goes on and meets life as it comes. There is nothing heroic about that. A man wants to run away, but because his fear of disgrace is greater than his fear of bullets he stays in the ranks and shuts his eyes and marches on. There is nothing heroic about that. A man is afraid as he sits alone and thinks about a task, but when he gets among his fellow-men, a mere contagious feeling takes possession of him and he is ready to fight and die because other men are fighting or dying, like a dog in a pack of dogs. That is " the courage corporate that drags the coward to heroic death." There is nothing heroic about that. Only when a man seizes the idea and meaning of some cause, and in the love and inspiration of that is able to forget himself and go to danger fearlessly because of his great desire and enthusiasm, only then is bravery heroic.

Ideality, magnanimity, and bravery then; these are what make the heroes. These are what glorify certain lives that stand through history as the lights and beacons of mankind. The materialist, the sceptic, the coward, he cannot be a hero. We talk sometimes about the unheroic character of modern life. We say that there can be no heroes nowadays. We point to our luxurious living for the reason. But oh, my friends, it is not in your silks and satins, not in your costly houses and your sumptuous tables, that your unheroic lives consist. It is in the absence of great inspiring ideas, of generous enthusiasms, and of the courage of self-forgetfulness. It may be that you must throw away your comfortable living to get these things; but your lack of heroism is not in your comfortable living, but in the absence of these things. Do not blame a mere accident for that which lies so much deeper. There are moments when you bear your sorrows, when you watch by your dying, when you bury your dead, when you are anxiously teaching your children, when you resist a great temptation, when your faith or your country is in danger; there are such moments with you all when you seize the idea of human living and are made generous and brave because of it. Then, for all your modern dress, for all your modern parlor where you stand, you are heroic like David, like Paul, like any of God's knights in any of the ages which are most remote and picturesque. Then you catch some glimpse of a region into which you might enter, and where, with no blast of trumpets or waving of banners, you might be heroic all the time.

And now we may turn to that which has been our purpose in all we have been saying. What we have had in our mind is the great work of foreign missions, and we have been led to speak of heroism in its three fold quality of ideality and magnanimity and bravery. Now no cause ever really takes possession of the world unless it puts on the heroic aspect, unless it shows itself capable of inspiring heroism. Christianity is subject to this law like every other cause. It, too, must show itself heroic or it fails to seize and hold mankind; and it is in the desire for universal extension, the desire to make its Master known to all men, the desire for foreign missions, that Christianity asserts her heroism.

It is true indeed that Christianity is itself heroic life. All that there is in human living becomes magnified and glorified to its best when it is put under the leadership of Christ. The deepest idea of life is brought out and proclaimed; the true generosity of life is uttered; its selfishness is broken up; and love, which is the power of the Christian life, casts out fear and makes the servant of the Savior brave. The Christian is the heroic man. Ah! as I say that, does there float across your mind the memory of many and many a time in history, or in the life that you have watched, or in your own life which you have lived, my Christian friends, when the Christian has not been the hero; when, even in the name of Christ, the Christianity which called Him its Master has seemed to forsake ideas and to give itself over to machineries, seemed to make life dwindle into a little system of economies for securing to privileged souls freedom from pain and a share in luxuries here and hereafter, seemed to make men cowardly instead of brave? I know it! I know it! Such things have been; such things have been and they still are, in the name of Christ. But such things are not Christianity. Look at Christ! The idealist, the generous, the brave! Anything that is mechanical, that is selfish, that is cowardly, coming into His religion, comes as an intruder and an enemy. Christianity in its essence is, Christianity in its long and general influence always has been, heroic; the power of ideality and magnanimity and bravery among men.

But if Christianity is heroic life, the missionary work is heroic Christianity. By this time I am sure that I have made it clear that if that is true at all it is true not from any mere circumstances of personal privation which attach to the missionary life, but because the missionary life has most closely seized and most tenaciously holds and lives by the essential central life-idea of Christianity. What is that idea? Out of all the complicated mass of Christian thought and faith, is there any one conception which we can select and say, " That is the idea of Christianity "? Certainly there is. What is it? That man is the child of God. That, beyond all doubt, is the idea of Christianity. Everything issues from, everything returns to, that. Man's first happiness, man's fallen life, man's endless struggle, man's quenchless hope, — they are all bound up and find their explanation in the truth that man was, and has never ceased to be, and is, the child of God. Therein lies the secret of the incarnation, all the appeal of the Savior's life, all the power of the Savior's death. It is the Son of God bringing back the children to their Father. Now we believe that, we love it, we live by it, all of us in all our Christian life. But when a man gathers up his life and goes out simply to spend it all in telling the children of God who never heard it from any other lips than his that their Father is their Father; when all that he has known of Christ is simply turned into so much force by which the tidings of their sonship is to be driven home to hearts that do not easily receive so vast a truth; to that man certainly the idea has become a master and a king, as it has not to us. Belief is power. By the quantity of power I may know the quantity of belief. He is the true idealist, not who possesses ideas, but whom ideas possess; not the man whose life wears its ideas as ornamental jewels, but the man whose ideas shape his life like plastic clay. And so the true Christian idealist is he whose conception of man as the redeemed child of God has taken all his life and moulded it in new shapes, planted it in new places, so filled and inspired it that, like the Spirit of God in Elijah, it has taken it up and carried it where it never would have chosen to go of its own lower will.

Here lies, I think, the real truth about the relation which the missionary life has to the surrenders and privations and hardships which it has to undergo. The missionary does give up his home and all the circumstances of cultivated comfortable life, and goes out across the seas, among the savages to tell them of the great Christian truth, to carry them the gospel. I am sure that often a great deal too much has been made of the missionary's surrenders, as if they were something almost inconceivable, as if they in themselves constituted some vague sort of claim upon the respect and even the support of other men. But we are constantly reminded that that is not so. The missionaries themselves, from St. Paul down, have never claimed mere pity for their sacrifices. It is other people, it is the speakers in missionary meetings, who have claimed it for them. The sacrifices of the missionary every year are growing less and less. As civilization and quick communication press the globe ever smaller, and make life on the banks of the Ganges much the same that it is on the banks of the Charles, the sacrifices of the missionary life grow more and more slight. And always there is the fact, which people are always ready to point out, that other men do every day for gain or pleasure just what the missionary does for the gospel, and nobody wonders.

12

The merchant leaves his home and goes and lives in China to make money. The young man dares the sea and explores the depths of Africa or the jungles of the islands for scientific discovery or for pure adventure. What is the missionary more than these? What do you say to me about his sacrifices? Only this, I think, that the fact that he is ready to do the same things — not greater, if you please, but the same things — for the Christian idea, which other men will do for money or for discovery or for adventure, is a great proof of the power of that idea. It takes at once what some people call a vague sentiment, and co-ordinates it as a working force with the mightiest powers the world knows; for there are none stronger than these, money, discovery, and adventure. And since men are to be judged not merely by the way in which they submit themselves to forces but by the quality of the forces to which they submit, not merely by their obediences but by their masters, not merely by their enthusiasms but by the subjects about which they are enthusiastic; it certainly is a different sort of claim to our respect when a man dares any kind of sacrifice for Christ and His gospel of man's divine sonship, from that which comes when a man dares just the same sacrifices for himself, or for his family which is but his extended self. Here is the true value to give to the often told and ever touching story of the missionary's sufferings. I resent it as an insult to him if I am asked to pity him because, going to preach the gospel of the Savior, he very often has to sleep out-doors and walk till he is footsore, and stand where men jeer at him and taunt him. But I rejoice in that story of suffering because I can see through it the clear strong power of his faith in that gospel for which he undertook it all. The suffering is valueless save for the motive which shines through it. The world is right when, seeing Paul and a whole shipload of other people wrecked upon the coast of Malta, it has wholly forgotten or never cared who the other people were, but has seized the shipwrecked Paul and set him among the heroes. It was not the shipwreck but the idea that shone through the shipwreck, that made his heroism. He was a martyr, a witness. The roar of the breakers and the crash of the ship were but the emphasis. The essential force and meaning was in the great apostle's faith. The poor wretches who suffered with him were on their own selfish errands, and the shipwreck could give no real dignity or beauty to what was not in itself dignified or beautiful.

It seems as if I need not take the time to show that with the supreme ideal character of the missionary's life there must go a supreme magnanimity and bravery.

Look at the point of magnanimity. No man can be magnanimous who does not live by ideas. But the higher and the more enthusiastic the ideas, the more complete will be the magnanimity they bring. Now the missionary idea that man is God's child gives birth to two enthusiasms; one for the Father, one for the child; one for God, one for man. The two blend together without any interference, and both together drown the missionary's self-remembrance, with all its littleness and jealousy. Who can tell, as the missionary stands there preaching the salvation to his dusky congregation, which fire burns the warmest in his heart ?

Is it the love for God or for his brethren? Is it the Master who died for him, or these men for whom also He died, from whom his strongest inspiration comes? No one can tell. He cannot tell himself. The Lord Himself in His own parable foretold the noble, sweet, inextricable confusion. " Inasmuch as ye have done it unto one of these ye have done it unto Me." But surely in the blended power of the two enthusiasms there is the strongest power of magnanimity. All that the mystic feels of personal love of God, all that the philanthropist knows of love for man, these two, each purifying and deepening and heightening the other, unite in the soul of him who goes to tell the men whom he loves as his brethren, about God whom he loves as his Father.

Of the courage of the missionary life I have already spoken. Its singularity and supremacy are not in the way in which the missionary dares physical danger; other men do that. It is not in his cheerful bearing of men's dislike and scorn. That we all know is too easy for us to wonder at it when a man is really possessed by a great idea. The real courage of the missionary is in the mixture of mental and moral daring with which he faces his great idea itself. A man dares to believe, in spite of all discouragement, in spite of all the brutishness and hateful life of men, in spite of retarded civilization and continual outbreaks of the power of evil, that man is still the child of God, and that the way is wide open for every man to come to his Father, and that the Christ who has redeemed us to the Father must ultimately claim the whole world for His own. That is the bravest thing a reasonable man can do, to thoroughly

believe that and to take one's whole life and consecrate
it to that truth.   A man may no doubt do it heedlessly
and thoughtlessly, just as a man may walk up to a cannon's mouth singing light songs, but when a man does
it with patient, calm, earnest thoughtfulness, it is the
bravest thing a man can do.   To face a great idea and,
owning its mastery, to put our hands into its hands,
saying, "Lead where you will and I will go with you;"
that is always a more courageous thing than it is to
fight with giants or to bear pain.

I have pleaded with you this morning for the heroism
of the missionary life.   Not because of the pains it suffers but because of the essential character it bears it is
heroic.   Pain is the aureole but not the sainthood.   So
they have marched of old, the missionaries of all the
ages of the religion of the Incarnation and the Cross,
idealists, believers, magnanimous and brave, the heroes
of our faith.   They were all this because they were missionaries.   They could not have been missionaries and
not have been all this.   You cannot picture mere ma-
chines or disbelievers or selfish men or cowards doing
what they have done.   They have lived in the midst of
infinite thoughts and yet not grown vague.   They have
worked with the tools of human life, but not grown
petty.   In one word, they have been heroes because of
their faith, because their souls supremely believed in and
their lives were supremely given to Christ.
If, as I believe with all my heart, the world's fullest
faith in Christ is yet to come; if, as I think, we are
just coming now to a simpler and deeper Christianity
than the world has ever known, who shall not dare to

hope that the missionary life, the heroism of Christianity, the heroism of the heroism of human life is not
dead, but is just upon the point of opening its true
glory and living with a power that it has never shown
before?

Let us have some such faith to-day. It is a little
heroic even to believe in foreign missions. If we may
not be among the heroes, let us, like the church of old,
hear the Holy Ghost and go with Paul and Barnabas
down to their ship and lay our hands on them and send
them away with all our sympathy and blessing. So,
perhaps, we can catch something of their heroism. So,
in our quiet and home-keeping Christian lives, the idea
of Christianity may become more clear, Christ our Lord
more dear, and we ourselves be made more faithful,
more generous, and more brave.

XI.

THE LAW OF LIBERTY.

"So speak ye, and so do, as they that shall be judged by the law of liberty."—JAMES ii. 12.

"THE law of liberty" is the striking expression of this verse, the one that provokes our curiosity.

Of all the qualities which great books and especially the Bible have, few are more remarkable than their power of bringing out the unity of disassociated and apparently contradictory ideas. One of the peculiarities of their use of common words is the way in which they take two which seem directly opposite and, carrying each out into its highest meaning, find for them a meeting-place in some larger truth. It gives us a glimpse of the final unity of all truth. We live down about the bases of the words we use; see them in their simply human relations; see them where they touch the ground. To us they seem to stand opposite, over against each other, ununited, ununitable. But we never must forget that every true thought outgoes its human relations, and for all true thoughts there must be some place of meeting. Inspiration is just the entrance of their complete meaning into human words; and then, filled with God, they are illuminated, and we can trace them all the way up and see that they are not isolated columns, but parts of a structure. They are not opposite and contradictory, but they meet together in an arch of one harmonious meaning. And then all language builds itself from being a wilderness of unconnected pillars, — about which we wander as an insect creeps from pillar to pillar across a vast cathedral floor, having no suspicion of its unity, — into one vast temple wherein intelligent men walk upright, looking upward to where the great roof collects and harmonizes all, and do intelligible worship.

Take these two words, "the law of liberty," Liberty and Law. They stand over against each other. Our first conception of them is as contradictory. The history of human life, we say, is a history of their struggle. They are foes. Law is the restraint of liberty. Liberty is the abrogation, the getting rid of law. Each, so far as it is absolute, implies the absence of the other. It is a contradiction of terms to speak of them together.

But the expression of our text suggests another thought, that by the highest standards there is no contradiction but rather a harmony and unity between the two; that there is some high point in which they unite; that really the highest law is liberty, the highest liberty is law; that there is such a thing as a law of liberty. This is the thing which we are to study and try to comprehend.

In the first place then, what do we mean by Liberty, that oldest, dearest, vaguest of the words of man? I have defined it often to you. I hold it to mean simply the genuine ability of a living creature to manifest its whole nature, to do and be itself most unrestrainedly. Nothing more, nothing less than that. Against all temporary and conventional ideas of freedom we assert that, that no man is a slave whose nature has power to express and use all of itself; that no man is free whose nature is restrained from such expression.

Now between this idea and our ordinary thought of law there must of course be an inherent contradiction. The ordinary laws of social and national life are special provisions made for the very purpose of restricting the natures and characters of their subjects. National law does not aim at the development of individual character, but at the preservation of great general interests by the repression of the characteristic tendencies of individuals. One man has a tendency to steal. The law sets itself against the freedom of his nature and says "You shall not." Another's character tempts him to murder. "No!" says the law, and cramps his liberty of action by the grasp of positive restriction. All national and social law, in the performance of its office, sets itself in struggle with the liberty of the individual, and binds his nature away from certain bad and harmful manifestations. And as law becomes despotic and supreme it goes on to restrict more and more the freedom of the personal nature. A tyrannical law, which has slaves for its subjects, restricts not only bad but good tendencies. A slave says, "I mean to learn to read." "No," says the master. "It is not good for the community you live in. Your individual freedom must yield to its requirements." And so the law shuts his book and takes it away. Another slave says, "I am going to run away; I am my own master;" but at once the law puts its fatal arm out and draws him back and says, "No! It is for our good that you should stay.

Your freedom must yield again;" and so it relocks the fetters.

Thus far, then, you see Law is the opposite of Liberty. Law between man and man, in its legitimate and its illegitimate aspects alike, is the law of constraint. It is always seen holding man back, repressing some tendency which, if the man were perfectly free, would be putting itself out to somebody's inconveniency. We say the word "law," and it has this repressive sound. We hear the noise of grating prison-doors, of heavy keys groaning in their locks. We see the lines of chains or lines of soldiers that bind the individual's freedom for some other individual's or for society's advantage. Law is constraint as yet, and is the foe of liberty.

This is the kind of law which always comes first. It was the first law of the world. Just as soon as Adam and Eve stood there free in the garden a law came down and bound itself about their liberty. " Of the tree in the midst of the garden ye may not eat." This is the first law of every family. The new life of the new child puts itself out into some one of its untried tendencies, and the mother's love, full of a supreme authority, draws it back, restrains it, says her first " No !" and thereby inaugurates, with her first denial, the struggle between liberty and law in her child's life. It is the law of all imperfect and immature life, the law of all the Old Testaments, this law of constraint, this law which contradicts the thought of liberty.

Now I make use of this last illustration of the parent and the child to show you how this law of immature life, the law of constraint, being preparatory, ceases ; and another, the law of liberty, takes its place. We

saw the child's liberty and the mother's law in conflict.
The child said "I will," and the mother said "You shall
not," and the mother's authority restrained the child's
free action. Now look at the relation of those same two
persons to each other twenty years after. Suppose
them to have grown into that higher and more beautiful
ideal of parental and filial life, which follows after the
age of bare authority and submission has passed away.
The child is a man. The mother is gray-haired. The
boy is free, his own master. The whole idea of command and mastery, the whole old notion of a law of
constraint, has drifted away from between them. But
is there nothing in its place? See the high dignity
with which the son honors himself by bending to the
mother's wish. See with what quicker instinct he has
learned to anticipate her will. You discern the whole
history of his education in any one act of filial love you
see him do her. His nature has become so full, so
impregnated with the spirit of love and obedience, that
just as soon as it is free, its tendencies set that way.
Its free tendencies become to it a law. Its liberty,
with a compulsion that is irresistible, makes him her
servant. The law of constraint which resulted from
their relations is over. The law of liberty which has
its source in his free, moral character takes its place.
He is obedience and so obeys. He is love, and so a
thousand loving acts strew the calm pathway where her
descending years must walk.

Now use the illustration. I do not know that I can
state it better. The law of constraint is that which
grows out of man's outward relations with God. The
law of liberty is that which issues from the tendencies

of a man's own nature inwardly filled with God. That is the difference. Just as soon as a man gets into such a condition that every freedom sets toward duty, then evidently he will need no law except that freedom, and all duty will be reached and done.

Here then, in a moral character which both desires and is able to attempt the right, have we not reached a meeting point of these two contradictions? Have we not gained already some conception of the meaning of a Law of Liberty? I have tried to describe it simply. Here is a law in liberty, a liberty in law. There is no compulsion, and yet the life, by a tendency of its own educated will, sets itself towards God. The man is perfectly free and yet he does God's will better than if he were chained to do it. The two pillars have met and joined into the arch of a self-deciding original moral life.

You see then what a fundamental and thorough thing this law of liberty must be. It is a law which issues from the qualities of a nature going thence out into external shape and action. It is a law of constraint by which you take a crooked sapling and bend it straight and hold it violently into line. It is a law of liberty by which the inner nature of the oak itself decrees its outward form, draws out the pattern-shape of every leaf, and lays the hand of an inevitable necessity on bark and bough and branch. All laws of constraint, whether in trees or men, are useless and cruel unless they are preparatory to, and can pass into, laws of liberty. My dear friends, if we understood this it would certainly show us the hollowness of a great deal of the life we live. We yield day after day, month after month, on through a long series of tiresome years, to the restraints of morality and religion. Morality says "You must not steal," and we do keep our fingers off our neighbor's goods. Religion says "You must pray to God," and we do say our prayers most toilsomely, morning and evening, summer and winter, as the years go by. It is of no use. It all comes to nothing unless these laws of constraint are passing into laws of liberty within us. Habits of honesty, habits of prayer, are mere bondages unless they are helping somehow the production of a free, honest, and prayerful character. The only object in bandaging and twisting a man's crooked leg is that some day it may get a free straightness into it which will make it keep its true shape when it is set free from bandages ; a law of liberty instead of a law of constraint. If that day is never coming, bandaging is mere wanton cruelty. Better take the bandages off and let it be crooked, if it is getting no inner straightness, and will be crooked as soon as they are removed. Now, just so, this discipline and education, all these commandments and prohibitions which God lays on us; they are mere cruelty, they merely torture and worry humanity, they come to nothing, unless within them some free law of inner rectitude is growing up. One looks across God's great moral hospital, sees crooked souls tied up in constraints, and wonders, as one might who looked through a surgeon's ward, behind how many of those bandages an inner life is gathering which some day will ask no binding up and need nothing but its own liberty to be its law. It is a strange question. Suppose to-morrow all the laws of constraint should be repealed together; nothing but laws of liberty left to rule the world ; all social penalties, all public restrictions lifted off together; nothing left but the last legislation of character. What would become of us? How, just as soon as our bandages were off, our unshaped lives would fall into their shapelessness. We should see strange sights tomorrow morning. The man whom social decencies had kept honest through many well-respected years, we should see how the long constraint with him had been just an outside thing, and his law of liberty, when it had leave to exercise itself, was only a thief's law born out of a thievish heart. Strange hands would find their way into their neighbor's treasure. Eyes all unused to glow with lust, would flame out into unholy fire when once the quality of the inner heart had leave to utter itself freely. I tell you, my dear friends, there are very few of us indeed who could stand being judged by the law of liberty. Could you? Would you dare, with the proper shame which a man feels before his fellow-men, would you dare to bid God lift the constraints away, and trust to the power of truth and love and holiness, to the amount of God's Spirit in your own heart, to carry you along His way to Him?

Thank God there are a few, rare lives that could abide the test. They come just often enough to re-assure our faith in human possibilities. Here and there a noble man, a true woman, from whom we feel sure that every last restraint of positive external law might be lifted off; and, just as it needs no hand to guide a sunbeam down the air, just as no heavy pressure has to hold down the round world into a sphere, so it would need nothing but the changed and perfected nature which is in them already to find the way and carry them along it, through every good, to the great final central good, in God.

It is of the first importance to our understanding of the gospel that we should understand the difference between the law of constraint and the law of liberty. It is by the law of liberty, not by the law of constraint, that the gospel establishes its standards. Hence comes that look of it which is the strangest to an outside spectator, the way in which it sometimes seems to depreciate morality and deal with spiritual and sentimental character. Christ took His stand in the midst of a sinning world and, leaving many a special sin unrebuked about Him, He just uncovered hearts with His question, "Dost thou believe in and love Me?" He went, that is, back to character. He knew that acts could be good for nothing except as they grew out of character. He knew that there could be no morality with any reliability or permanence about it, but what carried in it the enactment of a free live life. On this broad basis He founded Christian morality, not as a new code of laws; that would make Him only another Solon or another Numa; but as a new life in the world, as the manifestation of a new regenerated character. That made Him the world's Savior, that showed Him the world's God.

And again this doctrine of the law of liberty makes clear the whole order and process of Christian conversion. Laws of constraint begin conversion at the outside and work in. Laws of liberty begin their conversion at the inside and work out. Which is the true way? If you are a drunkard and I want to change you by God's help, how shall I go to work? I may restrain you if I

have the power, heap penalties upon you, shut up all
the drinking shops in town, tie you up in your room
day after day; I may try that way, and I try in vain.
All temperance history has proved it. Restrictive legislation may do something to keep sober men from
becoming drunkards, but it can never make sober men
out of those who are the slaves of drink already.
No; I must take another way. I must feel about the
drunkard just exactly as I must about the thief, about
the libertine, about the liar, that there is no chance of
his special sin being reformed unless the law for its
reformation comes out of his own soul, the law of a free
character there enacting the great "Thou shalt not!"
before which his wickedness must give way. I must
feel sure of that; and so I must strike right at the centre
and, no matter what sort of a sinner he is, — drunkard
or libertine or thief, — I must try somehow to get his
heart open to the power of Christ, the changer of hearts.
I must begin his reformation by trying after his conversion. Many men would call it, no doubt, a very
roundabout and unpractical sort of way; to go to preaching the gospel and talking about a change of heart to
some poor blear-eyed inebriate who came staggering to
you to get cured of his drunkenness. But still the fact
remains that if that poor creature's heart can be changed;
and if there is anything at all in the promise of a supernatural regeneration nobody can doubt its possibility; if
his heart can be changed, not merely this sin but all
sins must go down before the self-enacting law of the
new life which will be in him. Other methods of reform may be easier of application than this, but where
is any one which, once applied, sweeps the whole field
with such a perfect certainty of success?

There are, I doubt not, some among you who need just this radical and thorough truth. You have some one besetting sin. You have tried to get rid of it; you have struggled with it; you have set every law at work upon it; but there it is. It is not dead. It will not die. You have brought it up here to-night, and while I speak you are feeling how live it is all the time, that untruthfulness, that impurity, that selfishness, which no law of constraint has yet sufficed to kill. What you need is just the law of liberty; the law that comes freely out of a changed heart. You must be converted by God's Spirit before you can conquer down to the root that sin of yours. I do not offer you to-night another specific for its cure. I only spread before you the great offer of Christ, wherein he promises to save our souls and make them healthy, so that out of them nothing but healthy fruits can grow. "Whosoever will, let him come and drink of the water of life freely."

Again, this truth throws very striking light into one of the verses which precede our text, one of the hardest verses in the Bible to a great many people. "Whosoever shall keep the whole law, and yet offend in one point, is guilty of all," it is said. Why? Because the consistent, habitual breakage of one point proves that the others were kept under the law of constraint, not under the law of liberty. It proves that the tendency of the nature's liberty, which breaks forth in this one place, is a bad tendency and not a good one; that if the nature had its way, if all constraint was removed and it simply acted itself out, the nine points of obedience would be less powerful than the one point of disobedience. It takes only one volcano anywhere in

18

the earth to show that the heart of the earth is fire, and that some day it may burst through the thickest crust. It takes only one little quiver of flame, just leaking out between the shingles of a house, to prove that the heart of the house is afire, and that no part of all its safe-looking walls is genuinely secure. You see the flame along the shingles, and you speak of it as a whole; "The house is afire! There is fire in the house!" Just so you see the bad fiery nature which the law constrains breaking through, and again you speak of it as a whole. What particular shingle is burning is of no consequence. "The law is broken. The one whole law is broken by the one whole bad heart! The man has sinned; he is sin; his law of liberty is a law of wickedness." This is the tragedy of our single sins, dear friends; the tragedy of a fire that runs along the outline of the structure and, little as it is, proves that the whole is in danger; the tragedy of one break in the earth's crust down which we read the fearful possibility of the last great catastrophe. Down the crack which some one transgression makes in the fair face of a smooth and blooming life, we can see waiting for God's judgment-word, the fire before which that life shall be at last consumed with fervent heat.

The whole truth of the law of liberty starts with the truth that goodness is just as controlling and supreme a power as badness. Virtue is as despotic over the life she really sways as vice can be over her miserable sub- jects. Here is where we make our mistake. We see the great dark form of viciousness holding her slaves down at their work, wearing their life away with the unceasing labor of iniquity; but I should not know how to believe in anything if I did not think that there was a force in liberty to make men work as they can never work in slavery. You take a state that has been dependent and make it suddenly independent, free it from all the old obligations and tributes, and just let it be at liberty to develop its own self-reliant life. Does it stop working and settle back into barbarism? Does not the new liberty prove to it a new law? Does not inspiration come splendidly out of its independence, and the whole state lift itself up and answer the demands of its freedom with a before untried capacity of work?

So of the man as well as of the state. You take any slave to whom his liberty has been given. What is the result? Does he just sit down counting his liberty a mere liberty to do nothing, and, with hands folded before him, fall even far back beyond the listless labor of his slavehood's days? Ask the men who have been among the emancipated slaves. Sometimes, at first, they tell us such is the case; but almost always, when the truth of liberty gets in and settles on the poor dark brain, when the poor chattel really gets to know and believe that he is his own man, there comes forth from the new liberty a new law. There is a compulsion about the needs of his novel life which drives him harder and gets more work out of him than his master's frown or whip had ever used to do. He studies or digs or fights under the inner impulse of a new-found manhood, which is his law of liberty.

Now that is an illustration. It represents the incentive power of all freedom. There is one large presentation of the fact of sin which always speaks of it as a bondage, a constraint, and consequently of holiness as freedom or liberation. "The bondage of sin and death." ".The perfect liberty of the children of God." Those are the two terms. Now if our illustration includes a truth, it must be with every bondman just as with the black slave of the South, that his liberty will be a larger and more imperative compulsion to him than his slavery can be. This is what I want to believe. When I see a man toiling in some one of the slaveries of sin, I want to think: "Yes, he is working hard, but not half as hard as he would if he were free, and set on by an inner love to labor for the cause of holiness." I want to hold that in the nature of things right has a supreme control over its servants which the wrong can never win over its slaves. And I do hold it. I believe I see it. I believe there is no more splendidly despotic power anywhere than that with which the new life in a man sets him inevitably to do righteous and godly things. If there is one thing on earth which is certain, which is past all doubt, past all the power of mortal hinderance or perversion, it is the assurance with¹ which the good man goes into goodness and does good things, ruled by the liberty of his higher life.

The law of liberty! This is its manifestation. This is the picture of its meaning, this character of the regenerated man. Free, yet a servant! Free from external compulsions, free from sin; yet a servant to the higher law that issues forever from the God within him. In him is realized that high conception of the Collect in our morning service, which you and I utter Sunday after Sunday, and which he lives ·on from day to day. "O God, whose service is perfect freedom." He never says to himself "I must." God never speaks to him

"Thou shalt;" but straight across every temptation and expediency, across the prejudices of his own education and the perplexing standards of the world, across every social or national intimidation, he goes to do the thing he knows is right. He thinks right, and speaks right, and acts right, simply because he is right and is compelled to it by the liberty of his new nature. Liberty is a positive thing, not merely negative; it works and lives and struggles and is driven by a queenly compulsion to everything that is good.

O for such a liberty in us! Look at Christ and see it in perfection. His was the freest life man ever lived. Nothing could bind Him. He walked across old Jewish traditions and they snapped like cobwebs. He acted out the divinity that was in Him up to the noblest ideal of liberty. But was there no compulsion in His working? Hear Him: "I must be about my Father's business." Was it no compulsion that drove Him those endless journeys, footsore and heartsore, through His ungrateful land? "I must work to-day." What slave of sin was ever driven to his wickedness as Christ was to holiness? What force ever drove a selfish man into his voluptuous indulgence with half the irresistibility that forced the Savior to the cross? O my dear friends, who does not dream for himself of a freedom as complete and as inspiring as the Lord's? Who does not pray that he too may be ruled by such a sweet despotic law of liberty?

By this law we shall be judged. How simple and sublime it makes the judgment day! We stand before the great white throne and wait our verdict. We watch the closed lips of the Eternal Judge, and our hearts stand still until those lips shall open and pronounce our fate; heaven or hell. The lips do not open. The Judge just lifts His hand and raises from each soul before Him every law of constraint whose pressure has been its education. He lifts the laws of constraint and their results are manifest. The real intrinsic nature of each soul leaps to the surface. Each soul's law of liberty becomes supreme. And each soul, without one word of condemnation or approval, by its own inner tendency, seeks its own place. They turn and separate, father from child, brother from brother, wife from husband, each with the old habitual restrictions lifted off, turns to its own; one by an inner power to the right hand, another by a like power to the left; these up to heaven, and these down to hell. Do we need more? It needs no word, no smile, no frown. The freeing of souls is the judging of souls. A liberated nature dictates its own destiny. Could there be a more solemn judgment seat? Is it not a fearful thing to be "judged by the law of liberty"?

"So speak ye, and so do, as they that shall be judged by the law of liberty." Is this James, then, what foolish readers of the Bible call him, a shallow moralist and formalist? Is Paul or John more profound? How must they speak and do who live in sight of such a judgment? With what continual searching of their hearts! How solemnly they must speak! How solemnly they must do! What a deep reverence and awe and independence must be in them! How real the things of the soul, the things of right and wrong, the things of spiritual life, must be! Above all, how they must wrestle and pray to win from God that gift of the regenerating Spirit which can change their hearts down to the core; make them, like Christ's heart, the spontaneous source of every holiness; make their law of liberty a law of everlasting life!

XII.

FASTING.

A SERMON FOR LENT.

"Moreover when ye fast, be not as the hypocrites of a sad counte-
nance. . . . That thou appear not unto men to fast, but unto thy
Father which is in secret."—MATT. vi. 16, 18.

THE character of the time and place in which the
earthly life of Christ our Lord was lived, has certainly
had much to do in shaping the whole growth of Christianity. It was necessary that the incarnation should
stand at one special point in history and at one particular spot upon the earth. That period and spot must
have been chosen by Him who sent His Son to be the
Savior. And one consequence has been that the vices
and errors which peculiarly characterized the country of
Judea eighteen hundred years ago stand forever most
emphatically denounced, and their opposite virtues and
truths most enthusiastically praised, by the Master of
the Christian faith.

Among other things which had gone sadly wrong in
His time, there was what we may call the bodily treatment of the spiritual life, the treatment of the spiritual
life through the body in which it is enshrined. And so
Jesus is especially drawn to declare what the true
method of that treatment is. It shows us how naturally the evils which He encountered spring out of human nature, when we see that not even the clearness of

Christ's teaching upon the subject has prevented the
Christian world from dropping back into the same evils
over and over again. That there is such a bodily treatment of the soul's life is clear enough. Hardly anything can happen to our bodies that does not send some
influence in to the most spiritual part of us. The condition of the body tells immediately on the condition of
its inmate. And immediately the question comes, — the
question which has always come to those who cared earnestly for their soul's life, — since everything that happens to the body tells upon the soul, may we not treat
the body so as to help the soul? That idea runs
through the whole of man's religious history. It inspires alike the monk flogging himself in his lonely
cell, and the fresh young English believer in muscular
Christianity. Out of that idea sprang the whole theory
and practice of fasting, or the denial of any of the appetites of the body, with a view to the training of the cor-
responding appetites of the soul. That is what fasting
means. It is not mere abstinence from food or from
any other pleasure, in itself. It is abstinence with a
purpose. This idea of the soul in, and capable of being
treated through, the body, was essential to it. Now,
when Jesus came to those Jews He found the practice
still prevailing, but its purpose had passed out of it. It
was an honorable, almost a required thing, to practise
certain abstinences; but that care for the soul's life, out
of which the habit of abstinence had sprung, was gone.
Christ's whole endeavor, for the Jews and for the generations who, to His sight, stood crowding behind the
Jews, was to bring the purpose back into the practice.
A purpose is to every practice what an inhabitant is to

a house. A house can stand with no inhabitant, but it
soon becomes rotten and goes to decay. You can tell
in a day when a tenant has moved into a house which
has stood unoccupied. The house puts on at once the
look of life. Its breaks and ruins are repaired. It is
renewed and preserved by its new occupancy. So a
practice may stand after its purpose is dead, but it is
weak and soon grows rotten and decays. But if you
can bring its purpose back into it again, it assumes
once more the look of life. Its broken walls are re-
built, its windows mended, and its gates repaired.
Many men attempt to keep up a body of good habits
without any spiritual purpose of goodness to inhabit
them. It is as anxious and costly and hopeless an un-
dertaking as would be the attempt to keep in repair a
whole village of unoccupied houses. But put the purpose into the practice and let it live there, and it is
strange how the practice takes care of its own repairs
and is always sound and whole.

Lent begins this week, and the idea of Lent is spiritual culture, and always, as a part of that idea, there has
been associated with Lent the thought of abstinence.
We are looking forward to a soberer and quieter life,
a life which in some form or other is to fast from some
of its indulgences. And the old danger comes up with
the old duty, the danger lest the fasting should become
to us as dead a thing as it was to those Jews. To guard
against that danger, ought we not to try to put its highest
purpose into this practice to which we annually return?
Is it not well that on this Sunday before Lent we should
try to see what God designs by those Lents, those periods
of sobered life and abstinence from outward pleasures,

which both in His word and in the intimations of our own nature have His sanction and authority?

God has a reason for everything. Our best religious progress consists in large part of this, the coming by sympathy with Him to see the reasons of what have been to us bare commandments. The change from the arbitrary to the essential look in what God does is the richest and most delightful feature of the spiritual growth. God says that He will punish the wicked. I bow submissive, but am puzzled and depressed. He says so, and it must be right. But by and by I come to know that He must punish the wicked, that the wicked man punishes himself, and all is changed. The puzzle, the bewilderment, is gone. God says, " Love me and you shall prosper." It sounds like an arbitrary reward given to His own favorites; but we go on to see that to love Him is prosperity, and then the heart rests satisfied. So God says, " Curb and deny the body, and the soul shall thrive." Gradually again we come to see that this too is essential and not arbitrary, and to trace the principles under which physical mortification ministers to spiritual life. One of the greatest joys of heaven must forever be this deepening and deepening sight of the essential behind what seemed arbitrary in the ways of God.

Let us ask what is the use of fasting, for so we shall best come to understand the true methods and degrees of fasting. And let us begin with this. All bodily discipline, all voluntary abstinence from pleasure of whatever sort, must be of value either as a symbol of something or as a means of something. These two functions belong to it as being connected with the body, which is at once the utterer and the educator of the soul within.

Just suppose any great mental or moral change to come in a man's life. We will not speak of the great fundamental religious change of a man's conversion; but any change from frivolity to earnestness, from lightness to seriousness of life. He who has been careless, free, and irresponsible, taking life as it came, with no reality, no sense of duty, undertakes a different way of living, begins to study, begins to work, seeks knowledge, accepts obligations. The old life fades away and a new life begins. Self-indulgence is put aside. Self-devotion takes its place. This is a spiritual, an inward change. It is independent of outward circumstances. A man conceivably may live this new life, and everything external be still the same that it has always been. But practically this more earnest inward life suits the outer life to itself. Quickly or gradually the man who has begun to live more seriously within, begins to live more simply without. He comes instinctively to less gorgeous dresses and barer walls and slighter feasts. The outer life is restrained and simplified. And this restraint and simplicity is at once a symbol or expression of the changed inner life, and a means for its cultivation. If the change is one which involves repentance and self-reproach, the giving up of a life which never ought to have been lived at all for one that always has been a duty, then both of these offices of the outward self-denial become plainer. The stripping of the old luxury off from the life is at once an utterance of humble regret for a wrong past, and also an opening of the soul to new and better influences. It is as when an effeminate reveller at a banquet is suddenly summoned to a battle where he ought to be in the front rank. As he springs up from the couch in self-reproach, the casting away of his garlands and his robes means, first, his shame at having been idle and feasting when he ought to have been at work; and second, his eagerness to have his limbs free so that the work which he has now undertaken may be well done. His stripping off of his wanton luxuries is at once a symbol of his self-reproach for the past, and a means of readiness for the new work that awaits him. And that is the meaning of all voluntary mortification which has any meaning. You go to a monk in his cell, and say: " What brings you here? Why do you choose these bare walls, this hard bed, this meagre fare?" If he understands himself at all, and has any real right to be there in the cloister, his answer is: " I love them for two reasons. They are the symbols of my repentance for my sin. They suit this soul of mine, stripped bare of all its pride, and prostrate in humility. And then, besides, they help this new life of communion with my Lord. Through their blank emptiness the highest influences may come in to me. My soul is not muffled and hidden from the voice and touch of God." Both as a symbol of repentance and as a means of education he loves his dreary cell.

Now to take one step more, if what this monk's experience is made of must, in some form or other, come in the life of every growing spiritual man; if in every spiritual advance there must be a stripping off of pride and an opening of the nature by some new doors to some new power; then, in healthier and more human forms no doubt, but still the same essentially, there must be in every aspiring life the same symbol and the same means which he has in his cell. No man can be a better man save as his pride is crushed into repentance; and as the swathing, enwrapping mass of passions and indulgences that is around him is broken through, so that God can find his soul and pour Himself into it. There is no other way. You want to be a better man. Perhaps you cannot remember that you ever wanted it before. You have gone on, self-satisfied and self-indulgent. But at last this new wish has come to you. Now, what have you to do? Any merest tyro in the spiritual experience may tell. You have got to break your pride all to pieces with repentance; and you have got to say to these crowding passions of yours: "Stand aside. Leave my soul open, that it and God, it and duty, may come together." Pride and passion must be conquered. That is an inward struggle. But it reaches the outward life, and in the voluntary surrender of that in which the pride has gloried and on which the passions have fed there is the symbol of the humiliation and the means of the new life of the soul. Yes, the monk was all wrong when he thought that there was merit in his lonely life, all wrong when he forgot or despised the rich teachings and helps of God which come through bounty and not through poverty, all wrong when, trying to diet his soul, he starved it; but let not our brighter religion, our joy in all of God's good things, make us forget wherein the monk was right, in his earnest fight with pride and passion, and in his earnest desire to make the circumstances of his outward life his ally and not his adversary in that fight. That is the redeeming glory which often illuminates the inhuman brutality of his life, and makes his cell-walls glow with heroism.

This, then, is the philosophy of fasting. It expresses

repentance, and it uncovers the life to God. "Come down, my pride; stand back my passions; for I am wicked, and I wait for God to bless me." That is what the fasting man says. You see what I mean by fasting. It is the voluntary disuse of anything innocent in itself, with a view to spiritual culture. It does not apply to food alone. It applies to everything which a man may desire. A man may fast from costliness of dress, from sumptuous houses, from exhilarating company, from music, from art, considered as sensuous delights. There are times when some deep experience, some profound humility of repentance, rejects them all. Not they but their opposites become the soul's true utterance. In its sorrow for its sins, all sumptuousness jars upon it. The feast and the feast's music are out of place. By emptiness and not by fulness that self-contempt, that sense of the vanity of the spirit's search to find goodness in itself, must be expressed.

Now let us dwell upon these two in order. Let us think first about this first value of fasting as a symbol. It expresses the abandonment of pride. But it is the characteristic of a symbolic action that it not merely expresses but increases and nourishes the feeling to which it corresponds. Laughter is the symbol of joy, but as you laugh your laughter reacts upon the joy and heightens it. Tears are the sign of sorrow, but they feed themselves the sorrow out of which they flow. Cheers are the expression of enthusiasm, but as the crowd sends up its shouts its zeal deepens and glows the brighter. And so if abstinence is the sign of humility, it is natural enough that as the life abstains from its ordinary indulgences, the humiliation which is

so expressed should be deepened by its expression.
Thus the symbol becomes also a means. I know the
dangers to which this idea may lead. I know and I
dread as much as anybody that reversal of the true relation which begins the creation of feeling at the outside,
and tries to make the heart beat by mere moving of the
arms and opening of the dead lips. But with all its
possible misapplications it is a true principle still. The
utterance of an emotion increases that emotion. The
heart once beating, the outward exercise makes it beat
the more truly. And so it is no artificial thing, nothing
unreal or unnatural, when the soul, sorry for its sins,
ashamed of its poor bad life, lets its shame utter itself
in signs of humiliation, and finds in quick and sure
reaction the shame which it expresses deepened and
strengthened through the utterance which expresses it.
Take it all to yourself. Suppose that something some
day makes that real to you, which you know so well
now, that your life, made for a more than angelic purity,
is all blotted and stained with sin. Suppose that some
day that awful contrast faces you which changes a man's
whole thought of himself. You see yourself and you
see God. Your sin stands out against His holiness;
your darkness against His perfection. On such a day
as that, humbled and broken, tell me, what will your
outward life be? Do you think there will grow up in
you no repugnance to your easy luxuriousness? Will
it seem well and fitting that an inner life so bruised
and shamed should be carried about in a body pampered
and decorated, where men are crowding, where lamps
are shining, where all is gay and has no touch of anything but pleasure? Something so different from that.

That mortified, bewildered inner life will claim its symbol. Solitude, silence, soberness, plainness even to meagreness, will seem the true expression of its new experience. And then from that expression of it there will come back new vividness and depth into the experience itself; and the soul will gather a new humility out of the circumstances of humiliation which it has already gathered about itself. That is the constant reaction between the outer and the inner conditions. That is what all representative dress and habits mean. The nun's quietude, the priest's purity, the mourner's sorrow, the bride's joy, the soldier's glory, — all are first uttered and then deepened by the garments in which they are severally clothed. First you give the emotion its true symbol and then the symbol in its turn gives new strength back to the emotion.

And if then it be good to consecrate some special weeks to the especial recognition of the experience, it is surely good likewise to put the expressive and educating symbol into those weeks too. Lent is consecrated to self-knowledge, to the humbling of pride, and so to that fasting, that abstinence and soberness of life, by which the soul's humility is first expressed and then increased.

And then let us pass to the second value of fasting, its value directly as a means. The more we watch the lives of men, the more we see that one of the reasons why men are not occupied with great thoughts and interests is the way in which their lives are overfilled with little things. It is not that you deliberately dislike thought and study and benevolence. It is mainly that you are so busy with amusement and society and idleness that you are living such an unprofitable life. It is

not that you hate your soul that you never talk with it.
It is that your body lies so close to you that it occupies
all your thought.   It is not that you despise the highest
hopes and interests of your immortal nature that you
neglect them so.   It is mainly that your passions crowd
so thick about you that you are entirely occupied with
them.   It is no untrue picture of the lives of many of
us if we imagine ourselves, that is, our wills, standing
in the centre ; and close about each central figure, about
each man's self, a crowd of clamorous passions and eager
lusts ; while away outside of them there wait in larger
circle the higher claimants of our time and powers,
culture and truth and charity and religion, with all their
train.   This self stands in the centre listening to the
passions which crowd up so thick about it ; worried
and restless all the time because, though it cannot see
them, it is always conscious of that outer circle of more
worthy applicants.   It hears their strong remonstrance
with the passions which are shutting them out from the
soul that belongs to them.   It promises itself the time
when all these lower claimants shall have been satisfied,
and shall give way and let into their places those who
are more worthy than themselves.   That time does not
come.   The passions crowd and clamor as noisily as
ever.   What ought to come to pass is that those crowding passions should feel themselves the higher dignity
of those who wait behind them and should make themselves their ministers, and urge not their own claims but
the claims which surpass their own, upon the central
man.   If they will not do that, then the man sometimes puts out his hand, parts and pushes aside this
clamorous crowd, these physical appetites, these secular

ambitions. He says to them "Stand back, and at least for a few moments let me hear what culture and truth and charity and religion have to say to my soul." Then up through the emptiness which he has made by pushing these clamorers back, there pours the rich company of higher thoughts and interests, and they gather for a time around the soul which belongs to them but from which they have been shut away. By and by the old crowd may return. The passions will not be satisfied until they have girdled the man's life once more. But even when they hold him fastest afterwards, they cannot but remember how they have once been driven back; they cannot be as contemptuous as they used to be of that loftier circle of influences which still stands outside of them; perhaps some time or other they may come to take and rejoice in their true place as interpreters and messengers through which the power of these higher influences may reach the soul. That is the story of the true fast. That is the real Lent. It is the putting forth of a man's hand to quiet his own passions and to push them aside that the higher voices may speak to him and the higher touches fall upon him. It is the making of an emptiness about the soul that the higher fulness may fill it. It may be temporary. Once more the lower needs may fasten on us, the lower pleasures try to satisfy us; but they never can be quite so arbitrary and arrogant as they were, after they have once had to yield to their superiors. They will be conscious that the soul is not wholly theirs. Perhaps some day they may themselves become, and dignify themselves by becoming, the meek interpreters and ministers of those very powers which they once shut out from the soul.

A man whose very bodily appetites brought him suggestions of divinest things, whose most secular life had
playing freely through it the messages of God, he evidently would need no fast, no interruption of those
pressures on his life which, with whatever worldly-
seeming hands they touched him, all brought him influences from divinity. There will be no fasting-days,
no Lent in heaven. Not because we shall have no
bodies there, but because our bodies there will be all
open to God, the helps and not the hinderances of
spiritual communication to our souls.

Do you remember the Collect for next Sunday, the
first Sunday in Lent? — "O Lord, who for our sakes didst
fast forty days and forty nights, give us grace to use
such abstinence that, our flesh being subdued to the
Spirit, we may ever obey Thy godly motives in righteousness and true holiness, to Thy honor who livest and
reignest with the Father and the Holy Ghost, One God,
world without end. Amen." When we pray that prayer
next Sunday we shall begin with our Master's fasting,
we shall remember how He put the associations and
appetites of the earth aside that His Father might come
close to Him. We shall pray to Him then to help us,
too, so to let Spirit in where flesh is now, closest to
our wills and selves, that hereafter we may be more
full of spiritual influences always, more ready to do
what is right than to do what is pleasant, more sensitive
to the fear of God than to the fear of man. Is it not
indeed a noble and a thorough prayer? How earnest
must be the man who really prays it! How happy is
the man in whom it really is fulfilled!

Suppose you go, some one of you whose life is all

external, all animal, either in the grosser or the more elegant ways, — suppose you go to some lofty or beautiful thinker, to some philosopher or poet, and you say to him, "Speak to me; tell me your thought; make me the sharer in your ideas and visions." He looks into your face, he sees what manner of man you are, and has he not the perfect right to answer you, " I cannot. You must fast first. Wrapped round with soft physical indulgences, all padded and protected as you are, how shall I strike into your muffled intelligence and feeling? You must strip these coverings off. You must lay bare your pampered life. You must give up being a sybarite or profligate. You must make me an avenue through this throng of lusts. Then I can come to you and you can take me in"? It is not arrogance. He cannot speak to you until you open the way. Your frivolity is like a solid wall about you and you must break it down before he can come in. That is why fashionable society is neither intellectual nor spiritual; why any man or woman must break its chains and refuse to be its slave, or it is impossible to come to the best culture either of mind or soul. There is no nobler sight anywhere than to behold a man thus quietly and resolutely put aside the lower that the higher may come in to him. Every now and then a conscience, among the men and women who live easy thoughtless lives, is stirred, and some one looks up anxiously, holding up some one of the pretty idlenesses in which such people spend their days and nights, and says "Is this wrong? Is it wicked to do this?" And when they get their answer, " No, certainly not wicked," then they go back and give their whole lives up to doing their innocent little piece of useless-

ness again. Ah, the question is not whether that is
wicked, whether God will punish you for doing that.
The question is whether that thing is keeping other
better things away from you; whether behind its little
bulk the vast privilege and dignity of duty is hid from
you; whether it stands between God and your soul. If
it does, then it is an offence to you, and though it be
your right hand or your right eye, cut it off, pluck it
out, and cast it from you. The advantage and joy will
be not in its absence, for you will miss it very sorely,
but in what its loss reveals, in the new life which lies
beyond it, which you will see stretching out and tempting you as soon as it is gone. To put aside everything
that hinders the highest from coming to us, and then to
call to us that highest which, nay, Who is always waiting to come, — fasting and prayer, — this, as the habit
and tenor of a life, is noble. As an occasional effort
even, if it is real and earnest, it makes the soul freer
for the future. A short special communion with the
unseen and eternal, prevents the soul from ever being
again so completely the slave of the things of sense
and time.

Have we not then understood something of what the
essential values of fasting are? It is both a symbol and
a means. Every kind of abstinence is at once an
expression of humility and an opening of the life.
What then is Lent? Ah, if our souls are sinful and are
shut too close by many worldlinesses against that Lord
who is their life and Savior, what do we need? Let us
have the symbols which belong to sin and to repentance.
Let us at least for a few weeks, among the many weeks
of life, proclaim by soberness and quietude of life that

we know our responsibility and how often we have been false to it. Let us not sweep through the whole year in buoyant exultation, as if there were no shame upon us, nothing for us to repent of, nothing for us to fear. By some small symbols let us bear witness that we know something of the solemnity of living, the dreadfulness of sin, the struggle of repentance. Our symbols may be very feeble, our sackcloth may be lined with silk and our ashes scented with the juice of roses. But let us do something which shall break the mere monotony of complacent living which seems to be forever saying over to itself that there is no such thing as sin, that to live is light and easy work. Perhaps the symbol may strike in and deepen the solemnity which it expresses. Perhaps as we tell God of what little sorrow for our sins we have, our sorrow for our sins may be increased, and while we stand there in His presence the fasting may gather a truer reality of penitence behind it.

And let those same symbols be likewise the means of opening our souls to Christ. For a few weeks let these obtrusive worldlinesses which block the door of our hearts stand back; and let the way be clear that He who longs to enter in and help us may come and meet no obstacle. This is our lenten task. "If any man will hear My voice and open unto Me, I will come in and sup with him," says Jesus. To still the clatter and tumult a little so that we may hear His voice, and to open the door by prayer, that is the privilege and duty of these coming weeks.

I must not linger to draw out from these descriptions of what fasting is, the methods in which fasting may be best observed. I think that you will see them for your-selves. I am sure that if you have caught what I have said, you will not think that they are anything slight or fantastic or rigid or mechanical. It is the utterance of penitence and the opening of doors to Christ. It must be very sacred; not formal but alive and glorified with motive. It must be very personal; not imitated from any pattern but the utterance of each man's repentance and love and hope and fear. It must be very reason-able; not unfitting the body for any good work but making it a more and more perfect instrument for the soul.

May God be with us during this Lent. May we be with God. I dare to hope that there shall be among us much of that fasting which our Father loves; much penitence for sin and much opening of long-shut doors to Christ. O my dear friends, let us enter into it with earnestness that we may come out of it with joy!

XIII.

A WHITSUNDAY SERMON.

"And they said unto him: We have not so much as heard whether there be any Holy Ghost."—ACTS xix. 2.

IT is always strange to us to find other people entirely ignorant of what makes the whole interest of our own life. We can hardly understand how it is possible that men should live along year after year, it may be generation after generation, knowing nothing about what really makes life for us. If we did not have this or that resource we should die, we should not care to live. Here is a man who has it not, and yet his life seems to be worth a great deal to him. He goes on bright and contented. Apply this to your love of reading. What would it be to you if every book were shut? What would you do if all communication with great minds through literature were broken off, if all the stimulus which comes to your own mind were stopped? And yet there are plenty of these men whom you meet every day who never open a book! Or take the exercise of charity. You would find little pleasure in life perhaps if you were shut in on yourself and could do nothing for anybody else. At least there are people of whom that is true. To find some one whom you can help, and have him near you so that you can help him, is as necessary to you as your food and drink. But there are people enough who seem to thrive abundantly without one act of charity. No self-sacrifice breaks the smooth level of their selfish days. They live without that which is your very life. So of a multitude of things. To one man it is incredible that life can be worth having without wealth; another cannot understand how men can live without amusement; and another, with his social nature, looks at his friend who lives in solitude, and wonders how and why he lives at all.

But nowhere is all this so clear as in the matter of religion. One who is really living a religious life, one who is really trying to serve God, who is loving God and believes with all his heart that God loves him, who finds all through his daily life the thick-sown signs that he is not alone, that Christ is helping him and saving him, how strange and almost impossible it is for him to conceive of a life that has nothing of all that in it. How desolate it seems! How tame it looks! One man's days are full of "joy in the Holy Ghost." He is always looking up for inspiration and always receiving it. When he wants comfort there is the Comforter close beside him, nay, deep within him. And then he opens the gate into some brother's life and learns how he is living, and finds that there is nothing at all there of what is so dear to himself. That brother "has not so much as heard whether there be any Holy Ghost."

This was just the position in which St. Paul found himself at Ephesus. He had been a Christian now for many years. It was far back in the past, the time when Jesus had appeared to him at mid-day and made him His disciple. He had felt the powerful aid of the Holy

Spirit in many a difficult moment of his life. All that
he did and said was in the confidence and by the help
of this unseen Friend who was nearer to him than any
of his closest earthly friends. And now he came to
Ephesus where there were some people who called
themselves Christians, and looking for their sympathy
and fellow-feeling he inquired, "Have ye received the
Holy Ghost since ye believed?" And they said unto
him, "We have not so much as heard if there be any
Holy Ghost." What was everything to him, they knew
nothing at all about. No wonder that his soul yearned
over them and he stayed with them and taught them.
We can picture his joy as gradually they became sharers in his happiness. What greater joy can any man
desire than to bring any other man who has known
nothing of it into the knowledge and the power of the
Holy Ghost?

This is our subject for Whitsunday morning. What
is it to know and not to know "whether there be any
Holy Ghost?" Are there not many men among us
who, if Paul asked them the old question, would have
to give the old Ephesian answer? "Have you received
the Holy Ghost, my friend?" Be honest, and must
you not answer as they answered, "Indeed I have not
so much as heard whether there be any Holy Ghost.
The name indeed has sounded in my ears; but as a real
person I have not got any true idea of His existence?"
Indeed the element of personal experience is so involved with all our knowledge of the Holy Spirit, that
for any man to say "Yes, I know Him," is a vastly
profounder acknowledgment than the statement of any
other knowledge. That is the reason why it is often so

vague and hesitating; but just for the same reason there comes a time when a man certain of his experience can say "Yes, I have received, I do know the Holy Spirit" with a certainty and distinctness with which he cannot lay claim to the knowledge of any other thing or person.

In order to understand our question let us turn to this story of the Ephesians. They were Christian believers. They are called "disciples." They had been baptized after the baptism of John. They believed Christian truth and they accepted Christian duty. They had a knowledge of, a faith in Christ, but they had no knowledge of the Holy Spirit. The perception of a present God who should fill out belief in truth with personal apprehension, and who should make duty delightful by personal love, this they had not reached; no one had told them of it.

It was a strange condition. It is not easy to reconcile it with many of our Christian notions, but yet it is a condition which represents the state of many people whom we know, who seem to have just what they had and to be lacking in just what they wanted. I suppose a man — and it is not all a supposition, the specimens are all around us — who believes the Christian truths. That there is a God who made and governs everything, that this God has revealed Himself in Jesus Christ, that He has lived and taught among men, and that at last He died for men in all the torture of the cross, and rose out of the grave in all the inherent power of His immortality, — this they believe. And all that God requires, all that Christ commanded, they accept. The duties of a good life, purity, honesty, resignation, self-denial, all of these they acknowledge. They try to do these duties. Their lives are often wonderful with the severe and lofty standards that they set themselves. They work heroically to fulfil the Master's will. Do we not know such men? They often puzzle us. The aim of all their life is high. Perhaps as I describe them you know that you are such a man yourself. You know that Christ is the great Master. His truth and His commandments you receive. But all the time you know that something is lacking, — a vividness, a life, a spring, a hopefulness and courage which you hear of other people having, which you sometimes see suggested in the things you do, which you seem to be often just upon the verge of, but which after all you do not get, and for the lack of which you are forever conscious of a certain dryness in your belief and a certain shallowness in your duty. What is it that you lack? This lack which, if I speak to your consciousness at all, you recognize, this something which you want, I take to be precisely the Holy Spirit. I do not know any other way in which He can become so real to a true, earnest man, as in the realization of just this want.

Let us separate the two departments to which I have referred, and speak more particularly, first of Belief and then of Duty. We have all been familiar all our lives with the distinction between head-belief and heart-belief. We have been taught, sometimes in such a way that it puzzles us, sometimes in such a way that it was confirmed by all our deepest experience, that simply to know, even with the most unquestioning conviction, that certain things were true, was not really having faith in those things. We go up to the very limit of the belief that can come either by traditional acceptance or by the conviction which argument produces, and there we stand. We cannot advance one step farther. We seem to have exhausted all the power that is in us. But we are sure that out beyond there is a region which, though we cannot enter it, is real, and is the true completion of the region through which we have already travelled.

How familiar this is in our dealings with our friends! I meet a man whom I have heard of long. Every authority in which I trust has told me that that man is wise and good. I come to know him well, and for myself I see the evidence of his wisdom and goodness. He proves it to me by the things he does. I no more doubt it than I doubt the sun. I say that I believe in him and I do believe in him; but all the time I am aware that out beyond the limit of this belief which I have reached and on which I stand, there is a whole new country, the region of another sort of belief in him into which I have not entered, where if I could enter for an hour everything would be different and new. I may be helpless. I may not be able to drag my feet across the border. I may stand as if chained by magic on this line which separates the head's belief from the heart's confidence and trust; but, powerless as I may be to enter it, I know that all this other world is there, with the mists hanging over it and hiding it, but real and certain still, the land of personal friendship and communion.

And just the same is true of truths. I know that some great truth is true; our human immortality, let us say. Every one whom I trust has told me so. Those whose words are to me like gospel have assured me of it. I may even hear and believe that voice that speaks out of eternity itself. I may put full trust in the word of Christ which tells me that the dead are not dead but are living still. And my reason may be all convinced. I may be persuaded by every natural argument that the soul does not perish in its separation from the body, but goes on in its unbroken life. All this I steadfastly believe. But what then? Here I stand upon this clear sharp line. I am immortal. I say it over to myself and know that it is true. But still I am not satisfied. This certainty of immortality is nothing to me but a mere conviction. I get nothing out of it. It does not flow up into my duties and experiences. I am not stronger for it. I have not taken hold of it, nor has it taken hold of me. And, until this comes to pass, I feel a sense of incompleteness. I know in all my surest moments that there is an assurance which I have not reached. I know when my feet are planted the firmest on the outmost line of rational conviction that there is beyond that line a region of spiritual confidence which I have not entered.

Here then are the two kinds of belief in persons and in truths. What is the difference between them? The first is clear, definite, and strong. I know that he whom I believe in, be it man or God, is true and good. I know that the truth that I accept is certain and impregnable. But there is something hard, dry, literal, about my faith. I can write it all down and say all that I know about it in letters inscribed upon a book. I may contend for it vigorously, but I do not feed upon it. The other belief has in it just what this belief lacks. It has spirit. I cannot write it down in letters. My heart is full of it and it takes me right into the heart of the Being or the truth that I believe in.

Surely this difference is very clear. Surely we all know well enough that struggle after the heart and spirit of what our minds have accepted, which lets us understand it all. How often we have felt that disheartening certainty that we are holding tight the shells, the mere outside of our richest beliefs, and not getting at their soul and life. Sometimes have we not contended earnestly for our faith and told some unbeliever that he was losing precious truth because he did not hold it, and then gone off from our discussion saying to ourselves gloomily, " Yes, it is all true, but still, if he held it only on the outside as I do, would he be so much richer after all ? " How often do we seem to ourselves to be like starving men, holding fruits that we know are rich and nutritious within, but cased in iron rinds which no pressure of ours is strong enough to break.

We are then very often where these Ephesians were. What came to them and saved them was the Holy Spirit. What must come to us and save us is the same Holy Spirit. There they were holding certain truths about God and Jesus, holding them drearily and coldly, with no life and spirit in their faith. Paul came to them and said, "These truths are true, but they are divine truths. You can really see them only as you are sharers in divinity yourself, and look at them with eyes enlightened by the intelligence of God. God must come into you and change you. His Spirit must come into you and occupy you; and then, looking with His Spirit, you shall see the spirit of the truths you look at; full of the Holy Ghost, the ghost, the heart, the soul of these great verities shall open itself in all its holiness to you. You shall see Jesus. You shall lay hold on immortality not on the outside but on the inside, in the very heart and spirit. Is not this intelligible, my dear friends? If Raphael could enter into you as you stand before his picture, would you not see deeper than you do now? Would not the Raphael in the picture come out from depths which you have never fathomed? If a child can be filled with the father's spirit, will not the spirit of the household, the intention, the purpose of it all, come out from the hard skeleton of its structure to meet the new spiritual apprehension? And so if you can be filled with God, will not the soul of God's truth of every sort, as you stand face to face with it, open to you deeper and deeper depths, changing your belief into a more and more profound and spiritual thing?

This was what Paul prayed for and this was what came to those Ephesians. God the Holy Spirit came into them and then their old belief opened into a different belief; then they really believed. Do you ask what we mean by that? Do you insist on knowing in exact statement how God entered into these people? Ah, if you ask that, you must ask in vain. If you insist upon not receiving God until you know how His life comes to your life, you must go on godless forever. You must know more than you do know, more than any man knows, of what man is and what God is and what are the mysterious channels that run from one life into the other, before you can tell how God flows into man and fills him with Himself. Tell me, if you can, the real nature of your friend's influence, the inflow of his life on yours that makes you full of him. Only one thing I think we can know about this filling of man by God, this communication of the Holy Spirit, that it is

15

natural and not unnatural, that it is a restoral of communication, that it is a reënthronement of God where He belongs, that the prayer which invokes the Holy Ghost is the breaking down of an artificial barrier, and the letting in of the flood of divine life to flow where it belongs, in channels that were made for it. If we know this, then the occupation of man's life by God is simply a final fact. It is just like the occupation of the body by the soul. No man can tell how it is; but that it is, is testified by every form of human strength and beauty in which our eyes delight.

Pause then a moment and think what Whitsunday was, the first Whitsunday. We read the story of the miracle. We hear the rushing of the mighty wind and see the cloven tongues of fire quivering above the heads of the apostles. Perhaps we cannot understand it. It seems natural enough that when Jesus is born the sky should open and the angels sing; that when Jesus dies the skies should darken and the rocks should break. The great events were worthy of those miracles, or greater. But here at Pentecost what was there to call out such prodigies? If what we have said is true, was there not certainly enough? It was the coming back of God into man. It was the promise in these typical men of how near God would be to every man henceforth. It was the manifestation of the God Inspirer as distinct from and yet one with the God Creator and the God Redeemer. It was primarily the entrance of God into man and so, in consequence, the entrance of its spirit and full meaning into every truth that man could know. It was the blossom-day of humanity, full of the promise of unmeasured fruit.

And what that first Whitsunday was to all the world, one certain day becomes to any man, the day when the Holy Spirit comes to him. God enters into him and he sees all things with God's vision. Truths which were dead spring into life and are as real to him as they are to God. He is filled with the Spirit and straightway he believes; not as he used to, coldly holding the outsides of things. He has looked right into their hearts. His belief in Jesus is all afire with love. His belief in immortality is eager with anticipation. Can any day in all his life compare with that day? If it were to break forth into flames of fire and tremble with sudden and mysterious wind, would it seem strange to him — the day when he first knew how near God was, and how true truth was, and how deep Christ was? O have we known that day? O, careless, easy, cold believers! if one should come and ask you, "Have you received the Holy Ghost since you believed?" dare you, could you, answer him, "Yes"?

Let us take now a few moments to consider the other part of the Holy Spirit's influence, the way in which, when He enters into a soul, He not merely gives clearness to truth, but gives delight and enthusiastic impulse to duty. These Ephesians had not merely believed much Christian truth, they had been trying also to do what was right; they had accepted the Christian law so far as they knew it. We can think of them as very patient, persevering workers, struggling to do everything that they were told they ought to do. Now what did. Paul do for them here when he brought them the knowledge of the Holy Spirit? I think the answer will be found in that verse of the Savior's in which He described what the Holy Spirit's work should be. "He shall take of mine and shall show it unto you," Jesus had said. The work of the Spirit was to make Jesus vividly real to men. What he did then for any poor Ephesian man or woman who was toiling away in obedience to the law of Christianity, was to make Christ real to the toiling soul behind and in the law. He took the laborer there in Ephesus who only knew that it was a law of Christianity that he ought to help his brethren, and made it as personal a thing, as really the wish of Christ that he should help his brethren, as it had been to the twelve disciples when they were living under Christ's eye, while he was with them in Judea or while they were distributing the bread and fish at his command to the hungry men by the sea of Galilee. This was the change which the Holy Spirit made in Duty. He filled it with Christ, so that every laborer had the strength, the courage, the incitement to fidelity which comes from working for one whom the worker knows and loves.

And very often when our tasks are pressing on us is not this the change we need? Your Christian duties, the prayers you pray, the self-denials that you practise, the charities you give, — what is the matter with them? The temptations you resist, the good word that you speak to some brother, the way you teach your class, the way you condemn some prevailing sin, — what is the matter with them all? What is the reason why they are so dull and tame? Why are they not strong enthusiastic work? The reason must be that there is no clear person for whom you do these things. You serve yourself, and how clear you are to yourself; and so, what life there is in every act of your own service; but you serve Christ and how dim He has grown! and so, how listlessly the hands move at His labor! Now if the Holy Spirit can indeed bring Him clearly to you, is not the Holy Spirit what you need? And this is just exactly what He does. I find a Christian who has really "received the Holy Ghost," and what is it that strikes and delights me in him? It is the intense and intimate reality of Christ. Christ is evidently to him the clearest person in the universe. He talks to Christ. He dreads to offend Christ. He delights to please Christ. His whole life is light and elastic with this buoyant desire of doing everything for Jesus, just as Jesus would wish it done. So simple, but so powerful! So childlike, but so heroic! Duty has been transfigured. The weariness, the drudgery, the whole task-nature, has been taken away. Love has poured like a new life-blood along the dry veins, and the soul that used to toil and groan and struggle goes now singing along its way, "The life that I now live in the flesh, I live by the faith of the Son of God who loved me and gave Himself for me."

O my dear friends, have you received the Holy Ghost since you believed? Since you began to do your duty has any revelation come to you of Him who is the Lord of duty? Have you caught any sight of Christ, and begun to know what it is to do it all for Him? Has the love with which He lived and died for you been so brought home to you that you are longing only to thank Him by a grateful and obedient life? Have you so made Him yours that He has made you His? If so, the life of heaven has begun for you. Only to know Him more and more forever and so to grow into completer and completer service, there is your eternity already marked out before you. It stretches out and is lost beyond where you can see; but it all stretches in the one direction in which your face is set; deepening knowledge, bringing deeper love, forever opening into more and more faithful service. Go on into the richest developments of that life, led by the power of the Holy Ghost.

Both in belief and in duty then, this is the work of the Holy Spirit; to make belief profound by showing us the hearts of the things that we believe in; and to make duty delightful by setting us to doing it for Christ. O, in this world of shallow believers and weary, dreary workers, how we need that Holy Spirit! Remember, we may go our way, ignoring all the time the very forces that we need to help us do our work. The forces still may help us. The Holy Spirit may help us, will surely help us, just as far as He can, even if we do not know His name or ever call upon Him. But there is so much more that He might do for us if we would only open our hearts and ask Him to come into them. Remember, He is God, and God is love. And no man ever asks God to come into his heart and holds his heart open to God, without God's entering. Children, on this Whitsunday pray the dear God, the blessed Holy Spirit, to come and live in your heart and show you Jesus, and make you love to do what is right for His sake. Old men, aspire to taste already here what is to be the life and joy of your eternity. Men and women in the thick of life, do not go helpless when there is such help at hand; do not go on by yourselves, struggling for truth and toiling at your work, when the Holy Spirit is waiting to show you Christ, and to give you in Him the profoundness of faith and the delightfulness of duty.

Let us come to Christ's Communion Table and celebrate our union with Him and with one another, putting all fear and selfishness aside, and praying Him to show us there how rich a thing it is to believe in Him and how sweet a thing it is to serve Him by His Holy Spirit.

XIV.

CHRIST THE FOOD OF MAN.

"The Jews therefore strove among themselves, saying : How can this man give us his flesh to eat ? " — JOHN vi. 52.

ANY one who suddenly came upon a group of eagerly disputing men and overheard this question, unconnected, by itself, would see at once that he needed something more before he could understand it, that it must have a history; and if it interested him at all he would inquire how such a strange question came to be asked. The answer would be this : Yesterday, on the other side of the Sea of Tiberias, Jesus of Nazareth worked a miracle, and fed a crowd of five thousand men with five loaves of bread and two little fishes. During the night He crossed the lake. In the morning the people found that He was gone, and they took boats and followed Him. When He saw them, He told them that He was afraid they had come after Him not for His own sake, not because they loved or honored Him, but because they wanted another miracle and more bread. Then He goes on to tell them that the food they really need is food for the soul, not for the body. Then He offers them Himself as their Savior, their Master, their nourishment, their strength. And finally, led on into the strong figure by the first event which started his discourse, the flocking of the people after food, He makes·

this singular and impressive announcement: "I am the living bread that came down from heaven; if any man eat of this bread, he shall live for ever; and the bread which I shall give is My flesh, which I will give for the life of the world." Then came the question, tossed back and forth among the debating Jews, "How can this man give us his flesh to eat?"

From this simple sketch we can see that the discourse which the question interrupted was one of the most profoundly spiritual and solemn. The nurture of the soul of man by the communicated life of God, that is what Christ is talking of. Earth and man seem to lie open in their need, with all their ordinary concealments stripped away; heaven and God are open in their readiness to supply. All reserve is broken and the power of life, the manifested mercy of God, is offering itself to the want of man. In the very midst of this sacred offer comes in this question which at first only chills us and casts us back: "How can this man give us his flesh to eat?" We have been so carried on by the speaker's spirit that we have been ready to accept anything. The special form in which He clothed His offer has not staggered us. We have not stopped to analyze it, hardly to notice it. But here are some cooler or more captious Jews; nay, perhaps some Jews who, being more anxiously in earnest, do criticise and weigh every word in which the offer comes, and to them this form seems so strange as to be unintelligible, and so we begin to hear the murmur drifting round, "How can this man give us his flesh to eat?"

What was the spirit of the question? I have just suggested that there are different spirits in which it might be asked. There are two ways in which you may assent to any statement that you hear. You may not care much about it, and merely say "Yes" to it because it does not interest you enough to make you criticise it at all. Or, on the other hand, you may go down to the very bottom of it and believe it true with all your heart. And so there are two ways of questioning a statement, the superficial and the profound, the flippant and the earnest way. One man asks questions because he wants to prove the announcement false. Another man asks because he longs to see it prove itself true. There is the arrogant and wanton objector; and there is the eager questioner who so dearly loves the vision which the words he has just heard have raised before his mind that he hardly dares to ask about it lest he should lose it, but yet who must ask because it is too dear to be left in doubt. Both of these must have been present in the crowd which heard the words of Christ. Hence came the strife. One man said "I believe it," and you saw as he spoke that he had thought deeply and been deeply touched and really did understand and believe. Another said "Yes, I believe it," and you saw that he was a merely thoughtless partisan admirer of Christ, not having reached any true comprehension of his Master and not knowing what he was talking about. Another said "How can it be?" and his "How can it be?" evidently meant "It shall not be if I can help it." Another said "How can it be?" and you saw his face all wistful as he spoke, as if he said "It sounds like what I want. O, if I could only see just what He means and get hold of the truth and strength which I am sure there is in what He says! It eludes me, but

I am sure that it is there. How can it be?" These were all present in the crowd.

Now let us leave the company which was assembled on the shore of Gennesaret and come down to our own time and place. Still men are striving among themselves with the old question. Still the earnest believer, the flippant partisan, the captious objector, and the wistful inquirer, are busy with these words of Christ. These words have kept their hold upon the world. Now, just as then, they are not words to be ignored. Men will ask what they mean. Men are asking one another; nay, souls are divided within themselves and do not know how to think in seeking the answer to that old question, "How can this man give us His flesh to eat?"

What answer can we give? To the captious objector, in this as in every other question concerning Christ there is no answer really to be given. If a man wishes to find the religion of Christ untrue and asks you questions about it with the distinct desire of convicting your Master of folly or of fraud, then there is simply nothing for you to do but to turn off from him and go your way; not angrily, not with any idea of punishing him for his obstinacy by shutting him out of the truth. You have nothing to do with that. If such a terrible penalty as that can be inflicted, God must inflict it, and not you. You must get the truth in to any most closed soul where it is possible to send it; but if a man is wilfully obstinate and determined to find fault, you have to turn away simply because it is impossible by the very nature of the things to make him see and believe. For whatever the announcement of Christ may mean, it means something whose understanding must be experimental certainly; it declares something which the heart must feel before the mind can comprehend it. It is a law of spiritual action and so appeals to the spiritual function for its recognition. If that spiritual function is closed and bolted against its access by the heavy will there is no hope that it can enter in another way. If you hold a rose up before a man and he shuts his eyes tight and just holds out his hands and says "Here, I am ready to be persuaded; convince me by touch that your rose is red;" then you are helpless. If you hold a spiritual power up to the conscience and the heart, and the conscience and the heart are shut tight, refusing to obey and love, then you are hopeless even if the intellect does cry "Convince me." Christ in every claim is spiritual demand as well as mental conviction, and so the willing heart must go with the open mind. Nothing is harder or more painful than to try to tell a man who is simply interested in Christianity as a curious problem, what Christ is to you as Savior and Master and Friend; and to see not merely that he utterly fails to understand you but that he thinks all such accounts of your own experience and such appeal for a new spiritual sense in him to be thoroughly unreal, irrational, and absurd.

We must speak then mainly to others; to those who do not want to disbelieve, those who are willing to believe. Some of them do believe already. Having long made Christ a spiritual study, kept their lives close to His for years, He has borne witness of Himself to them and they have drawn much up from Him. He has fed them richly; but still, when the full words are put before them, about "eating his flesh," it seems as if there were still something a great deal deeper than they have known yet, and they begin to ask with vivid anticipation of some new experience of the Savior, made delightful by all their recollection of the old, " How can He give me His flesh ? I would know all if there is more to know, now that I have known so much and found it so full of joy and strength."

And then there are others who do not believe but who want to; who cannot claim any personal experience of Christ but who long for it; who hear others telling what He has done for them and who wish that they might know something of all this; who hear His own account of what He can do, outgoing any story that any ripest saint has to tell of what He has done; those, in one word, who want a Savior and feel that this must be their Savior though they cannot see just how His work is to be done. These are the people that I want to speak to especially to-day, for there are no people in the world in whom Christ must feel so deep and tender an interest, none of whom we are so sure that He would say as He said of the scribe in the Gospel, " Thou art not far from the kingdom of God."

And the very first thing that one wants to say always to such people is this; that although they cannot get the assurance which they need out of the reported experience of other people, yet the experience of others may give them an assurance of the possibility of gaining what they want and so may help them very much. It does not make you warm, perhaps it makes you feel all the colder, to see other men walking off there in the full sunlight; but it may let you know that your case is not hopeless, that if you sit and wait a little longer the light that is shining on them may move on until it reaches you ; or, what is better still, that if you will you may get up and go into the sunlight which will then warm you as much as them. Either way the sight of their comfort gives you hope and courage, which is what you need. So it is in religious things. A verse of Scripture may be all dark to you, but you know that multitudes have found in it the revelation of light and life. You cannot possibly take their comfort in it for your own. All spiritual culture is a great deal too individual for that. But you can believe that there is comfort in it and search after it more hopefully because they found it there. It must signify something to you that, though it seems so unintelligible to you, there have been hundreds of thoughtful men and women whose soul's life has run deep and strong as a river, who have looked for truth with eyes quickened by much knowledge of life and human need, who, if you had asked them for the secret of human existence, would have done nothing, but turn and lay their hand upon this chapter and say : " Except I eat His flesh and drink His blood I have no life. That is my only life. I feed on Him." You may say it proves nothing and explains nothing. It makes us believe at least in the possibility of proof and explanation.

And one thing more. Notice how Christ receives this doubting question : " How can this man give us His flesh to eat ? " " Except ye eat the flesh of the Son of Man and drink His blood, ye have no life in you." That is His answer. It reminds us of another scene. In the third chapter of St. John, Jesus says to Nicodemus, " Except a man be born again he cannot see the kingdom of God;" and Nicodemus answers, "How can a man be born when he is old?" and Jesus answers him, "Except a man be born again he cannot enter into the kingdom of God." You see the similarity of the two cases. In each of them Christ says "It must be;" and in both cases the answer comes, "How can it be?" and in both again the answer is, "It must be;" nothing more. What does it mean but this, that you cannot know how it is done except by doing it? You ask me "How?" The answer is, "I cannot tell you. Go and do it and you shall learn." It may seem strange, but it is no new law. It is a law which runs through all life in application to the highest things. I cannot tell you how to meet sorrow. Go and meet it and you shall learn the sweet lesson out of the bitter education. I cannot tell you how to meet joy so that the head shall not be turned. It is when the head is tempted to be giddy that it learns soberness in prosperity. I cannot tell you how to meet death. Who ever did tell his brother? Nay, can even God tell us so that we can know beforehand what we shall say to the king of terrors when at last he stalks across our path? But, going straight up to him, what beautiful sights have we not seen of old men greeting him as their friend, and strong young men letting him take their burden off of their yet unbent backs, and little children laying their hands trustingly in his to go down the dark way which he knows, which leads into the Father's light. Of all these highest trials there can be no previous experiment to see how it is done. You must do it. So only can you learn how to do it. "How can I?" cries the poor bereaved heart sitting in the darkened room alone; "How can I live my dreary life alone ? " " Go on and live it " is the answer. And as he goes it is not dreary and he can live it bravely in Christ's strength. So it is with being a Christian. Be one; so only can you know how. " How can I eat His flesh ? " " Except you do you have no life." It seems hard and unreasonable, this inexorable demand for the unintelligible and impossible; but it is only the principle of all experimental truth ; that in no other way than by experience can it be learned. It seems to involve a contradiction but yet it is the method of much of the very best progress which we make, and we all act on it constantly.

> " You must love Him, ere to you
> He shall seem worthy of your love."

But now after all these preliminary words, let us go on and see if we can understand the question and at all see its answer. " How can this man give us His flesh to eat ? " The whole expression which called out the question is a figure. It is figurative through and through. Even the most literal Romanist who applies it all to the sacrament of the Lord's Supper and treats that sacrament in the most material way still must own something of a figure in it. The bread even though turned into the sacred flesh is still eaten by the bodily mouth for spiritual purposes, and it seems impossible to bridge over the gap in the idea between the physical and spiritual nourishment without some intrusion of analogy or figure. The figure is very vivid and graphic, so clear and sharp that it sometimes seems as if there were no figure there, as if it were the statement of the baldest material fact, but it is figurative nevertheless.

And the general spirit of the figure is clear ; it means support or strength. That is the idea of food. Only food means a certain kind of strength. It is strength in a man, not strength without a man. It is strength incorporated and not strength applied. You see the difference. If a wall is tottering upon the street the men come with their timbers and wedge them in and brace the bulging building back and hold it up. If a man is weak so that his legs tremble under him, you give him food, and the strength of the food enters into him and becomes his strength, and he stands firm. There is the strength of a buttress which sustains a tower, or a rock in which a tower is set. That is outward strength. There is the strength of food which supports the man by becoming the man. Evidently that is something different. That is inward strength. And this last is the sort of strength which Christ promises in the gift of Himself. Thus much is clear in the word "eat."

We easily distinguish everywhere between the two sorts of strength, and the last is more valuable in so far as it is more intimate and personal. The outer strength is the strength of the prop and the buttress ; the inner strength is the strength of the life-blood in the veins. You have a hard duty to do to-morrow morning, something which you thoroughly hate to do. Your reluctance makes you weak. But you must do it because it is God's will and so your duty. You do not expect or try to escape, but you cry out to God to strengthen you, and He has two ways of answering your prayer, one better than the other, which He uses according as He finds you open and fit for the lesser or the larger mercy. He may bring all His commandments and penalties and lay

16

them up like buttresses against the weak wall of your resolution and crowd you into duty by the pressure of compulsion and of fear. Or He may fill you so with Himself, make you love Him so that you shall, as the Collect beautifully prays, "love the thing that He commands," and so grow into duty by the inspiration of His character, His standards, His life, become yours by love. Or again, you are too weak for your sorrow. What does He do to give you strength? He may perhaps take the sorrow off; or He may give you something to beguile it, something that makes you proud to suffer, or some strong friendship that is brought out by your suffering and almost makes you forget your agony. Those are external strengths. Those are buttresses against the walls. He may do something better. He may give you that unutterable certainty of His sympathy which does not abolish pain but transforms and transfigures it, so that you would not let the suffering go if with it you must lose this precious nearness of God. He may make suffering, by some such exquisite mixture, the source of rich delight and holy deeds, so that the suffering itself becomes the central pillar of the life, and does not have to be held up, but holds. That is the inner strength. That is the strength of food.

And notice how this last alone is vital. It alone makes life. It lives. The buttress keeps the dead wall standing, but the sap makes the live tree still more alive with growth. So compulsion and fear keep us true to duty, but love makes us larger and fit for greater duty every day. Every vital strength must be the strength which incorporates itself with the very being of the thing that it supports. Except we eat we can have no life in us.

Now we must remember that the great trouble of life with which religion has to do, the only weakness that really can give a man the most deep and poignant sorrow, must be moral trouble, must be sin. There alone can self-reproach come in; and if a man has nothing to reproach himself with he can bear anything. But when we are speaking of the weakness of sin then it is evident that the only strength that can be sufficient for it must be the strength that enters into and becomes part of and changes the sinful nature. You have done wrong, you are wrong, and in your wickedness you are weak as the wicked always are. You are tottering and trembling under the fear of punishment, under the sense of broken harmony with God, but most of all under the consciousness of a corrupted and perverted nature in yourself. What does Christ do for you? First, He declares forgiveness. That takes away the fear of punishment. He calls on you to believe that you are pardoned. He asks of you that faith which, laying hold of His great love, shall see the penalty of broken law broken itself and trodden under foot by triumphant grace. He reveals God's love to you. He shows you a Deity not angry but infinitely pitiful. Against the wall tottering with a sense of divine displeasure He builds the strong buttress of an assured love of the Father you have sinned against, and so keeps you from falling. These are external strength. If they stood by themselves they would be only external. The soul, sure that the past is forgiven, feeling above it the pitying presence of a grieved but loving God, has every outward strength for holiness that it could ask. But what then? If still the sinful nature stays within, if the whole loved and forgiven man is still full of the old bad impulse, what is there still but weakness? Some new strength must come, and it must be inward and not outward. It must enter in and change the nature. It must mingle itself with the soul itself and make that holy which was unholy, set that right which was wrong. It must be a new birth of goodness in the man as well as a new world of mercy about the man. It must be not only buttress to sustain but food to change; not only a Christ to stand outside and support with the strong hands of His forgiveness, but a Christ to come in and strengthen by the power of His incorporated life.

The two indeed are not so separate as we seem thus to describe them. They must come together. The outer and the inner, forgiveness and regeneration, are inseparable halves of one single mercy, given not separately but by one single act of pitying love. They cannot come separately. God does not forgive a soul and leave it still hopeless in its unchanged native sinfulness; nor does God change a soul and leave its new life crushed under the burden of its old unforgiven sin. He does both, or He tries to do both, for every soul. But in our thinking about the great mercy there appear these two aspects of it, and we think of them separately. Christ is the Staff we lean on, the Rock we stand on, the Light that leads us, the Master on whose breast we lie; but He is also the Bread of Life. He is many things outside of us, — Wisdom, Righteousness, Redemption. He is also something inside of us, Sanctification. He says " Lean on Me, stand on Me, take hold of Me and walk." But when He takes up His deepest word it is this, — "Feed on Me; unless you feed on Me you have no life in you." He says "Look and see how good God is; touch Me and feel God's mercy; hear Me and I will tell you how He loves you." But at the last this comes as the commandment of the deepest faith, the promise of the highest mercy, — "O taste and see that the Lord is gracious."

My dear friends, how noble and how beautiful it is. Great is the work that Christ does for us. Greater, deeper still, because without it all the other would be purposeless and useless, is the work that Christ does in us. How wonderful it is. The world glows with the assurance of redemption. Heaven opens, and there the saints and elders are prostrate before the throne. The whole spiritual universe trembles with the new spiritual life which has come to it out of the marvellous death. In the midst of it all lies one soul, dead and incapable of action, though intensely alive with desire for a share in all this glorious vitality. It knows that all this is for it, and yet it cannot rise up and lay hold of it. The world about it is strong with the promise and temptation of holy things. The soul itself is weak with its own unholiness. Then comes the better, perfect, completing promise of a change of soul. The Christ who has done all this offers to do one thing more, to make the dead soul alive and able to enjoy and use it all. He will come into us, not merely stand without us. He will come in and be Himself the power which lays hold of His own invitations. We may feed on Him. Nay, let us take His own strong word and say, "He that eateth Me, the same shall live by Me." That is the inner life, Christ in the soul rising up and laying hold of the infinite possibilities which redemption has prepared. Forgiveness is not too great a boon, earth is not too sacred or solemn, heaven is not too glorious, for the soul which, alive with Christ, claims all the spiritual life that Christ has created for its own.

To feed on Christ, then, is to get His strength into us to be our strength. You feed on the cornfield and the strength of the cornfield comes into you and is your strength. You feed on the cornfield and then go and build your house, and it is the cornfield in your strong arm that builds the house, that cuts down the trees and piles the stone and lifts the roof into its place. You feed on Christ and then go and live your life, and it is Christ in you that lives your life, that helps the poor, that tells the truth, that fights the battle, and that wins the crown.

But what is this strength of Christ that comes to us? There can be only one answer. It is His character. There is no strength that is communicable except in character. It is the moral qualities of His nature that are to enter into us and be ours because we are His. This is His strength, His purity, His truth, His mercifulness, — in one word, His holiness, the perfectness of His moral life. It is not that He made the heavens; it is not that He is the Lord and King of hosts of angels, cherubim and seraphim, who do His will and fly on errands of helpfulness to laboring souls all through the world at His command. Those are the external strength which Christ supplies. In unknown, countless ways He furnishes it. Even the powers of nature He can mould to most obedient servantship to His disciple's needs. He helps us as the divine can help the human, by supplies of power coming from without and laying themselves against the tottering life. But this is not the strength which enters in and, by a beautiful incorporation with the disciple's weakness, becomes his strength. That must be a strength of which the human disciple too is capable, as well as the divine Master. It must be that holiness which was in Jesus of Nazareth and which we, because we are of the same humanity that He wore, are capable of possessing and developing. This is the strength of which we eat, and which like true food enters into us and becomes truly ours while it is still His.

And this brings us to the understanding of that word "flesh." We are to eat His flesh. Now the flesh was the expression of the human life of Jesus. It was in His incarnation that He became capable of uttering those qualities in which man might be like Him, which men might receive from Him and take into themselves. Think of it. God had stood before men from the first, and they had looked with awe and adoration upon Him throned far above them. They had worshipped Him, they had feared Him, they had loved Him. Now and then some ardent and ambitious spirit soaring to the highest dream of the soul, or some patient and humble nature purified to deeper insight by its humility, had conceived that man ought not only to worship and fear and love God, but to be like God, to reflect in his own obedient nature the perfectness that he adored. But how? What was it that he should reflect? What was there in the Deity that could repeat itself in man? Not His majesty, not omnipotence and not omniscience, surely.

Men were bewildered; and either vague and impious attempts to match the inimitable glories that belong only to divinity, like Eden or Babel; or else reckless discouragement and brutal despair, as if nothing that was in God could be restored in man, as in the countless Sodoms and Gomorrahs of the ancient world, — these were the terrible results of the blind craving. Then came the incarnation. Here was God in the flesh. Solemnly, that of the divine which was capable of being wrapped in and of living through the human, was brought close within that wondrous human life lived in a human body. There was the God we were to imitate, to grow like to, to take into ourselves until He filled us with Himself. It was the incarnate God; it was the God in the flesh that was to enter into man. This was the flesh we were to eat and by which we were to live.

Do you not see this? God in the heavens, the eternal unseen God, is true. His truth is the pillar of the universe. But can man win that truth? It is too vast, too mighty, too bound up with omniscience. But behold here! Here in the flesh is truth as perfect, as divine, yet truly human. Listen to the truth as it is shown to Pharisee and publican, to His disciples and His judges, to the young man who wanted to be His follower, and to Judas Iscariot who was to betray Him. That is the truth, that truth incarnate, the divine truth in the flesh, that we are to take and eat and make it truth in us. So of purity. It was awful as it flashed in solemn indignant judgments from the clouded skies. It was gentle, gracious, and human, though none the less divine, as it defied and cowed the devil in the temptation in the desert. So of pity, even. It awes us and consoles us when it comes to us out of the unseen heart of God by the revelations of nature or our own experience. But it enters into us and makes us pitiful when it falls upon us in the soft tear-drops of the pitying Savior at the tomb of Lazarus. These are the acts that Jesus did. Take the yet more wonderful being lying behind them all which Jesus was, and see how that, in its perfect consecration, in its consecrated perfectness, became clear and imitable to men; how men began to believe that they might be that divine thing too when they saw it in the incarnate God, in Christ; and then, I think, you can understand something of how only in the flesh could God thus present Himself for the most intimate entrance into man; so can know something of what Jesus meant when He bade the hungry human soul eat of His flesh.

How high that hunger and its satisfaction is. You long for God to come and be within you, to rule you, to fill you; nay, in the words that sound so mystical but are so real to multitudes who seek in vain for other words to tell the strange experience, for God to be you and to live your life. That is a vast desire. How every other wish grows insignificant beside it. Do you know anything of it? I trust you do. You look on high and God is too mighty. You look close by your side and Jesus Christ, the God incarnate, has the very words you need: "He that eateth My flesh and drinketh My blood dwelleth in Me and I in him." "This is the bread that came down from heaven." "He that eateth of this bread shall live forever." Then there is nothing left but to cry, "Come, come, Lord Jesus."

But there is one thing more that I must say. This

giving of His own flesh for our food is always spoken of
in connection with the great sacrifice of the flesh in
which He gave it for us.   There is always this association between the reception of the strength of the incarnate Christ, and His crucifixion in which He willingly
gave Himself up that He might furnish that strength
to His people forever.   The great Christian sacrament,
which embodies this idea of which we have been treating, the idea of the feeding of the soul upon the flesh of
Christ, is all filled full of memories of the agony in
which the flesh was offered.   What does this mean ?
Does it not mean this, — that however man longs for
his God; however man sees that in the incarnate
Christ there is the God he needs and whom his nature
was made to receive; it is only when man sees that
Divine Being suffering for him, only when he stands by
the cross and beholds the love in the agony, that his
hungry nature is able to take the food it needs, that is
so freely offered ?   The flesh must be broken before we
can take it.   This is what Christ says, and the history
of thousands of souls have borne their witness to it,
that it is the suffering Savior, the Savior in His suffering, that saves the soul.   Eager and earnest men may
have gone beyond what is written, beyond what is possible for us to know, in their attempts to analyze that
suffering and in telling just how it works most wonderful effects.   I believe they have.   But do not let that
make you lose sight of what the Bible tells you, that it
is the death of Christ that saves the world ; nor of what
your own heart must tell you if you let it speak, that it
is only when you see this Savior whom you honor, whom
you love and try to serve, dying to show a love for you

which nothing short of death could utter; only then that the soul opens wide enough with gratitude to take Him in completely to be its life and its salvation.

The suffering Savior inly known, and through His wounds letting out His life into the starved lives of those who hold Him fast, that is the Gospel. It is not what church you belong to or what work you do, but what you know of, how deeply you are fed by Him — the suffering Savior. That is the question for the soul.

Before His cross the lesson must be learned. Stand there until you are grateful through and through for such a love so marvellously shown. Let gratitude open your life to receive His Spirit; let it make you long and try to be like Him; let love bring Him into you so that you shall do His will because you have His heart. That entrance of His life into you shall give you strength and nourishment you never knew before. Then you shall know in growing, dependent, delighted strength, more and more every day, the answer to the old ever new question, "How can this man give us His flesh to eat?"

How can He? Certainly He can if you will go to Him and pray to Him and love Him and obey Him and receive Him. And what a strength comes of that holy feeding! Where is the task that terrifies the man who lives by Christ? Where is the discouragement over which he will not walk to go to the right which he must reach? You may starve him but he has this inner food. You may darken his life but he has this inner light. You may make war about him but he has this peace within. You may turn the world into a hell but he carries his inner heaven safely through its fiercest fires.   He is like Christ himself.   He has meat to eat that we know not of, and in the strength of it he overcomes at last and is conqueror through his Lord.   It is possible, and may God make it real for all of us.

XV.

THE MANLINESS OF CHRIST.

"Handle me and see, for a spirit hath not flesh and bones as ye see me have." — LUKE xxiv. 39.

IN these words Christ after his resurrection appeals to His disciples to bear witness that He is a true living man, and not a disembodied spirit. He bids them use their human senses to discover that He is truly human like themselves. The words therefore may represent to us the perpetual appeal which Christ makes to our human consciousness and to the perceptions of mankind to recognize His true humanity. As He then offered His human body for the inspection of His disciples, and bade them own that it was truly a man's body, so He is always offering His whole human nature and calling on men to witness that He is truly human in thought and feeling and character, the pattern and fulfilment of humanity.

I want to speak this morning of the Manliness of Christ. It is a subject of which many thoughtful men are thinking. A recent book of Mr. Thomas Hughes, whom one may almost call a student and connoisseur of manliness, has dwelt with very great force and beauty upon the manliness of Christ, and has turned many people's thoughts that way. He frankly accepts the challenge that if Christ is really the perfection of our humanity He must present our human nature in such a shape and action that we men shall be able to recognize it by our best human standards as the truest and the best; not weak, timid, sentimental; but strong, brave, vigorous, full of feeling but also full of conscience; full of reason; patient by abundance not by lack of life; tolerant, forgiving, meek, not from superficialness but from the depth of insight and emotion. So does this writer, with his genius for manliness, describe the manly Christ. He holds His picture up and as it were cries anew " Ecce Homo," " Behold the Man." But at the same time he owns that somewhere, somehow, there has grown up a certain distrust of Christ's manliness, a certain misgiving that the man of the four gospels does not completely match with the standard of manly life which is most popular and current among men. There are actions of His, there are features of His character, which men need to study, which perhaps they need to grow to. before they can see that they are the types of truest manliness. It is from these two facts that I wish to start in what I have to say. First, the fact that the character of Christ does satisfy the highest conceptions of our humanity; and second, the fact that it is only the highest conception of our humanity which it satisfies, that the lower, the current, ordinary, commonplace notions of manliness are puzzled by it. Both of these facts are true and both are important. At first sight they may seem contradictory; but out of a consideration of both of them together I think that we must reach a true idea of the nature and mission of the manliness of Jesus.

And let me add one remark more. The very word

" manliness " has a certain ambiguity about it. I think it is a word which many men are beginning to hesitate at using though they hardly know the reason why. It has a touch of cant. What does it mean ? It surely ought to mean the sum of the best qualities which characterize our humanity, joined in their true proportion. That is what manliness ought to mean. And evidently if it did mean that, then if our manhood is continually changing, rising, opening new possibilities, revealing new qualities, it must follow that manliness must be not one single invariable quality, but a constantly advancing and enlarging ideal of character, never completely and permanently settled until manhood shall have reached its best. It is necessary to bear in mind, I think, that manliness, in its truest definition, must be this ever changing and developing idea; even while we feel ourselves at liberty to use the word in the popular and ordinary way, as if it were one fixed and constant and clearly recognizable condition of human life. At any rate it is only with this fullest conception of what manliness means that we can rightly understand the nature and influence of the manliness of Jesus.

The Incarnation, then, the beginning of the earthly life of Christ, was the fulfilment, the filling full, of a human nature by Divinity. We do not ask, we do not dare to hope to know, what was the influence upon Divinity of that mysterious union. But of what was its influence upon humanity there certainly can be no doubt. It made the man in whom the miracle occurred, absolutely perfect man. It did not make Him something else than man. If it had done that, all His value as a pattern for humanity, all His temptation of men to be like Him would be gone. Whenever He says to men " Follow Me ; " " Be like Me," He is declaring that He is man as they are men, that the peculiar Divinity which filled Him, while it carried humanity to its complete development, had not changed that humanity into something which was no longer human. Can we picture that to ourselves ? Is it not just as when the sunlight fills a jewel ? The jewel throbs and glows .with radiance. All its mysterious nature palpitates and burns with clearness. It opens depths of color which we did not see before. But still it is the jewel's self that we are seeing. The sunlight has made us see what it is, not turned it into something different from what it was. Or to take another illustration which perhaps comes nearer to our truth. A man becomes a scholar. He learns all rich and elevating truth. As that truth enters into him, his human nature opens and deepens and unfolds its qualities. He becomes " more of a man," as we say in one of our common phrases. But that very phrase, "more of a man," implies that he becomes not something different from man, but more truly and completely man. His manhood is not changed into something else ; it is developed into a completer self by the truth which he learns.

In both these cases one thing evidently appears ; which is that the developing power which brings the being into which it enters to its best has essential and natural relations to the being which it develops. The jewel belongs to the light. The man belongs to the knowledge. And this must always be the truth which must underlie all understanding of the Incarnation. Man belongs to God. The human nature belongs to the Divine. It can come to its best only by the entrance and possession of it by Divinity. The Incarnation, let us always be sure, was not unnatural and violent but in the highest sense supremely natural. It is the first truth of all our existence that man is eternally the son of God. No man who forgets or denies that truth can really lay hold of the lofty fact that God entered into man.

We may pass on then, with this truth clear in our minds that the Christhood was a true development and not a distortion of humanity, we may pass on to study the working of the law of development under other illustrations.

Human nature, we say, is developed by the advance of civilization. Man civilized is man filled out, carried along towards his completion. True civilization does not make man something else than man. It makes his manhood more complete. It gives him no new powers of thought or action. It sets free the powers that belong to him as man. It makes him truly manly. But when we say this we at once remember what different views different men have always had of the effects of civilization. In general men have believed that civilization was an advance. The civilized man has seemed in general to be completer than the savage man. But always, alongside of this opinion, there has run a more or less distinct remonstrance. Always there have been men who have dwelt upon the loss which civilization has involved. Civilization has seemed to some men to mean deterioration. A certain freshness, freeness, breadth, spontaneousness, has seemed to make the savage a completer man than he who had been trained in many arts, and evolved through a long complicated his-

17

tory. The protest has not been clear or strong enough to shake the general conviction that the civilized man was the more truly human man ; but there is surely meaning, as there is deep pathos, in the way in which men have always looked back from the heights of the highest culture, and felt that they had lost something in the progress, longed for some charm of youth which the race remembered but found no longer in itself.

And what is true of the race is true also of the individual. The boy grows up to be a man, and as he ripens he becomes more manly. His human nature, filled out with more knowledge and experience, completes more nearly the full figure of humanity. But who is not aware of that strange sense of loss which haunts the ripening man ? With all that he has come to, there is something that he has left behind. In some moods the loss seems to outweigh the gain. He knows it is not really so, but yet the misgiving that freshness has been sacrificed to maturity, intenseness to completeness, enthusiasm to wisdom, makes the pathos of the life of every sensitive and growing man.

We stop a moment to observe how full the Bible is of this idea. The New Jerusalem with which it ends is greater and better than the Garden which blooms at its beginning. A more complete and manlier man walks on the sea of glass mingled with fire than walked in the shade and light of Eden. The whole story is of an education and a progress. And yet all through the Bible runs a tender and live regret for that lost imperfect manhood. Better things may come in the great future, but it seems as if there were something gone in the great past that never could come back. The edu-

cation and progress are haunted by the memory of a
fall. There is no thought of going back. The true
completion of humanity always in the Bible lies before
and not behind. And yet the flaming sword of Genesis
always seems to shut man out from a tree of life which
he never can forget even while he presses forward to
the completer tree of never-failing fruit which grows by
the side of the river of the water of life in the Apoca-
lypse.

It would seem then as if this truth were very general,
that in every development there is a sense of loss as
well as a sense of gain. The flower opening into its
full luxuriance has no longer the folded beauty of the
bud. The summer with its splendor has lost the fascinating mystery of spring-time. The family of grown-
up men remembers almost with regret the crude dreams
which filled the old house with romance when the men
were boys. The reasonable faith to which the thinker
has attained cannot forget the glow of vague emotion
with which faith began. The enthusiast, devoted to and
filled out by his cause, misses the light and careless life
he used to live. It is not that the progress is repented
nor that the higher standard is disowned. Rather it
seems to be a certain ineradicable charm that belongs
to incompleteness, inherent in its consciousness of promise and of hope, which lingers even when the promise
has been fulfilled and the hope attained, and makes us
sometimes almost seem to be sorry for the fulfilment
and attainment.

And now, after all this, let us come back to the
manliness of Christ. I think that it all applies there
and may give us some help. Suppose exactly that

to take place which the doctrine of the Incarnation assures us has taken place. Suppose that God should come and perfectly occupy a human life. That life like every human life belongs to Him. He occupies it with a certain supernatural naturalness. And what impression will that life, fully developed, developed completely by the indwelling God, make on the men who see it? Will it not open to them views of their own possibilities which they never had before? Will they not say, "Here for the first time is a man"? Will they not see that all their old standards were poor and partial? Will they not own that it is the supremely manly life? This they will certainly do if by manliness they mean that which before I said they ought to mean, the full ideal of manhood, if they have not stopped short and formalized their notion of manliness at some incomplete attainment of human nature. And yet, will they do this readily and easily? Will there be no clinging to the old standards; no sense of loss in the abandonment of lower ideals; no reaching back here too after the brilliancy of incompleteness, of partial unsymmetrical development; no missing of the morning that came before this full noontide of character which is flooding their souls?

This is precisely what I think we see. Men call Christ the crown of manhood, the perfect man, and yet they need a book, yea, many books, to teach them that He is manly. They have given that name so long to brilliant incompleteness that they find it hard to carry it over to the complete life when it appears. The name of manly has become a certain fixed definite thing, not pliable and capable of advancement and enlargement to some new manifestation of what is worthiest of man, what it is noblest for a man to be.

This seems to me to be the real state of the case. Men own that the human character of Christ is the completest human character that the world has ever seen, and yet they give their admiration to incomplete characters; and, not yet lifted to the full revelation of the Lord, they call that manly which they know all the while is something less than the full-orbed attainment of the perfect man. Here is a Christian boy who loves Christ, honors Him, wants to please Him, wants to serve Him, and yet that boy carries in his mind a distinctly inferior type of character to which he gives this name of manly. He knows that Christ was and is tender and patient. Nay, it is because Christ has revealed to him that tenderness and patience are the consummate utterances of our manhood, that he has recognized the tender, patient Christ as being supremely man. And yet that boy's soul is haunted by the sense that in giving himself up to these new standards and making it the prayer and struggle of his life to be tender and patient, he would be losing something which he cannot bear to lose, the sternness and hardness and quickness to resent an insult, which all the earlier standards of life have agreed upon as the proofs of manliness. It is a strange condition, but is it not just exactly the condition which we have found in all the instances of progression and development of which we spoke? The acceptance of the higher standard is haunted by a reluctance to let the lower go. Many a man, as I believe, is to-day just in this condition. He knows that the humanity of Jesus is the type of all humanity. He ought, if he knows that, to go right on and say, "Then Jesus is the manliest of men, and what He would do under any given circumstances must be the manliest thing that under those circumstances it is possible for any man to do. If He would not resent an injury but forgive it, then forgiveness, not resentment, must be true manliness." Does he say that? No, he draws back and cannot let the charm of the old spontaneous unchristian resentment go, and strikes his revengeful blow and says, "I know it is not Christian, but it is manly," and so abandons his conviction that Jesus is the perfect man.

This is not a mere question of the meaning of a certain word. It is something far more real than that. It seems to me very clear that while men recognize in Christ a true and high humanity, so that they are willing in all their better moods to own Him as the pattern man, there yet lurks underneath this acknowledgment a quiet, half-conscious misgiving and questioning whether His manliness is one that the human heart can cordially accept and love. The reason is convinced, and the heart hesitates; just the condition of the subject of any development where the heart still looks back with longing to the undeveloped state. This is the philosophy of that which we see everywhere, that of which I spoke at the beginning of my sermon; the mixture of profound admiration for the character of Christ with a misgiving, a suspicion of some weakness in Him and in the life that implicitly follows Him; a disposition to hold back the name of manly from the perfect man and His disciples.

If this be true, then, it points us at once to what is

most important, which is that the manliness of Christ has a double mission in the world. It is at once authentication and revelation. It must at once appeal to me to recognize it by the human instinct that there is in me already, and so trust Him for all He has to do; and also it must enlarge, enlighten, and refine the instinct of humanity by which it has first been recognized. I know Christ because I know manhood; and then, knowing Him, He makes me know manhood anew and far more deeply. In other words, it is the work of the human Christ at once to satisfy and to reconstruct our notions of manliness. Alas for us if it were not so. Alas if, coming in among our ordinary human lives, His human life so absolutely fitted in with them that it offered them no suggestion, gave them no lesson or rebuke. The real truth about the manliness of Christ seems to be this: that He is so like us that He makes us know that we may be like Him, and so unlike us that He makes us know that we must be unlike our present selves before we can be like Him. His life fits in among our human lives like a jewel which is so adapted to the gold into which it is set that nobody can doubt that they were made for one another, and yet which so far fails of suiting its place perfectly that we can see that the gold has been bent and twisted and must be twisted back again in order to accommodate it perfectly. He is at once our satisfaction and our rebuke. He has our human qualities; He feels our human motives; but in Him they take new shapes. It is with Him as it is with our best and noblest friends. They all first claim us by their likeness, and then shame and instruct us by their unlikeness. So it is with the manliness of Jesus.

Therefore there will always be a point where we shall fail if we depend simply upon the evident manliness of Jesus to make men believe in Him. If we say to men, "You have the standard in your own manhood to judge Him by," there will always come a time when, before the judgment of their imperfect manhood, He will fail. But what we may say is: "You have the standard in your hearts to recognize Him by. Recognize Him by that and make Him your Master and it will be His work to develop and refine the nature which first knew Him by His likeness, so that by and by it shall see that in the things in which He seemed to be most unlike to it, He still is and has always been the pattern and completion of its truest self."

I should like, if there were time, to turn and see with you how in His life on earth, which is recorded in the gospels, Jesus did for the men with whom He came in contact just this same double work. I can only suggest to you the many illustrations of it. There are three things perhaps, above all others, by which men think that they can recognize true manliness. The first is independence; the second is brávery; and the third is generosity. Now look at the life of Jesus as I hope that you remember it in the gospels. There is independence there certainly. He stood almost alone. A little group of disciples who only half understood Him were His company. The rest of the people grew more and more hostile as His career advanced. He more and more outwent His friends and more and more enraged His enemies. Yet still He stood unmoved. Men, whether they loved or hated Him, saw that He carried within Himself the convictions and determinations by which He lived. It was this, first of all, that made them feel His strength. "He speaks as one that has authority," the people cried one day when His discourse was finished. Another day the Pharisees came to Him and said, "Master, we know that thou art true, neither carest thou for any man, for thou regardest not the person of man." In all this there was something very powerful. This independence must have impressed the finest young spirits of Capernaum and Jerusalem as very manly. And then, when they were yielding to its influence and gathering round Him, think how they must have been staggered and thrown back at hearing this same independent Master declare as the very central secret of His life and power that He was utterly dependent on a nature which was above His own. "I can of mine own self do nothing; as I hear I judge." "He that taketh not his cross and followeth after Me cannot be My disciple." Only the very finest spirits among His followers were able to stand firm and loyal while the manliness which had attracted them at the beginning first seemed to fail them, and then opened before their eyes into a yet nobler type of manliness, of which dependence upon God lay at the very heart.

This same is true of Christ's courage. Men saw Jesus stand on the hill at Nazareth among a crowd of hooting enemies. They saw Him stand calmly in the boat on the stormy midnight lake and never tremble. They saw Him face the gibbering maniac among the tombs. They saw Him set His face toward Jerusalem and go up thither quietly, knowing that there He would be crucified. They said to one another, "See how brave He is. He does not know anything like fear. Behold, what manliness!" And then, full of this enthusiasm, some of them witnessed Gethsemane. They heard Him pray to be released from the approaching pain. They watched Him in the days before Gethsemane, as the horror of the coming death gathered around Him. " Father, save me from this hour," they heard Him cry. It is impossible not to believe that their conception of manliness underwent first a shock and then an enlargement, as their Master showed them that sensitiveness to pain is a true and necessary element in the loftiest courage.

Or yet again, think of Christ's generosity. An open, tolerant, and kindly temper, that welcomes confidence, that overlooks faults, that makes much of any good in other men, that easily forgives wrong ; that is a part of any ordinary notion of manliness. And this the men of Palestine found unmistakably in Christ. His life was always open. Whatever He had He would share with any man. " If any one shall speak a word against the Son of Man, it shall be forgiven him," He said. " Come unto Me, come unto Me," He kept saying as He went up and down the land. And to this frank, bright, open summons men did come. They recognized a man and gathered round His manliness. And then how often, just as they were crowding closest to Him, He said some word or did some action which let them see that, much as He loved them and wanted to welcome them, He loved something else behind them more, and could not welcome them completely unless they met Him in the broad chambers of truth and self-devotion. When Nicodemus comes to Him, Christ turns quickly in the midst of His generous greeting and says, " Except a man be born again he cannot see the kingdom of God." When the eager young man comes running to give himself to the new Master, the Master meets him almost with a blow. "Foxes have holes, and birds of the air have nests, but the Son of Man hath not where to lay His head." Men must have been perplexed and staggered by such words. "Is He then not generous, not cordial? Does He not love us? Does He not want us?" they must have said to one another; and only slowly, as they dealt with Him, the deeper law of generosity must have opened to them, that no man loves his brethren completely unless he loves the truth better than any brother; that no man desires generously for his brethren unless he desires the best things for the best part of them, and will willingly sacrifice the poorer things which belong to the poorer part of them to secure that loftier attainment.

In all these instances, and they might be multiplied indefinitely, the same thing, I think, appears; and that is the way in which Christ's manliness first claims men; and then, because it is a completer manliness than they have ever seen, it puzzles and bewilders men, and if they are not truly in love with it, repels and casts them off; and only finally, He refines and elevates their idea of what it is to be manly by the deeper revelation of Himself. This is a truth which it seems to me we never can lose sight of when we talk or think about the manliness of Jesus and its power over men. All through the history of Christ's presentation to mankind He has attracted men and He has repelled men. He has satisfied and He has puzzled men's standards of human life. Both of the two are true and natural phenomena. If I could take Christ to-day — take Christ Himself and not merely some man's feebly told version of His story — if

I could take Christ Himself out into the midst of a group of Western roughs, and set His calm presence in their midst, what should I see? What would be His effect on them? They would know His manliness certainly. But would they apprehend how thorough and complete His manliness was? They would call Him strong. But would they not also call Him weak? He would meet and satisfy the best of the standards and instincts which He would find all ready in those rugged hearts; but He would certainly disappoint them too; and only through disappointment, and the revelation of Himself to hearts whose confidence in the completeness of their own first perceptions had been shaken, would they come finally to see that He was most manly in those very things in which He had seemed to them at first to be unmanly.

And so it is that Christ has always come to men. I think that it is very like the way in which He came to the Jews. Christ's relation to Judaism always seems to me to be a sort of miniature and illustration of the relation in which He stands to humanity. He was a true Jew. Any Jew with a true Jew's heart must have owned Him for a fellow-Jew without a doubt. But He was too true a Jew to satisfy completely the stunted and imperfect Judaism of his time. A Judaism so far below the actual realization of its own best idea could not but be puzzled by Him. Only the best of the nation was able gradually to be taught by Him the full meaning of the national history, the full depth of the national idea. The life of St. Paul, and the Epistle to the Hebrews, show what the complete conception of Judaism was capable of reaching when it was filled out and interpreted by the complete Jew, Christ.

Let this be the picture and parable of what the man Christ may do for humanity. So truly man that all mankind must know His manliness, He is yet so much truer man than all other men that it is only by the revelation of our humanity which He himself makes to us that we ourselves can know how thoroughly manly He is. Just see then what is the conclusion to which the end of our long study brings us. Is it not this; that there are two knowledges of Christ, one lower and one higher? There is one knowledge by which, just with our ordinary standards, if we are only sincere and true, we may know that this Man is a man above all other men, and take Him for our Master. When, with that knowledge, we have put ourselves into His power so that He may teach us and complete our incomplete conceptions, then another deeper knowledge comes. We learn to know not merely that He is manly because there are in Him those things which we as men most ardently admire; but also that we can be truly manly only as we come by love and admiration and obedience to share the completeness of character which is in Him. The first knowledge brings us to obedience. The second knowledge is the power of spiritual growth.

Into that higher knowledge may we all advance; making Christ ours first, that in the end He may make us His. With reverent hands may we handle Him and see that He is truly manly, that He really wears our humanity, that so we may through His humanity come to the Father God whom He reveals.

XVI.

HELP FROM THE HILLS.

"I will lift up mine eyes unto the hills, from whence cometh my help."—
PSALM cxxi. 1.

MANY people seem to think that the escape from
trouble is everything, without regard to the door by
which escape is made; and that the finding of help in
need is everything, no matter who may be the person
of whom the help is sought. But really the door by
which we escape from trouble is of more importance
than the escape itself. There are many troubles from
which it is better for a man not to escape than to escape
wrongly; and there are many difficulties in which it is
better to struggle and to fail than to be helped by a
wrong hand. In these first words of one of the greatest
psalms of David, the nobleness which we immediately
feel seems to lie in this, that David will seek help only
from the highest source. "I will lift up mine eyes unto
the hills, from whence cometh my help." Nothing less
than God's help can really meet his needs. He will not
peer into the valleys. He will not turn to fellow-men,
to nature, to work, to pleasure, as if they had the relief he
needed. "I will lift up mine eyes unto the hills from
whence cometh my help. My help cometh from the
Lord who hath made heaven and earth."

How instantly we feel the greatness of a man who

could write such words as those. He is great in his
understanding of his own essential human greatness.
Not every man is able to think so loftily of himself as
to realize that in every true sorrow of his there is something which only God "who hath made heaven and
earth" can comfort; and that in every weakness of his
there is something which only God "who hath made
heaven and earth" can help. This is what we mean, I
think, in large part, when we so often say that trouble
tests men and shows what sort of men they are. It is
the time of need that lets us see what men think of
themselves, how seriously they contemplate their own
existence, how they estimate their need, by letting us
see where they seek their help. Have you never been
struck by it? One mourner in the hour of bereavement
rushes into society or to Europe; another turns to self-
forgetting charity and spiritual thoughtfulness. One
bankrupt begins to abuse the world for prospering while
he is failing; another rejoices, and finds the relief of his
own misery in rejoicing, that some part of the world, at
least, is better off by the action of the same forces which
have ruined him. One man turns instinctively to the
lowest and another to the highest, in his need; and so it
is that, in their own way, our hours of need become our
judgment-days.

I want to speak this morning of the duty of every
man to seek help from the highest in every department
of his life. I will not say only from the highest, for
we shall see, I think, how the lower helps come in in
their true places; but we need to be reminded that no
trouble is fully met and no difficulty thoroughly mastered unless the trouble is filled with the profoundest

consolation and the difficulty conquered with the greatest strength of which its nature makes it capable.　It is the forgetfulness of this truth, I think, which causes a large part of the superficialness and ineffectiveness of all our lives.

For the truth rests upon another truth which we are also always ready to forget, which is that the final purpose of all consolation and help is revelation.　The reason why we are led into trouble and out again is not merely that we may value happiness the more from having lost it once and found it again, but that we may know something which we could not know except by that teaching, that we may bear upon our nature some impress which could not have been stamped except on natures just so softened to receive it.　There stands your man who has been through some terrible experience and found relief.　Perhaps it was a terrible sickness in which he was drawn back from the very gates of death.　Perhaps it was some mighty task which the world seemed to single him out to do, to fail in which would have been ruin, and in which it seemed at one time certain that he must fail.　Perhaps it was a midnight darkness that settled down over all truth, so that it seemed hopeless ever again to know anything truly of God or man.　Whatever it was, the experience has come and passed.　There stands your man, relieved, released, out in the sunlight on the other side of it. What do you ask of him as he stands there ?　Is your sense of fitness satisfied if he is only relieved, released ; if he is only like a man who, after a hard fight with the waves, has got his footing once more just where he was when he was swept away ?　Certainly not.　The human

sense of fitness asks more than that. He must have
seen something in the dark, or in the transition from the
dark back to the light again, which pure, unclouded
light could not have shown him. Into this kneaded
and tortured life there must have been pressed some
knowledge which the life in its best health was too
hard and unsensitive to take, some knowledge which
the life, restored to health, shall carry as the secret of
inexhaustible happiness forth into eternity. Without
these revelations the midnight and the torture would
be inexplicable and hideous. But these revelations
depend upon the way the soul's eyes look for help. A
man may stand in the darkness looking at the ground,
and when the dawn gathers round him he will only be
glad of the light, but will have no perpetual and precious memory of sunrise. This is the real reason why
no release from difficulty or trouble is all that it might
be to us, unless we have sought it from the highest and
thank the highest for it when it comes. The eye comes
out of the darkness trained by looking up. Let yourself be helped by the noblest who can help you, that
you may know the noblest with that intimate knowledge with which the helped knows the helper, and that
the power of knowing nobleness may be awakened and
developed in you.

1. But we shall understand this better and feel it more
strongly if we pass at once to special applications of our
truth and see it in its workings. Take first the everlasting struggle with Temptation. Every man who is
more than a brute knows what it is. All men whose
consciences are not entirely dead engage in it with some
degree of earnestness. But how perfectly clear it is that

18

any man who undertakes that struggle may look either to the valleys or to the hills for help, may call the lower or the higher powers to his aid. Suppose a man is wrestling with his passions. Some miserable dissipation which he never hates and despises so much as just when he is ready to yield to it, is haunting him all the time. His lust is all awake. His appetite is one day smiling and persuasive, the next day arrogant and brutal. "You must, you shall give way to me," it seems to cry to him. But still he fights. And in his weakness he looks round for help. Where shall he find it? It seems to lie close by him, in the very structure of the body in which the lust is raging. There are the laws of health. Shall not they be his safeguard? Let him be convinced that if he gives himself the bad indulgence which he craves, he will feel the quick answer in certain pain and drag a miserable body through a wretched life to a dishonored grave. Let him know that, and will it not give him the strength for resistance that he needs? No doubt it will help him, though it will not be his highest help. Many a man is held back to-day from iniquity which his whole heart desires by the inevitable prospect of the pain, the sickness, the misery, the death, that an indulgence will incur. Indeed it seems as if some people thought that herein lay the gospel for the coming age; that just as soon as men had learned the laws of health completely, vice would be all abolished, and temperance and purity reign where the passions have so long trodden them under foot. Or take another case, and see a man tempted to dishonesty in some dealings with his fellow-men. Where shall he turn for strength to his integrity? Let him picture to himself the dis-

grace that must come if he is found out, the loss of reputation and of his fellow-men's esteem. Let him imagine
himself walking the streets a despised, avoided man,
with scornful fingers pointed at the detected cheat.
Such visions, such fears as those, may help him, and he
may resist the temptation to fraud, and keep his integrity unsoiled. Or yet again when a man is tempted to
cruelty or quarrelsomeness he may resist because he
considers that, after all, the discomfort of a quarrel is
greater than the satisfaction of a grudge indulged. Or
one who feels the weakness of indolence creeping over
him may put himself into the midst of the most active
and energetic men he knows and get the contagion of
their energy and be kept alive and awake by very
shame. All these are perfectly legitimate helpers for
the man beset by his temptation. The fear of pain, the
fear of disgrace, the fear of discomfort, and the shame
that comes with the loftiest companionship, — we may
have to appeal to them all for support in the hours,
which come so often in our lives, when we are very
weak. But, after all, the appeal to these helpers is not
the final cry of the soul. They are like the bits of wood.
that the drowning sailor clutches when he must have
something at the instant or he perishes. They are not
the solid shore on which at last he drops his tired feet
and knows that he is safe. Or rather, perhaps, the man
who trusts them is like a dweller in some valley down
which a freshet pours, who drives the stakes of his im-
perilled tent deeper into the ground; not like one who
leaves the valley altogether and escapes to the mountain where the freshet never comes. "I will lift up
mine eyes unto the hills," says David. Not until a

man has laid hold "behind and above everything else" upon the absolute assurance that the right is right and that the God of righteousness will give His strength to any feeblest will in all His universe which tries to do the right in simple unquestioning consecration; not until he has thus appealed to duty and to the dear God of whose voice she is the "stern daughter;" not till then has he summoned to his aid the final perfect help; only then has he really looked up to the hills.

I have already said that when a tried and tempted soul thus flees to God and to the absolute righteousness, he does not cast the lower helps away. Still as he looks up to the hills his eye is led there along the gradually rising ground of lower motives. The man who keeps his purity and honesty and strength because he is God's child and must do his Father's will, may still care for his health and his reputation and cultivate a healthy shame before his fellow-men. But these are not the king he serves. They are only, as it were, the servants who bring him the king's orders; to be heeded and obeyed, but not for themselves but for their king who sends them.

This will seem clear enough if we remember how there come times in all the deepest lives when the servant has to be disobeyed in order that the obedience to the king may be complete. The preservation of health, the care for reputation, cannot be the final safeguards and citadels of purity and integrity, because there come times in which, just in order that purity may be kept, health and even life have to be cast away. Just in order that a man may still be upright he has to walk directly across his fellow-men's standards and forfeit their regard.

But the time never comes when a man to be good has to disobey God. Therefore it is that obedience to God is the only final and infallible help of the soul in its struggle with temptation. The rest are the fortifications around the city. Sometime their destruction may be the only way to save the city which they were meant to guard; but the heart of the city itself, the citadel where the king sits, the city cannot perish so long as that is safe; and when that falls, the city's life is over.

I beg you, my dear friends, old men and young men, all surrounded with temptations which will not give you rest, to know and never to forget that there is no safety that is final and complete until your eye is fixed upon the highest, until it is the fear and love of God that is keeping you from sin. It is good for every man to care for his life and his reputation. Let the doctors show us more and more how every wrong we do our bodies shortens and impairs our life. Let experience teach us more and more that he who is mean and base will surely some day find himself despised. But these are not enough. The rectitude which they alone protect is not the highest rectitude. It is a selfish, calculating thing. And it is wholly possible that they may themselves become the betrayers of the rectitude which they are sent to guard; so that a man, to keep his life, may do his body wrong, and to keep his reputation may go down into the most miserable meanness. You are never wholly safe until your eye is fixed on God, and until it is because He is so awful and so dear that you will not do the sin which tempts you.

2. I pass on to speak about another of the emergencies of life in which it makes vast difference whether the

soul looks to the hills for help or to the valleys. Not
merely in temptation but in sorrow a man may seek the
assistance of the highest, or of some other power which
is far lower. What does it mean when, the blow of some
great grief having fallen on a man, his friends gather
round him and dwell upon the blessed relief that time
will bring him ? Nay, the man speaks to his own heart
and says : "Let me drag on awhile and time will help
me. It will not be so bad when the days have made
me used to it. Let me live on and the burden will
grow lighter." As these words are often said, they are
unutterably sad and dreadful. If they mean anything
distinct, they mean that by and by the poor man will
forget. The face he misses now will grow more dim
before his memory. The sweet music of the days that
he has lost will grow fainter and fainter in the distance.
How terrible that comfort is. How the true soul cries
out against it : " I do not want relief which comes by
forgetting. I will not seek comfort in the thought that
my affection is too feeble and brutish to keep its vividness forever. Let me remember forever, even though
everlasting memory only means everlasting pain. You
add a new pang to my sorrow when you tell me that
some day I shall escape it by forgetfulness." That is
the cry of every noble soul. And no less does it break
out in remonstrance when the other relief, the relief or
distraction, is offered to it. " Come, busy yourself in
some absorbing occupation, take some exacting work or
some fascinating pleasure, and so your pain shall lose its
hold on you." That is only the same thing in another
form. That is only offering the man escape by a side
door instead of by the far off gate through which the

other offer promised him that he should some day go forth into forgetfulness of his grief. No wonder that the heart, with such relief set before it, grows jealous of the proffered distraction and morbidly shuts itself in upon its sorrow and will have nothing to do with those occupations which it is told are to dissolve and melt away the pain which, with all its painfulness, still has at its heart the preciousness of love. All this is looking to the valleys and the depths for comfort. " I will lift up mine eyes unto the hills," says David. By and by the soul, vexed and distressed by its poor comforters, turns away from them. They have bid it avoid its grief, and the very horror which their advice has brought has shown the soul where its real relief must lie. It must be somewhere in the grief that the help of the grief is hidden. It must be in some discovery of the divine side of the sorrow that the consolation of the sorrow will be found. It is a wondrous change when a man stops asking of his distress, "How can I throw this off?" and asks instead, "What did God mean by sending this?" Then, he may well believe that time and work will help him. Time, with its necessary calming of the first wild surface-tumult, will let him look deeper and ever deeper into the divine purpose of the sorrow, will let its deepest and most precious meanings gradually come forth so that he may see them. Work, done in the sorrow, will bring him into ever new relations to the God in whom alone the full interpretation and relief of the sorrow lies. Time and work, not as means of escape from distress but as the hands in which distress shall be turned hither and thither that the light of God may freely play upon it; time and work so acting as servants of God, not as substitutes for God, are full of unspeakably precious ministries to the suffering soul. But the real relief, the only final comfort, is God; and He relieves the soul always in its suffering, not from its suffering; nay, he relieves the soul by its suffering, by the new knowledge and possession of Himself which could come only through that atmosphere of pain.

There are no times in life when opportunity, the chance to be and do, gathers so richly about the soul as when it has to suffer. Then everything depends on whether the man turns to the lower or the higher helps. If he resorts to mere expedients and tricks, the opportunity is lost. He comes out no richer nor greater; nay, he comes out harder, poorer, smaller for his pain. But if he turns to God, the hour of suffering is the turning hour of his life. Opportunity opens before him as the ocean opens before one who sails out of a river. Men have done the best and worst, the noblest and the basest things the world has seen, under the pressure of excessive pain. Everything depended on whether they looked to the depths or to the hills for help.

3. Again, our truth is nowhere more true than in the next region where we watch its application, the region of doubt and perplexity of mind. A man is uncertain what is true, what he ought to believe, especially about religion, the most important of all subjects, and, as he thinks sometimes, the most uncertain as it is the most important. He wants help. He wants some power to lead him into certainty. Where shall he turn? At once the lower resource presents itself on every side. He is offered authority. Close by his side starts up some man, some church, which says, "I have the truth. It

has been given to me to tell to you. Believe what
I declare simply as I declare it and your doubt is
gone. The trouble is all over." It seems an easy thing
to do. Nothing is stranger than the satisfied way in
which men who, on every other subject, use their own
minds and seek the truth by its own proper methods,
here in religion only seem to ask that some one shall
speak with overwhelming positiveness and they will believe him. Indeed here, in religion, men seem to bring
forth their most wanton credulity and their most wanton
scepticism. Here, in religion, is where you can find men
believing without any evidence at all; and, again, disbe-
lieving against all the evidence which the nature of the
case admits. A very large part of the power of the
Church of Rome to-day comes simply here, that men,
bewildered and perplexed, demand an infallible authority upon religious things; and since the Church of
Rome stands forth the loudest and most confident and
most splendid claimant of infallibility, they give themselves to her. It is not that they have convinced themselves that she is infallible. It is rather that she alone
really claims to be; and they have started with the
assumption that an infallible authority they must have,
and here is the only one that offers. Now of such an
escape from doubt as that what shall we say? The
deepest, truest thing that we can say about it is that it
is not a real escape, because that into which it brings
the soul is not really and properly belief. "What
should we think," says a wise writer, "of any man who
knew Euclid, but only accepted the demonstrations on
the authority of the book?" He who holds a truth of
religion, not because he himself has found it to be true

but because some trusted friend here by his side, or some great father in the ancient church, or some council which voted on it once, has told him it is true, does not really and properly hold the truth. He has no more escaped from doubt than you have escaped the rain when you have crept under some other man's umbrella who for the moment is going your way, but who may any moment turn aside, and whose umbrella in the mean time is not big enough for two.

And, beside this, even if the condition which is reached by pure submission to authority could properly be called faith, it would still be weak by the lack of all that personal effort after truth, that struggle to be serious and fair, that athletic, patient, self-denying life which is the subjective element of faith; as true and necessary a part of the full act as is the acceptance of any most perfectly proved objective truth. No; he who looks to authority for his religion is not lifting up his eyes unto the hills. That comes only when a seeker after truth dares to believe that God Himself sends to every one of His children the truth which that child needs; that while God uses the Bible, the church, and the experience of other souls as channels for His teaching, He Himself is always behind them all as the great teacher and the final source of truth; that He bids each child in His family use the powers which belong distinctively to him, and apprehend truth in that special form in which the Father chooses to send it into his life. It is this directness of relationship to God, it is this appeal of the life directly to Him, it is this certainty that no authority on earth is so sacred but that every soul may — nay, that every soul must — judge of its teachings by its own God-given faculties enlightened and purified by devout consecration to God ; it is this which makes the true experience of faith. What comes to the soul in such an experience is not infallible certainty on all the articles on which man craves enlightenment, but it is something better. It is an hourly communion with the Lord of truth. It is a constant anxiety to turn the truth which He has already shown into obedience, and a constant eagerness to see what new truth He may be making known. It is a thorough truthfulness. I beg you, my dear friends, not to believe, because of the supposed need of infallible certainty in all religious questions, that therefore religion is a matter of authority. There is no authority short of God. Look up to Him. Expect His teaching. And though between you and the hill-tops clouds of uncertainty may come, never let them make you turn your eyes away in discouragement, or think that on the earth you can find that guidance which is not a thing of earth but which must come to us from heaven.

4. I want to speak in very few words of only one more application of our truth. It is with reference to man's escape from sin. There is a need of help which, when any soul has once felt it, seems to surpass all others. " What shall become of the wickedness that I have done ? How shall I cast my sin away and be once more as if I had not sinned ? " And then there always have stood up, there always will stand up, two answers. One answer says, " God will forgive your sin. He will remit its penalties. He will not punish you. In view of this or that persuasion every penalty of sin is lifted off and you are free." The other answer says, " You cannot be wholly free from sin till you cease to be sinful.

No taking away of penalties can free you. You must be another creature. God will give you a new heart if you will be obedient to Him. Every release from punishment has value only as it wins your grateful soul for Him who pardons you and makes you ready to receive the new heart which He has to give." No doubt both answers have their truth. But no doubt also, the second answer promises a more divine and perfect mercy than the first. The help of transformation is a loftier benefit than the help of remission. I can picture to myself the first without the second. I can image a soul with all its penalties removed, but yet not saved. I cannot picture to myself the second without the first. I cannot imagine a soul in any region of God's universe, turned from its wickedness and made holy by His grace and yet bearing still the spiritual penalties of the sins which it committed long ago. Therefore it is that the best spiritual ambition seeks directly holiness. It seeks pardon as a means to holiness. So it lifts its eyes up at once to the very highest hills. I wish that I could make the thoughtful men, especially the young men who are just deep in perplexity about Christianity, see this. You must not think of Christ's redemption as a great scheme to save you from the punishment of sin. That is too negative. That is too low. It is the great opening of the celestial possibilities of man. Expect to escape, know that you can escape, from the consequences of having been wicked, only by being good. Crave the most perfect mercy. Ask for the new life as the only real release from death. So only can your religion glow with enthusiasm and open into endless hope.

In these four illustrations then I have tried to enforce the message that I wanted to bring. O for that spirit which is content with nothing less or lower than the highest help. To turn in temptation directly to the power of God; to cry out in sorrow for God's company; to be satisfied in doubt with nothing short of the assurance that God gives; to know that there is no real escape from sin except in being made holy by God's holiness, — these are what make the man's complete salvation. I turn to Jesus, and in all His human life there seems to me nothing more divine than the instinctive and unerring way in which He always reached up to the highest, and refused to be satisfied with any lower help. In the desert the Devil offered Him bread, good wholesome bread. Apparently He could have had it if He would; but He replied, " Man shall not live by bread alone but by the word of God." At Jacob's well His disciples brought Him food and said, " Master, eat; " but He answered, " I have meat to eat which ye know not of. My meat is to do the will of Him that sent Me." On the cross they held up to Him the sponge full of vinegar; but the thirst that was in Him demanded a deeper satisfaction, and He gave His soul to His Father and finished His obedient work. So it was everywhere with Him. The souls beside Him found their helps and satisfactions in the superficial things of earth. They laid hold on petty distractions, outside ceremonies, superficial assurances, and so seemed to forget their cares and questionings. He could not rest anywhere till He had found God His Father, and laid the burden which was crushing Him, into the bosom of the eternal strength and the exhaustless love.

It is your privilege and mine, as children of God, to be satisfied with no help but the help of the highest. When we are content to seek strength or comfort or truth or salvation from any hand short of God's, we are disowning our childhood and dishonoring our Father.

It is better to be restless and unsatisfied than to find rest and satisfaction in anything lower than the highest. But we need not be restless or unsatisfied. There is a rest in expectation, a satisfaction in the assurance that the highest belongs to us though we have not reached it yet. That rest in expectation we may all have now if we believe in God and know we are His children. Every taste of Him that we have ever had becomes a prophecy of His perfect giving of Himself to us. It is as when a pool lies far up in the dry rocks, and hears the tide and knows that her refreshment and replenishing is coming. How patient she is. The other pools nearer the shore catch the sea first, and she hears them leaping and laughing, but she waits patiently. She knows the tide will not turn back till it has reached her. And by and by the blessed moment comes. The last ridge of rock is overwashed. The stream pours in; at first a trickling thread sent only at the supreme effort of the largest wave; but by and by the great sea in its fulness. It gives the waiting pool itself and she is satisfied. So it will certainly be with us if we wait for the Lord, however He delays, and refuse to let ourselves be satisfied with any supply but Him.

XVII.

THE CURSE OF MEROZ.

"Curse ye Meroz, saith the angel of the Lord, Curse ye bitterly the inhabitants thereof; because they came not to the help of the Lord, to the help of the Lord against the mighty."—JUDGES v. 23.

DEBORAH and Barak had gained a great victory in the plain of Esdraelon and along the skirts of the mountain of Little Hermon. Their enemy Sisera had fled away completely routed, and the wild, fierce, strong woman who "judged Israel in those days," and the captain of the Israelitish army, sang a splendid proud song of triumph. In it they recount the tribes who had come up to their duty, who had shared the labor and the glory of the fight. And then, in the midst of the torrent of song there comes this other strain of fiery indignation. One town or village, Meroz, had hung back. Hidden away in some safe valley, it had heard the call which summoned every patriot, but it knew it was in no danger. It had felt the shock of battle on the other side of the hills, and nestled and hid itself only the more snugly. "Curse ye Meroz, saith the angel of the Lord; curse ye bitterly the inhabitants thereof, because they came not to the help of the Lord, to the help of the Lord against the mighty." It is a fierce vindictive strain. It bursts from the lips of an exalted furious woman. But it declares one of the most natural indignations of the human heart.

Meroz is gone. No record of it except this verse remains. The most ingenious and indefatigable explorer cannot even guess where it once stood. But the curse remains; the violent outburst of the contempt and anger which men feel who have fought and suffered and agonized, and then see other men who have the same interest in the result which they have, coming out cool and unwounded from their safe hiding places to take a part of the victory which they have done nothing to secure. Meroz stands for that. It sometimes happens that a man or a town passes completely away from the face of the earth and from the memory of men, and only leaves a name which stands as a sort of symbol or synonyme of some quality, some virtue or some vice, forever. So Meroz stands for the shirker; for him who is willing to see other people fight the battles of life, while he simply comes in to take the spoils. No wonder Deborah and Barak were indignant. Their wounds were still aching; their people were dead and dying all around them; and here was Meroz, idle and comfortable, and yet, because she was part of the same country, sure to get the benefit of the great victory as much as any.

It was not only personal anger. This cowardly and idle town had not come " to the help of the Lord." Deborah knew that the cause of Jehovah had been in terrible danger. It seemed as if it had only barely been saved. She was filled with horror when she thought what would have been the consequences if it had been lost. And here sat this village, whose weight perhaps might have furnished just what was needed to turn the doubtful scale; here it had sat through all the critical and dreadful day, looking on and doing nothing. It was all her passionate sense of the preciousness of God's government and the danger in which it had stood which burst from her lips when she cursed Meroz.

There are many people always who are in the community and in the world what Meroz was in Palestine. For there is an everlasting struggle going on against wickedness and wretchedness. It never ceases. It changes but it never ceases. It shifts from one place to another. It dies out in one form only to burst out in some other shape. It seems to flag sometimes as if the enemy were giving way, but it never really stops; the endless struggle of all that is good in the world against the enemies of God, against sin and error and want and woe. And the strange and sad thought which comes upon our minds sometimes is of how few people after all are really heartily engaged in that struggle, how few have cast themselves into it with all their hearts, how many there are who stand apart and wish it well but never expose themselves for it nor do anything to help it.

Look at the manifest forms in which men show their will to work for God and goodness. Those of you who have had any occasion to observe it know full well by what a very small number of persons the charitable and missionary works of the church and all operations which require public spirit in a community are carried on. If there is a reform to be urged; if there is an abuse to be corrected in the administration of affairs; if there is some oppressed and degraded class whose rights, which they cannot assert themselves, must be asserted for them; if there is a palpable wrong done every day upon

19

our streets, — most of you know how very few are the
people in this city, who, apart from any private interest
in the matter, are looked to as likely to take any con-
cern for the public good. The subscription papers
which one sees passing about for public objects might
almost as well be stereotyped as written, so constantly
do they repeat the same limited list of well known
names.

These are superficial signs. But ask yourself again,
How many of the people among us who are in the posi-
tions of influence in various occupations, feel any kind
of responsibility for the elevation of their occupation,
feel any desire of making it a stronghold against the
power of evil? How many merchants feel that it belongs to them to elevate the standards of trade? How
many teachers value their relation to the young because
they have the chance to strengthen character against
temptation? How many men and women in social life
care to develop the higher uses of society, making it
the bulwark and the educator of men's purer, finer,
deeper life? Every occupation is capable of this profounder treatment, besides its mere treatment as a
means of livelihood or of personal advancement. In
every occupation there are some men who conceive of it
so. How few they are! How the mass of men who
trade and teach and live their social life, never get beyond the merely selfish thought about it all! The lack
of a sense of responsibility, the selfishness of life, is the
great impression that is forced upon us constantly.

It is so even in religion. To how many Christians
does the religious life present itself in the enthusiastic
and inspiring aspect of working and fighting for God?

How almost all Christians never get beyond the first thought of saving their own souls! I think I am as ready as any man to understand the vast variety of forms under which self-devotion may be shown, and not to impute selfishness to that which simply is not unselfish in certain special forms. But, making all broad allowances, I think there is nothing which so comes to impress a man as the way in which the vast majority of men hold back and, with no ill-will but all good wishes, let the interests of their fellow-men and of goodness and of God take care of themselves. I should like to speak to-day of the curse of Meroz, the curse of uselessness, the curse of shirking; and I should rejoice indeed if I could make any young man see how wretched it is and inspire him with some noble desire to do some of the work, to fight some of the enemies of God.

Notice then first of all that the sin for which Meroz is cursed is pure inaction. There is no sign that its people gave any aid or comfort to the enemy. They merely did nothing. We hear so much about the danger of wrong thinking and the danger of wrong doing. There is the other danger, of not doing right and not thinking right, of not doing and not thinking at all. It is hard for many people to feel that there is danger and harm in that, the worst of harm and danger. And the trouble comes, I think, from the low condition of spiritual vitality, from the lack of emphasis and vigor in the whole conception of a man's own life. A man who is but half alive, a poor helpless invalid shut up in his room, hears the roar of human life going on past his windows, and it causes him no self-reproach that he is not in it, that he has no part or share in all this work. He does not expect it of himself. He recognizes still the positive sins. He knows that he has no right to commit murder, or to forge, or to lie as he sits there. His helplessness has not released him from any of those obligations. But he does feel released from enterprise and activity. He is not called upon to do a well man's work. His task is only to keep himself alive. Now the spiritual and moral vitality of many men is low. What can revive it? What can put strength and vigor into it? There is a verse of St. John which, among many other things which it tells, tells this, I think. "He that hath the Son hath life," John says, "and he that hath not the Son of God hath not life." That is a great declaration. It says that if a man takes Christ, that is to say if a man loves and serves Christ because Christ has redeemed him into the family of God, he really lives, vigor comes into him, responsibility lays hold upon him. The work of the world becomes his work. God's tasks become his tasks. The enemies of God become his enemies. This is the meaning of countless passages which people make to mean so much shallower, so much smaller things. "God sent His only begotten Son into the world that we might live through Him," John says again. When Christ has redeemed a man, and the man knows his redemption and wants to serve Christ in gratitude, then the invalidism of the soul is gone. The man lives all through and through, and wherever Christ needs him he is ready; which merely means that wherever there is any good work to be done, he does it.

Now there are in all our cities, and this city has its full share of them, a great multitude of useless men, and of men perfectly contented in their uselessness. Many a man looks back upon his life, and save for the kindly offices which he has rendered to his immediate associates, he cannot remember one useful thing he ever did. He never stood up for a good cause. He never remonstrated against an evil. He never helped a bad man to be better. A merely useless man! His life might drop out of the host to-morrow and none would miss a soldier from the ranks. No onset or defence would be the weaker for his going. I know not how he reconciles it to himself. It may be that the palsy of a fashionable education has been on him from his birth. Perhaps he grew up, as you perhaps are bringing up your children now, to think that because his life was plentifully provided against necessity, therefore it was free from duty. There is nothing so pitiable as to see a boy in some self-indulgent household, who evidently came into the world with faculties to make him be, and make him enjoy being, a strong and helpful worker for God and man, having all chance and taste for using these faculties quietly, steadily crushed out of him by the constant pressure of a fashionable home. It is the child of God being slowly made into the man of the world. But however it came about, let us take the only too familiar phenomenon of the useless man who excuses his uselessness, and let us see what are some of the various forms which his uselessness assumes. I shall speak of three; cowardice, and false humility, and indolence. Let us see how dead they make a man; and how the Son of God is the true life of all of them.

1. The first source then of the uselessness of good men,

or, if you please, of men who are not bad, is moral
cowardice. Cowardice we call the most contemptible
of vices. It is the one whose imputation we most indignantly resent. To be called a coward would make
the blood boil in the veins of any of us. But the vice
is wonderfully common. Nay, we often find ourselves
wondering whether it is not universal, whether we are
not all cowards somewhere in our nature. Physical
cowardice all of us do not have. Indeed physical cowardice is rarer than we think. A war or a shipwreck
always .brings out our surprise when we see how many
men there are that can march up to a battery, or stand
and watch the water creep up the side of their ship to
drown them, and never quail. But moral courage is another thing. To dare to do just what we know we ought
to do, without being in the least hindered or distorted
by the presence of men who we know will either hate
or despise or ridicule us for what we are doing, that is
rare indeed. Men think they have it till their test
comes. Why, there is in this community ; nay, there is
in this congregation to-day, an amount of right conviction
which, if it were set free into right action by complete
release from moral cowardice, would be felt through the
land. A man is deeply assured of Christianity. He is
trying to serve Christ. He is always trying to be spiritual. If he can creep up at night and drive a spike
into some cannon of infidelity or sin when no one sees
him, there is something in his heart that makes him do
it. He will give his anonymous dollar or thousand dollars to religious work. But he never stands out boldly
on the Lord's side, never declares himself a Christian
and says that the work of his Master shall be the work

of his life. Is it cowardice? He says there is no man he is afraid of; and there is none. The fear is concentrated on no individual. But is there not a sense of hostile or contemptuous surroundings that lies like a chilling hand upon what ought to be the most exuberant and spontaneous utterance of life? Have not the long years of living in such an atmosphere enfeebled the power of the native will? One sees it in old men continually, the fear which keeps the best and most enthusiastic hopes and wishes chained. One has but little expectation of the breaking of that chain in them. But it is sad to see those same chains fastening themselves on younger men. The mere boy feels them growing. He wants to be generous, pure, devoted, Christian. Everything urges him to put his life from the first upon the side of righteousness and Christ. And what hinders him? He early learns to cloak it under various names, but the power itself is fear. Cowardice wrings the foul or profane word from the lips that hate it while they utter it. Cowardice stifles the manly and indignant rebuke at the piece of conventional and approved meanness of the college or the shop. Cowardice keeps the low standards of honor traditional and unbroken through generations of boys. Cowardice holds the young Christian back from a frank acknowledgment of his Lord.

It is easy to make an argument with such a moral cowardice. It is easy for the boy or man who finds that he is losing his best life out of fear of his fellows to reason with himself. "Come," he says to himself; "1 am failing of my duty, I am dishonoring my best convictions, I am living a lie; and all because I am afraid of whom? Of a boy or a man, or of a company of boys or men whom I cannot respect. I know that he whom I fear is mean and low in his judgments. He is wicked, and in his heart there is no doubt the misgiving of wickedness. He probably distrusts and only half believes in his own abuse or his own sneer. And yet I am afraid of him. And what am I afraid that he will do? Why, either that he will detest me or ridicule me. Suppose he does. What is the value of these missiles? Do I really care for his praise so much that to lose it would really give me pain? And then am I not wrong in thinking that he cares enough about me to waste upon me either his hate or his contempt? Do I not over-estimate the space which I fill in his thoughts? Am I not doing myself wrong in order that a man or a world may think well of me, which in reality never thinks of me at all?" This is the argument which the conscious coward holds with himself. It is unanswerable. It ought to break the chains instantly and set the coward free. A man ought to cast his fears to the winds when he comes to realize that he is fearing contemptible people, and fearing that they will do to him contemptible things which in all probability they will never care enough about him to do at all. That is what many a man does realize about his cowardice; and does it set him free? Almost never, I believe. Almost never is a man made independent and brave by having it proved to him that it is a foolish thing to be afraid. No, men do not escape from their cowardice so. Nothing except the inflow of a larger consecration which oversweeps and drowns their cowardice can really put it out of the way forever. Nothing but the knowledge of God's love, taking such possession of a man that his one wish and thought in life is to glorify and serve God, can liberate him from, because it makes him totally forget, his fear of man. "I will walk at liberty because I keep Thy commandments." O those great words of David! What an everlasting story they tell of the liberty that comes by lofty service. They tell of what you young people need to save you, at the very outset of your life, from cowardice. Not by despising men will you cease to fear them. People's worst slavery very often is to things and people that they despise. Only by loving God and fearing Him with that fear whose heart and soul is love; only by letting Christ show God to you so that you must see Him; only so shall you tread your cowardice under your feet and be free for your best life.

2. We must go on to the second of the causes of the uselessness of men who might be useful, which I called false humility. Humility is good when it stimulates, it is bad when it paralyzes, the active powers of a man. It may do either. We have noble examples of humility as a stimulus; the sense of weakness making a man all the more ardent to use all the strength he has. But if conscious weakness causes a man to believe that it makes no difference whether he works or not, then his humility is his curse. Perhaps this was part of the trouble of Meroz. The little village in the hills, poor, insignificant perhaps, lay listening to the gathering of the tribes. She saw the signal fires and heard the summons of the trumpet run through all the land. She knew the summons was for her as well as all the rest. But who was she? What could she do? What strength could she add to the host? What terror could she inspire in the foe? What would Barak care for her sup-

port, or Sisera for her hostility ?   So she lay still and
let the battle fight itself through without her.   Do you
not recognize the picture ?   Whenever men hide behind
their conscious feebleness ; whenever, because they can
do so little, they content themselves with doing nothing ;
whenever the one-talented men stand with their napkins
in their hands along the roadside of life, — there is
Meroz over again.   Once more the argument is clear
enough ; as clear with humility as it is with cowardice.
Listen, how clear it is !   You who say that you can
do so little for any good cause that there is no use of
your doing anything ; you can give so little that it is not
worth while for you to give anything ; your word has
so little weight that it need not be spoken for the Lord,
— consider these things.   First, what do you know about
the uses of the Lord, of this great work which the Lord
has to do ; what do you know of it that gives you the
right to say that your power is little ?   God may have
some most critical use to put you to as soon as you declare yourself His servant.   Men judge by the size of
things ; God judges by their fitness.   Two pieces of iron
lie together on a shelf.   One is a great clumsy plough-
share ; and the other is a delicate screw that is made to
hold the finest joint of some subtle machinery in place.
An ignorant boor comes up and takes the great piece
and treasures it.   The little piece he sees is little, and
throws it away.   Fitness is more than size.   You can see
something of your size ; but you can see almost nothing
of your fitness until you understand all the wonderful
manifold work that God has to do.   It is a most wanton
presumption and pride for any man to dare to be sure
that there is not some very important and critical place

which just he and no one else is made to fill. It is almost as presumptuous to think you can do nothing as to think you can do everything. The latter folly supposes that God exhausted Himself when He made you; but the former supposes that God made a hopeless blunder when He made you, which it is quite as impious for you to think.

And remember, in the second place, what would happen if all the little people in the world held up their littleness like a shield before them as you hold up yours. Grant that you are as small as you think you are, you are the average size of moral and intellectual humanity. Let all the Merozes in the land be humble like you, and where shall be the army? Only when men like you wake up and shake the paralysis of their humility away, shall we begin to see the dawn of that glorious millenium for which we sigh; which will consist not in the transformation of men into angels, nor in the coming forth of a few colossal men to be the patterns and the champions of life, but simply in each man, through the length and breadth of the great world, doing his best.

Remember, too, that such a humility as yours, the humility that enfeebles and disarms you, comes, if you get at its root, from an over-thought about yourself, an over-sense of your own personality, and so is close akin to pride. It has run all around the circle in its desire to escape from pride, and has almost got back to pride again. Now pride is the thickest and most blinding medium through which the human eye can look at anything. If your humility is not transparent but muddy, so that you see things not more clearly but less clearly because of it, you may be sure there is pride in it. O my friends, there is a humility which some men are too humble to feel, a distrust of self which some men are too forgetful of self ever to experience.

The argument, then, against allowing any sense of weakness to keep us from doing all that we can do, is perfectly conclusive. But, once again, does this argument dispel the paralysis and set men free to work? Almost never, I believe, again. Not by studying himself, but by forgetting himself in the desire to serve his Lord, does a man exchange the false humility which crushes for the true humility which inspires. What has become of the self-distrust and shyness of that gentle scholar who has turned into a Boanerges of the truth; or of that timid shrinking woman who goes unmoved through the hooting of a rabble to the stake? Both have lost themselves in their Lord. Both have learned the love of Christ till that became the one fact of their existence; and then the call of Him who loved them has drawn the soul out of all self-consciousness. They have forgotten themselves, forgotten even their humility, and are wholly His. And there is the door through which all morbid self-distrust, all the despair of conscious weakness, must find escape.

3. I shall not need to say much upon the third of the causes for men's shirking the duties and responsibilities of life. Not that it is not important, but that it is so simple. It is mere indolence, mere laziness. Perhaps Meroz was not afraid. Perhaps she was not shy and self-distrustful. Perhaps she simply believed that the work of God would somehow get itself done without her, and so waited and waited and came not to the help of the Lord against the mighty. Ah, we are

always giving elaborate and complicated accounts both of the virtues and the vices of our fellow-men which are really as simple and explicable as possible, as clear as daylight. A man does a good thing and we are not content to say that he does it because he is a good man, but we must find strange obscure motives for it, some far-off policies and plans, some base root for this bright flower. Another man lets his duty, his clear duty, go undone, and again we set our ingenuity to work to guess why he does not do it. He misconceives his duty, he is too modest, he is waiting for something; when the real trouble is in a simple gross laziness, a mere self-indulgent indolence, which makes him indifferent to duty altogether. Let me go back to the picture which I tried to draw at the beginning of this sermon; a man who was born in luxury has lived in luxury, and now is coming on to middle life with the habits of his youth about him. He belongs to that strange, undefined, and yet distinct condition of life which is called society or fashion or respectability. That is a strange condition. It is not characterized by remarkable intelligence, not by peculiar education, not always by the most perfect breeding; but the main thing about it is that over it there hovers a vague air of privilege. The men and women who live in it are not looked to by other people, and do not look to themselves, for the active energetic contributions to the labor of life. It does not furnish the workers to the state or to the church. With this condition many of you are perfectly familiar. To it many of you belong, and feel its influence. Nothing is expected of you, and you do nothing. A well-bred, good-natured selfishness fills up the life of such a man. Duty? It seems as if he never had heard

the word ; or as if he thought that it belonged, like those
other two words, poverty and work, to beings of another
order from himself. Now is there any hope for such a
man ?   O, if he were only a fancy sketch !   O, if he were
not real and actual all through the city !   O, if there were
not whole hosts of boys, with the capacity in them to be
something better, who are growing up with him as the object of their admiration, and becoming year by year more
and more like him !   Is there any hope of such a man
coming to understand that it is not for such a life as he is
living that God has made him ?   I own the only chance I
see is in his coming to understand, in some real sense and
meaning of those words, that God did make him.   I think
that is the real knowledge that is needed in our parlors
and our clubs; needed there, lacking there, often quite
as much as in our drinking saloons and dens of thieves.
That a man's life is not an accident, that we are here
because God put us here as the master mechanic puts
each bolt and shaft of the engine into the place where
it is wanted ; is not that the quickening, the transform-
ing knowledge ?   That physical strength, those strong
arms and nimble hands, are not accidents ; not an accident, that quick perception and that power of endurance ;
not an accident, that easy temper and careless acceptance
of the things of life which might be elevated into faith.
Let a man know .this, and his sense of fitness must be
outraged every day as he hears the life, which he was
made for, claiming him, and yet goes on in uselessness.
But there is only one way to really know this deeply.
The only way to really know that God made us is to
let God remake, regenerate us.   The only way to be
sure that God gave us our physical life is to let Him

give us the spiritual life which shall declare for the physical life an adequate and worthy purpose. The only way to realize that we are God's children is to let Christ lead us to our Father. That is the only permanent escape from indolence, from self-indulgence; the grateful and obedient dedication to God through Christ which makes all good work, all self-sacrifice, a privilege and joy instead of a hardship, since it is done for Him.

The curse of Meroz is the curse of uselessness; and these are the sources out of which it comes — cowardice and false humility and indolence. They are the stones piled upon the sepulchres of vigor and energy and work for God, whose crushing weight cannot be computed. Who shall roll us away those stones? Nothing can do it but the power of Christ. The manhood that is touched by Him rises into life. I have tried to show you what that means. O my friends, it means this, that when a man has understood the life and cross of Jesus, and really knows that he is redeemed and saved, his soul leaps up in love and wants to serve its Savior; and then he is afraid of nobody; and however little his own strength is, he wants to give it all; and the cords of his self-indulgence snap like cobwebs. Then he enters the new life of usefulness. And what a change it is! To be working with God, however humbly; to have part of that service which suns and stars, which angels and archangels, which strong and patient and holy men and women in all times have done; to be, in some small corner of the field, stout and brave and at last triumphant in our fight with lust and cruelty and falsehood, with want or woe or ignorance, with unbelief and scorn, with any of the enemies of God; to be distinctly on God's side, though the weight of the work we do may be utterly inappreciable, — what a change it is when a poor, selfish, cowardly, fastidious, idle human creature comes to this! Blessed is he that cometh to the help of the Lord, to the help of the Lord against the mighty. There is no curse for him. No wounds that he can receive while he is fighting on that side can harm him. To fight there is itself to conquer, even though the victory comes through pain and death, as it came to Him under whom we fight, the Captain of our Salvation, Jesus Christ.

XVIII.

THE MYSTERY OF LIGHT.

A SERMON FOR TRINITY SUNDAY.

"Who coverest Thyself with light as with a garment."— PSALM civ. 2.

THE Psalms of David have two different descriptions
of the way in which God offers Himself to the knowledge of man. They are both figurative. Each of them
is drawn from one of the two great aspects in which the
world of nature stands before men's eyes. They seem
at first to be quite contradictory of one another. But,
as so often is the case, the more we think of them the
more we see that both are true, and going back to their
meeting-point we find, lying there, the deepest and the
fullest truth concerning God. In the eighteenth Psalm
David sings of God, "He made darkness His secret
place; His pavilion round about Him were dark water
and thick clouds of the skies." And again in the nine-
ty-seventh Psalm, "Clouds and darkness are round
about Him." And then in this verse of the one hundred and fourth Psalm, which I have quoted for my
text, "Who coverest Thyself with light as with a garment." Darkness and light! The two opposites which
divide the world! The two foes which are in perpetual
fight throughout all nature! Behold they both are
made the mediums of the utterance of God. "Darkness

20

is round about Him ;" and yet He stands before the world, " clothed with light as with a garment."

When we try to reach the ideas which are included in these two pictures, so as to see whether we can hold them both in our minds at once, the first thing of which we wish to be sure is that the difference between them is the difference not between mystery and no mystery, but between two kinds of mystery. It is not that the figure of the darkness presents to us a Being all obscure and hidden, whom no intelligence can understand, and then the figure of the light throws open all the closed doors of this Being's nature so that whoever will may enter in and understand Him through and through. God is forever mysterious to man. The infinite is forever infinitely past the comprehension of the finite. None but another God, the equal of Himself, could fathom what God is. He not merely does not, He cannot, make to us a revelation of Himself which shall uncover all the secrets of His life and leave us nothing for our wonder, nothing to elude us or bewilder us. What then ? What is it that He does do when He changes the figure of His presentation and, instead of standing before our awe-filled vision wrapped in the robes of darkness, stands forth radiant, " clothed with the light as with a garment ?" This is one of the questions which lie at the root of any true understanding of revelation ; one of the questions men's confusion with regard to which keeps their whole idea of revelation misty and confused ; one of the questions therefore which we want to answer as carefully and truly as we can.

The answer to the question lies in the fact that there

are two kinds of mystery, a mystery of darkness and a
mystery of light. With the mystery of darkness we are
familiar. Of the mystery of light we have not thought,
perhaps, so much. Some object which we would like
to study is hidden in obscurity. We cannot make out
its shape or color. We strain our eyes, but it eludes
us still. We know that the way it looks to us may be
quite different from the reality. We know that the
cloud is jealously hiding some of its features without
the knowledge of which no man can truly say that he
knows the object. We struggle with our ever baffled
vision, saying all the time, "How mysterious!" "What
a mystery it is!" But now supposing that the object
of our scrutiny, being something really rich and profound, were brought out of the darkness into a sudden
flood of sunlight, would it grow less or more mysterious?
Suppose it is a jewel, and instead of having to strain
your eyes to make out the outline of its shape, you can
look now deep into its heart; see depth opening beyond
depth, until it looks as if there were no end to the
chambers of splendor that are shut up in that little
stone; see flake after flake of luminous color floating up
out of the unseen fountain which lies somewhere in the
jewel's heart. Is the jewel less or more mysterious
than it was when your sight had to struggle to see
whether it was a topaz or an emerald? Suppose it is
a landscape. One hour all its features are vague and
dim in twilight; hill, field, and stream in almost indis-
tinguishable confusion. Six hours later the whole is
glowing in the noonday sun, the streams burning with
silvery light, the colors of the fresh spring hillsides
striking from far away upon the senses, filling them with

delight and wonder. Everything is thrilling and bursting with manifest life. Has not the mystery increased with the ascending sun ? Suppose it is a friend. A man about whom you have heard conflicting and bewildering accounts, whom you have been unable to make out as he stood off at a distance, has drawn near and touched your life. You have grown intimate with him. You have traced his ideas and actions back into his character. You have seen him on many sides, and out of many impressions the roundness and completeness of his nature has become clear to you. Is it not true that the more you see of him the more you wonder at him ? If you are worthy to see him and he is worthy to be seen, familiarity breeds not contempt but reverence. The more light there is upon the greatest and best men, the more mystery they show to their wondering fellows. There is no mystery of character to any man like that of his father and his mother, whom he has known all his life in the constant clear light of home. And so we might proceed with many illustrations. Is a great idea, a great study, a great cause, more deeply mysterious to the superficial or to the thorough student ? Was not the mystery of mathematical truth more truly mysterious to Professor Peirce than it is to you or me ? Does not the mystery of color or the mystery of form grow more intense to Raphael and Michael Angelo as they surpass the mere gazer of the galleries ? Africa looks mysterious to the mere tourist who sails into the harbor at Alexandria. Has it lost or deepened its mystery for Livingstone and Stanley when they have toiled up the long nameless rivers into the heart of the dark continent ?

This is the mystery of light. With all deep things the deeper light brings new mysteriousness. The mystery of light is the privilege and prerogative of the profoundest things. The shallow things are capable only of the mystery of darkness. Of that all things are capable. Nothing is so thin, so light, so small, that if you cover it with clouds and hide it in half-lights it will not seem mysterious. But the most genuine and profound things you may bring forth into the fullest light, and let the sunshine bathe them through and through, and in them there will open ever new wonders of mysteriousness. The mystery of light belongs to them. And how then must it be with God, the Being of all beings, the Being who is Himself essential Being, out of whom all other beings spring and from whom they are continually fed? Surely in Him the law which we have been tracing must find its consummation. Surely of Him it must be supremely true that the more we know of Him, the more He shows Himself to us, the more mysterious He must forever be. The mystery of light must be complete in Him.

Shall the time ever come when God shall be so perfectly understood by man that the mystery shall be gone out of His life, and man feel that he knows Him through and through and can tell his brother-man about Him; as the father stands by the steam-engine and explains it to his boy, so that what used to be a beautiful wonderful thing which seemed almost alive, becomes only an ingenious arrangement of steel and iron, which the boy goes off to imitate in his workshop, making a little steam-engine which repeats the big one which he has been studying? Shall the time ever come when man shall understand God like that? Men often talk as if such a time would come. Nay, men often talk as if such a time had come; as if their theologies, their descriptions of God, had eliminated mystery from Deity and made the infinite perfectly intelligible to the finite. This is the danger which haunts the popular theology and often makes the devotional meeting and the religious controversy and the revival hymn and the statement of religious experience very unpleasant and sometimes very harmful. Very many good people seem to think that in order to make God seem dear and capable of being loved and trusted by His children, they must make Him seem perfectly simple and comprehensible; they must take away from the thought of Him all that is awful and mysterious; as if awe and mystery were not essential elements in the highest loveliness; as if our deepest and most trustful love were not always given to the things which are awful and mysterious to us; the love of the little child for his father who embodies for him omniscience and omnipotence; the love of the patriot for his country; of the philanthropist for his race; of the poet for nature. There was a time when men seemed to be so busy in wondering at God that they forgot to love Him. Sometimes now it seems as if they so longed to love Him that they dared not remember how wonderful He is. When the full religion shall have come, men will know that the more wonderful they find Him to be, the more completely they may love Him; and the more He gives Himself to their love, the more He will be wonderful to them forever.

For to those who stand nearest to Him He is most mysterious. We talk with ready understanding of the death of Christ, before which the angels stand in awe.

" No angel in the sky
Can fully bear that sight,
But downward bends his wondering eye
At mysteries so bright."

Mysteries so bright! The more bright the more mysterious! Heaven is to be full of mystery. The nearer we stand to the Lamb upon His throne, the deeper depths we can discover in His majesty and love, the more wonderful shall He be to us forever. Revelation — it is a most important thing to know — revelation is not the unveiling of God, but a changing of the veil that covers Him ; not the dissipation of mystery, but the transformation of the mystery of darkness into the mystery of light. To the Pagan, God is mysterious because He is hidden in clouds, mysterious like the storm. To the Christian, God is mysterious because He is radiant with infinite truth, mysterious like the sun.

I have dwelt long on this because I wanted to make it as clear as I could, and because it seems to me to be what we want first and most of all to remember when we are thinking of the New Testament revelation of God, which we call the doctrine of the Trinity. To us to whom that revelation seems to be clear, God stands forth in it with amazing light. Behold He who hid Himself in darkness has come forth into the region which our most dear affections and our loftiest thoughts keep forever flooded with brightness. He is our Father, our Brother, our Inspiring Friend. Father, Brother, Friend! These are words of light. In the clear atmosphere of the relations which those words represent our life is lived, our most familiar interests and hopes and occupations go their way, walk up and down, and do

their several business. When God then sheds around
Himself the revelation of these three relationships, and
declares Himself to be Father and Son and Spirit, it is
surely a vast access of light. We know Him as we
have not known Him before, while our whole knowledge of Him was wrapped up in the undefined, unopened
majesty of that one name, GOD. And what then? In
the new light of this great revelation has the mystery
of God grown less or greater? Surely not less but
greater. Nothing could be more misleading than for
the believer or for the doubter of the doctrine of the
Trinity to talk about that doctrine as if it claimed to be
the solution, the dissipation, of the mystery of God. I
say "God" to the religious heathen who has gone so
far as to believe that there is one God and not many
gods in the universe; I say "God" to him and he
gazes into the darkness of that great idea and says, "I
do not know what God is; I do not dare to ask. A
million questions come buffeting me like bats out of the
darkness the moment that I dare even to turn my face
that way. Let me hear His commandments and go and
do them. For Himself I dare not even ask what He
is." That is the mystery of darkness. That is Moses
on Mount Sinai. That is the Egyptian in the desert.
That is the pure worshipper of the one unknown god-
hood everywhere. Then I say "God" to the Christian
and he looks up and says, "Yes, I know; Father, Son,
and Spirit; my Father, my Brother, my inspiring Friend.
I know Him, what He is, for He has shown Himself to
me." But with each word, Father, Brother, Friend,
there come flocking new questions, not like bats out of
the darkness, but like sunbeams out of the light, bewil-

dering the believing soul with guesses and insoluble suggestions and intangible visions of the love, the truth, the glory of God, which were impossible until this clothing by God of Himself with radiance in Christ had come. That is the mystery of light. That is St. John in Patmos. That is the Christian saint and thinker and questioner of all the ages standing before "the light of the knowledge of the glory of God in the face of Jesus Christ."

I am anxious to assert that the revelation of God in Jesus Christ is not the dissipation but the change, the transfiguration of mystery. The doctrine of the Trinity is not an easy, ready-made, satisfactory explanation of God, in which the inmost chambers of His life are unlocked and thrown wide open that whoso will may walk there and understand Him through and through. Often men's disappointment comes just here. The believer in the doctrine of the Trinity says, "I thought that with my acceptance of this truth all doubt, all questioning would be over. But lo! the questions which I knew before were nothing to the questions that come flocking around me now. My heart is full of wonder. Christ, who reveals God to me, seems to escape me and elude me. The mystery of my religion is increased a hundredfold since God shone on me in the light of the gospel revelation." It is often an anxious and discouraging discovery. There is a strange confused consciousness that all is right, and yet a haunting suspicion that something is wrong, when the humble, puzzled believer thus declares the perplexity of his faith. And on the other hand the doubter and denier of the Trinity declares, "See how simple my pure doctrine is, and how

complicated and hard to understand your teaching
makes the nature and life of God. It has lost simplicity and clearness." There is no answer to either of
them, my friends, save the one great sufficient answer
which lies in the truth of the mystery of light. There
is a mystery concerning God to him who sees the richness of the Divine life in the threefold unity of Father,
Son, and Holy Ghost, which no man feels to whom God
does not seem to stand forth from the pages of his Testament in that completeness. Not as the answer to a
riddle, which leaves all things clear, but as the deeper
sight of God, prolific with a thousand novel questions
which were never known before, clothed in a wonder
which only in that larger light displayed itself, offering
new worlds for faith and reverence to wander in, — so
must the New Testament revelation, the truth of Father,
Son, and Spirit, one perfect God, offer itself to man.

The figure of our Psalmist's verse seems to me to be
full of beauty and significance in connection with what
I am now saying. "Thou coverest Thyself with light
as with a garment," he cries to God. The garment at
once hides and reveals the form it clothes. The man
among men puts on the king's robe, and the purple
which he wears at once declares his dignity and starts
a hundred new questions concerning him. So when
God tells us any new thing about Himself, that new
revelation, that new light, is like a garment. It utters
and it hides His majesty. Through it we see what He
is ; and yet a hundred new questions about how He can
be that, and what it means for us that He should be
that, and what more which He must also be His being
that involves, come crowding on us.

Think how it must have been in the disciples' intercourse with Jesus. Their earliest life with Him was
very simple. They seemed to understand Him wholly.
They thought that they knew perfectly what He was
and what He had come to do. They learned to love
Him dearly and intimately in this familiarity. Now
and then in those first chapters of the gospels He says
some deep word or does some unexpected action which
seems to startle them and brings a puzzled question
which is like the first drop before the tempest of puzzled questions concerning Christ which has come since
and which is still raging around us, but generally in
those earliest days they have very few questions to ask;
they seem to understand Him easily. By and by, however, to any one who reads the Gospels thoughtfully,
there seems to come a gradual change. Jesus does
not withdraw Himself from them. He comes nearer
and nearer to them constantly. He tells them deeper
and deeper truths about Himself. He opens remoter and
remoter chambers of His history. "Before Abraham
was, I am," He says. "I and my Father are one," He
says. As He speaks, He is ever growing more and
more wonderful to His simple-hearted followers. The
love which they had given Him in those first bright
transparent days is not taken back or lessened; it is
ever deepening and increasing; but it is also ever being
filled with mystery and awe. By and by comes the
night of the Passover with its abundant revelation. As
we watch Jesus sitting there and telling the disciples
truth after truth about Himself, what words like the
old words of the Psalmist describe the scene, He is
"clothing Himself with light as with a garment." We

can seem to see the lustrous raiment of truth gathered about His familiar form, at once revealing it to, and hiding it from, His amazed disciples; revealing it to their love, hiding it from their understanding. He grows dearer and more mysterious to them every moment as He speaks. Then comes Gethsemane, and then the Cross, and then the Resurrection, and then the Pentecost. He, their Lord, is "clothing Himself with light as with a garment," all the while; more light and more mystery and withal more love perpetually, until at last the John who had once questioned Jesus as if He were a scribe or teacher, "Master, where dwellest Thou?" is seen writing His reminiscence of it all in words that burn with mysterious reverence, words that make us think He wrote them on His knees. "The Word was made flesh and dwelt among us, and we beheld His glory, the glory as of the only begotten of the Father."

Men sometimes shrink from following the disciples of Jesus in this developing apprehension and adoration of their Lord. There are some readers of the New Testament who cling to its first chapters, and love to picture to themselves over and over again the scenes in which Christ, sitting on the mountain or wandering by the lake, talked like a gentle, noble master to the simple-hearted men who never dreamed of the majesty which they were dealing with. Before such readers the last deep chapters of St. John and the expanse of the epistles seem to stretch like a great ocean, over which hang thick clouds, from which come solemn sounds that distress and frighten them, and on which they do not like to launch away. And yet the epistles are a true part of the same revelation with the gospels. The fact is clear beyond all doubt that the disciples who had walked with Jesus by Gennesaret were the same disciples who preached throughout Judea and far abroad the power of the Son of God, the mysterious salvation by the life and death of Christ, the crucified and risen Savior. Such change, beyond all doubt, came to those men as Jesus revealed Himself before them, as in their presence He clothed Himself with light as with a garment.

And is a progress such as theirs, a deepened knowledge of the mystery of Christ such as was given to them, possible for men to-day? Indeed it is! If there is any man or woman here this morning who has honored Jesus Christ, loved Him, believed Him, called Him the noblest of men, the perfect man perhaps; and taken pride in the simplicity, the definiteness, the completeness of such a notion of Christ; pointed to it and said, "Behold how clear it is; how free from all bewildering mystery;" if there is any such Christian here to-day to whom it can be made known that absence of mystery may be a sign not of abundance but of lack of light, to whom then his Christ, his teacher, his model man, may open the depths of His life and manifest the higher nature on which the perfection of His humanity rested; if there is any Christian who, ready and glad to see his Christ become more mysterious before his eyes as He robes Himself in fuller light, can take with joy the word of that Christ as He declares Himself the Son of God, to such a Christian the exact experience of the disciples may be repeated. Such repetitions are not rare. Continually Christ, trusted in His humanity, is making known His divinity. It is the effort, the tendency, of His whole nature to do that if men will let Him, if only they do not, fascinated with the simplicity of His manhood, refuse to go on and in into the deeper truth which He has to give them about Himself.

I have dwelt to-day on this one point. I have tried to show that there is such a thing as a mystery of light, and what is its true nature. I have tried to show that if God shows man new and more profound truth regarding Himself the result will certainly be a deepened mysteriousness and a growth of many questions too hard to answer; and therefore that the fact that the doctrine of the Trinity is full of mystery and overruns with questions before which the mind stands helpless, is not an objection to its truth, but is rather what man ought to look for in any revelation which proceeds from God.

And now in one last word, dear friends, what will this be to us? Only, I hope, a new encouragement to trust ourselves frankly and gladly to whatever revelation God may have to make to us. I am afraid that there are many Trinitarians who, in all their faith, are yet staggered and troubled because of its mysteriousness. I am afraid that there are many Unitarians who close their eyes to the deepest words of the New Testament because they too distrust the presence of mystery in the conception of God. I am not pleading with you now to believe this or that concerning God, but only, without prejudice or prepossession, to be willing to believe whatever He shall show you of Himself. Be sure that for such as we are to know such as God is must be for us to enter into a realm where mystery shall fill the air. Above all, be sure that it is only by completest willingness to know His completest truth that we can rightly know anything regarding His surpassing nature.

With such convictions fastened in your souls, O give yourselves, my friends, to Him. Ask Him to be your Savior. Ask Him to forgive your sins. Ask Him to take your sins out of you and make you pure. Ask Him to show you His holiness so that you shall love it and make it your own, growing holy like Him. Ask Him to save you in all the unknown wants of your poor broken life, where you are not even able now to know that you need salvation. Ask Him to do this and He will do it all. And as He does it, let yourself believe, without a hesitation; let yourself believe in the divinity of Him who alone could do so divine a work as the forgiveness and salvation of a soul. That is the only way in which men ever come really and truly to believe in the divinity of Jesus Christ.

XIX.

THE ACCUMULATION OF FAITH.

"Behold, He smote the rock, that the waters gushed out, and the streams overflowed. Can He give bread also? Can He give flesh for His people?"— PSALM lxxviii. 20.

BELIEF in God is such a large action of our human nature, and appears in such a multitude of ways, that unbelief also, its opposite, must have many forms. God is so vast, and for man to lay hold on Him is so complete an action, that it is no wonder if that hold may fail at any one of many points; and no two unbelievers, as no two believers, can be perfectly alike. In the Psalm from which I take my text the singer is telling the old story of the national history of the Jews. All the escape from Egypt and the journey through the desert is recounted; and in this twentieth verse the peevish and complaining Israelites are heard in the wilderness, doubting whether God, although he had done much for them, can still supply the new needs which are coming into sight. "Yea they spake against God; they said, Can God furnish a table in the wilderness?" And then — to quote the Prayer Book version of the Psalm — "He smote the stony rock indeed that the water gushed out and the streams flowed withal; but can He give bread also, or provide flesh for His people?" You see what kind of unbelief is here. It does not deny the past fact. It acknowledges that God has done one miracle of mercy.

But in that miracle it finds no such revelation of God Himself and His perpetual character and love as gives assurance that He will again be powerful and merciful. These Israelites have no accumulated faith. They are just where they were before the last miracle relieved them. That miracle stands wholly by itself. It does not promise or imply another. The old bright scene comes up before them ; the sparkling water tumbling out of the hard, sunburnt stone. They revel in the recollection ; but then they turn back to their present hunger, and the chance of bread and flesh seems only the more desperate because of the mocking and tantalizing remembrance of the water from the rock.

The power of accumulation of life differs extremely in different men. Some men gather living force, wisdom, faith, out of every experience. Other men leave the whole experience behind them and carry out with them nothing but the barren recollection of it. And the difference, when we examine it, depends on this; on whether the man has any conception of a continuous unbroken principle or personal association running through life, and bringing out of each experience its soul and essence to be perpetually kept. It is something like this. Two fields of wholly different soils lie side by side. Neither is mingled with the other. The traveller who simply tramps across them leaves one behind him as he climbs the stile and enters on the other as a wholly new experience. But let a stream flow through them and it binds their life together. It takes the essence out of the soil of the first and mixes it with the soil of the second. The second not merely remembers the first as something that lies next to it, something that it has seen across

21

the wall. It receives that first field into itself and mod-
ifies its own life by its presence through the ministry of
that stream, which is common to them both. Now so
it is, it seems to me, with some event of your earlier life.
You look back to something which happened to you or
which you did when you were fifteen years old. That
event may be to you to-day a mere recollection, merely
a relic which stays in your memory; or it may be the
source of a power which pervades your life. What will
decide which it shall be? Will it not depend upon
whether you understand that event and see in it the
exhibition of principles in whose power you are still
living; or whether it is merely an accident, unintelligible,
with no perceptible cause, with no reasonable explanation? A living principle, a deep continuous conviction
of the meaning of life, is the stream that makes the new
fields gather and keep the richness of the old. Suppose
you had a sickness ten years ago. If you understand
what it was that cured you, then the memory of that
sickness is a power, and you see a new sickness of the
same sort coming with less fear. Suppose you escaped
in some great business crisis five years ago. If your
escape seems to you a lucky accident, you tremble when
you see a new business crisis coming, for it is not
likely that such a lucky accident can happen twice. " I
escaped once," you say; "but I cannot hope to get off
safe again." But if you know how you escaped; if
that old struggle was to you a revelation of great perpetual principles that rule the business world and which,
as a new need of them occurs, come back to you famil-
iarly, then the old recollection is a power. Filled with
its inspiration you go on bravely to meet the now intel-

ligible danger. Or if you are a public man, and it seems to you nothing but a series of happy chances that the country has thus far weathered the storms and kept off the rocks that have beset her voyage through the century, then no wonder that you look forward with dread and feel that it is only a question of time how soon she goes to pieces. But if you have studied your country's past history deeply and wisely enough to see that in every emergency it has been her essential principles that have saved her, then you are able to look all coming dangers in the face and devote yourself not to planning how you and your fellow voyagers can be saved from the wreck when the ship has gone to ruin; but how the ship can be kept most purely and directly in the power of those first essential principles on which her safety in any emergency must rely and which, if they can have free play, will always save her.

Let these be illustrations, and now turn and think of God. He is the great first principle. He is the under-power, the abiding base and background of our human life. His will, uttering His nature, is the stream that flows from field to field of our existence and binds them all together. The things that have to do with Him must have to do with one another. Now, once again, something came to you twenty years ago, something very rich and beautiful, something which has made life bright and wonderful ever since. It may have been your birth; perhaps you are only twenty years old. Life began for you twenty years back. It may have been a great affection. It may have been a great new truth. It may have been the sight of a character which revealed the possibilities of humanity to you. Whatever it was, the great question about that acquisition to-day is, Do you indeed know that God gave it to you? As you feel it, do you feel, down through it, God? Does it reveal, has it all along through these years been revealing, God to you? You know that I mean something more by this than merely whether you have learned to say piously about it, "It is God's gift." I mean this, Has its value for you become lodged in this, that it is a token of God's love for you and a revelation of His nature; just as the picture on your walls, which a friend gave you years ago, shines with the perpetual brightness of his kindness and his taste. The Jews, you know, in our verse said, "He," that is God, "He smote the stony rock indeed, and the water gushed out;" but really they did not completely know and believe that He, that God, had done it. They did not know and believe it so that with the memory of it GOD came up in their remembrance and filled their life. If that had been, they could not have asked any question about any future manifestation of His power. This is the question then, Does the joy of living which makes you rejoice that you were born; does the joy of thinking, the joy of honoring your humanity as some great man exhibits it to you; does each of these joys reveal God to you? If it does, it becomes a fountain of faith. If it does not, it becomes only a beautiful memory. There is all that difference. It is the difference between a thicket of ferns lovely with their exquisite leafage, and another thicket up into which gushes and wells perpetually the cool water from the exhaustless cisterns underneath for the refreshment of thirsty men.

The unbelief then of which we have to speak is one

which so fails to find in the past events of life a revelation of God, that those past events have no strength or divine assurance to give to the new problems and emergencies of life as they arise. This kind of unbelief, I think we shall see, is very constant. See how it comes in to break up the unity of life. A boy passes through his boyhood. It is full of happiness and a boy's healthy pleasure. Happy at home, happy in the playground, happy at school, those bright and breezy years slip by. When they are gone the boy stands on the brink of manhood and looks over into the untrodden years. Are the problems, the difficulties, the temptations which he sees there, just what they would be if he had not already passed through boyhood? Certainly not, if boyhood has given him anything of a real faith in God. Certainly not, if all these happinesses which have come to him are recognized as God's gifts, and if through the gifts he has known God the Giver. Then, though he must leave the gifts behind, he carries the Giver with him into the manhood that he is entering. That is the true unity of life. It is the unity of a long journey in which, though the quick railroad is constantly compelling you to leave each new scene behind you, the wise kind company of the friend whom you are travelling with, and who in each new scene has had the chance to show you something new of his wisdom and kindness, has been continually with you and bound the long journey into a unit. This is the sort of life that Wordsworth was imagining when he sang :—

"The child is father of the man;
And I could wish my days to be
Bound each to each by natural piety."

We can see how this must come when underneath
the habits of any period of life we recognize and find
the revelation of God. The habits are rigid, uniform
and untransferable. But God is infinitely various. His
great arms can hold the infant like a mother, and build
a strong wall about the mature man who is fighting the
noonday fight of life, and lay the bridge of sunset over
which the old man's feet may walk serenely into the
eternal day. If the issue of any period of life is merely
certain habits, we must lay them aside as we go on. If
the issue of any period of life is a certainty of God, that
we may freely carry over for the enrichment of the new ;
just as the clothes which you wore when you were a boy
you have outgrown, but the health which filled you then
is in you now.

And this is so not merely as one passes from youth to
age, but also as one sees any new occupation or duty
opening before him. You have been in one business
and you are going into another. You have weighed all
the chances. You have used all the discretion and judgment that you possess. You believe that you are fit for
the larger work. And yet, as you sit thinking it over
the night before the new shop is to be opened and the
new advertisement is to stand in the papers, you are full
of your misgivings. Shall I succeed ? Am I not leaving a certainty for an uncertainty ? I know that God
has prospered me thus far, but will He, can He, help me
here ? And then, just in proportion to the purity and
absoluteness of your confidence that it has really been
God who has helped you, and the simplicity and completeness with which you resolve that, in the new business as in the old, you will be His obedient servant and

put no obstacle in the way of His helping you still, just in proportion to your faith and consecration, will be the courage with which you see the dawn of the new day that is to bring to you the untried task.

Take one step more. Suppose a human soul looking out into the mysterious and unrevealed experiences of the everlasting world. The window of death is wide open, and the shivering soul stands up before it and looks through and sees eternity. No wonder that it trembles. The warm, bright, familiar room of earthly life, where it has dwelt so long, lies there behind it; and before it, outside the window, the vast, dim, pathless, unknown world of immortality. How shall the soul carry with it the sense of safety and assurance in God, which it has won within His earthly care, forth into this unknown, untrodden vastness whither it now must go? Only in one way; only by deepening as deeply as possible its assurance that it is God — not accident, not its own ingenuity, not its brethren's kindness — that it is God who has made this earthly life so rich and happy. God is too vast, too infinite for earth. He is too vast for time, and needs eternity. Wrapped into Him the soul may be not merely resigned; it may be even impatient to explore those larger regions where the power which has made itself known to it here shall be able to display to it all the completeness of its nature and its love. As the child of the sailor may wish to go to sea that he may see the father whom he believes in do his supreme work in fighting with the midnight hurricane; as the child of the soldier may wish to see his father on the battle-field; and the child of the statesman may wish to see his father in the senate; so the child of

God may wish for eternity, sure that there upon the vaster fields he shall see vaster exhibitions of that power and grace which he has learned completely to believe in here.

And yet here, I think, if a man does really know that God is giving him more and more revelations of Himself every day, increasing his faith by all the various treatments of his life, all that is necessary for him is that he should simply accept that constant growth in faith, rejoice each day in the new certainty of God which is being gathered and stored within him, and not look forward, not even ask himself how he will meet the large demands of death and immortality when they shall come. He may be sure that when they come this strength of faith which now is being stored within him will come forth abundantly equal to the need. So a soul need not even think of death if only life is filling it with a profound and certain consciousness of God. The ship in the still river, while its builder is stowing and packing away the strength of oak and iron into her growing sides, knows nothing about the tempests of the mid-Atlantic; but when she comes out there and the tempest smites her, she is ready. So shall we best be ready for eternity, and for death which is the entrance to eternity, not by thinking of either, but by letting life fill us with the faith of God.

There is one great and perpetual illustration of the truth which we are studying in the history of the Christian church and of religious thought. There the kind of unbelief of which I have spoken is continually coming out. It is often very strong in men who think themselves supremely faithful, very champions of the faith.

The Christian church lives through one period of her career; she conquers the enemies that meet her there; she makes the hard rock yield her water; she keeps herself alive and feeds her children. Then she passes on into another period with its new needs, its call for other methods and for other miracles; and always there is a spirit in the church which trembles and has not learned, from the way in which God has cared for His church in the past, that He, the same God, is able to take care of her in the future also. This is the fault of all retrospective Christianity, of all Christianity which is anxious to abide in the old days, to fight over and over again the battles of the past, and to ignore or to avoid the modern battles, the special difficulties which the faith of Christ is called upon to meet in our own times. This is the fault of all the Christianity which is panic stricken before the enemies which it sees that faith in Christ must certainly be called upon to meet in the near future. I think I hear the voices of that panic from many quarters now. "He smote the stony rock indeed, and the water gushed out, but can He give bread also, and provide flesh for His people?" He answered the scepticism of the old centuries, but can He answer the subtler, finer sceptics of to-day? He overcame the worldliness of the eighteenth century, but can He conquer the materialism of the nineteenth? He saved His church when she was persecuted with fire and the rack; can He save her also when she is tempted with the corruptions of prosperity and fashion? He stood by her in the days when Luther lifted up his voice for spiritual truth; will He stand by her also now when it is evident that not Luther nor any other reformer has fathomed the truth of Christ completely, or brought the last message from the lips of God? Will He stand by her still as she in all humility tries to learn yet more truth and, by an inevitable necessity, by a necessity that she cannot escape and must expect to encounter, meets in the attempt to learn profounder truth the danger of profounder error? These are the questions that one hears. According to the answers which men and churches give to them they go forward hopefully or go back timidly. The man who sees in all the history of the Christian church one great assurance that Christ is always with His people, and will always help any soul which reverently and really wants to know deeper things concerning Him, and will lead it through many blunders and errors into truth, — that man goes forward. The man who sees in the history of the Christian church only the record that in the primitive ages, or in the reformation ages, Christ let His people see certain truths concerning Him and His ways, — that man goes back, lives in what seemed to him the finished revelation of those days, tries, by the imitation of their habits and the constant repetition of their phrases, to keep himself in their shadow; deserts his own age, in which God seems to him to be less present and less real, and lives among dead issues in which he knows was once a living fire. But oh, if God is not really a living God in the world to-day, we have no God. How little it would be — nay, truly it would be nothing to you and me, called, driven as we are to meet the hard temptations, to answer the hard questions of this very present day — to know that once a God had answered other questions and made men conquerors over other temptations in other days. Only when all I read

about that presence of His life among our human lives
makes me know Him and, making me know Him, makes
me absolutely certain that He is such that on to the very
end no servant of His can meet a temptation which He
can help His servant to subdue and the help not be
given; no disciple of His can ask a question which it
is possible for Him to answer and the answer be with-
held; only when the old history of all the Christian ages
opens its heart to me and gives me an assurance such as
this, only then have I attained to its true use and its
richest blessing.   With such a power as this, not merely
the men of the past with whom I agree, but the men
from whom I most profoundly differ, help me.   It is not
their opinions which I adopt; it is their spirit; it is the
presence of God's Spirit in and with their spirits that
makes me glad and hopeful.   I may see, I do see, a hundred times, how it was that, even with God's Spirit in
them, they came only to partial truth, to truth mixed
and clouded with mistake.   So while I am made hopeful of God's presence, I am made also conscious of my
own responsibility, and watchful over the condition of
the mind into which I bid that Spirit welcome.   Alas
if it were not so.   Alas for us if we were compelled to
assent to all the theology of Calvin or of Channing, before we could thank Christ for the guidance which His
Spirit gave both to Calvin and to Channing in their
search for truth, and gather from it strong assurance
that His spirit would help us too.   Forever the past
of the church is to us but a great curiosity-shop, into
which we go to steal a bit of bric-a-brac which suits our
fancy and which we can stick up incongruously in our
modern homes, unless out of it all there issues one great

assurance that Christ has always been with every soul
which would receive Him; in different ways according
to each soul's circumstances and nature; in different degrees according to each soul's receptivity; but that always
and everywhere He has given Himself to every soul that
would receive Him and that therefore, if we will receive Him, He will give Himself to us. When we
gather from it that assurance, the past of the church
becomes to us the fountain of strength and the oracle
of truth.

The Church is led into new ways of work and worship. The State adopts new policies. Society puts on
new manners. Nay, even the Faith asserts her doctrines in new forms. And yet in all of them there must
be continuity and unity. The Church, the State, Society, the Faith, they are not perishing, and new churches,
states, societies, faiths, taking their places every year.
They are the same continuously. How can one know
this and understand it? Only by apprehending the
spiritual power which is the soul of each, and seeing
how that remains the same through everything. It is
like the freedom which a workman gains when he has
mastered the principles of the trade he is engaged in.
So long as he is only familiar with its methods and its
tools he is slavish and uniform. He cannot imagine
the thing that he does being done in any but one way.
Those who are doing his thing in other ways than his
seem to him not to be doing it. But as soon as he has
grasped its principle he is flexible and free. He values
not the method but the thing; and then there is true
unity between him and all others who, in most distant
times and places, are doing what it is the business of

his life to do. Every man's business, whatever it be, becomes a liberal education to him just as soon and just as far as he lives not in its methods but in its principles. Now God is the principle which underlies all this business of human living. The methods of living are manifold. The principle of life is one. The man who lives in the methods loses the freedom and the unity of life. The man who lives in the principle, in loving, grateful, obedient communion with God, grows free with a divine liberty, and is a true brother of all the working children of God throughout the ages and throughout the world.

In the few moments which remain, let me try to come close to your personal religious life and see how there the unbelief of which we have been speaking is always trying to creep in. You look back over the years in which you have been trying to serve your Savior, and what do you see? Many a temptation conquered by His strength; many a sin forgiven and turned by gratitude for His forgiveness into an inspiration; many a hard crisis where Christ your Lord has been all sufficient for you. Why is it that to-day, in your present temptation, in your present need, you feel so little sure of Him? A new desert opening before you frightens you even while you remember with thanksgiving how He led you through the old. The thanksgiving dies away upon your lips for the past mercy as you come in sight of the new emergency for the brave meeting of which it would seem as if that past mercy ought to have fitted you completely. "He smote the stony rock indeed, that the water gushed out and the

streams flowed withal." There, as brightly as if you
still were revelling in their refreshment, the fresh springs
sparkle and sing before your recollection. "But," and
then you turn to the hunger and weariness that seem to
be awaiting you; "but, can He give bread also, or provide flesh for His people?" O, to how many souls all
that has come with a terrible surprise and disappointment! They thought that they were ready for anything. They thought that out of all the rich blessing
of the past they had gathered a strength that nothing
could break down, a courage that nothing could dismay.
But now they stand in front of the new temptation or
the new pain and tremble like children, just as if they
had never seen a temptation or a pain before. What
does it mean? It must mean that out of the old mercy
they had not gathered God. They have come out of it
with thankfulness for release, with soberness, with hope,
with joy; but they have not brought a deep and abiding fellowship with Christ, a firm, immovable confidence that they are His and He is theirs, to take with
them into the midst of the new need which they have
reached. If their terror, as the new trial comes, means
anything more than that instinctive shrinking from
pain which is part of our very physical humanity and
which has no taint of spiritual weakness in it, this must
be what it means. There is such a difference between
coming out of sorrow thankful for relief, and coming
out of sorrow full of sympathy with and trust in Him
who has released us. Nine lepers hurry off to show
themselves with their white skins to the priest. One
leper only waits to cast himself at the feet of Jesus and
worship Him. Tell me, will not those nine be different

from that one if ever a new disease should fall upon them all ?

Let that one leper be the type of the soul to whom the whole blessedness of a blessing from Christ has come. Not only the health but the Healer he delights in. Not only the salvation but the Savior is his glory and his joy. Such souls there are. I know that some of yours are such; souls to which all the deliverances and the educations that have filled their past lives are precious, not merely for the safety and the instruction which they have brought, but far more for the personal knowledge of the Deliverer and the Teacher which has been won in them, and in whose strength the soul looks on and faces all that the future has to bring without a fear. "He smote the stony rock and the water gushed out. Therefore I know He can give me bread and flesh; He will give me bread and flesh if bread and flesh are what I ought to have."

So to the soul that finds in all life new and ever deeper knowledge of Christ, the Lord of Life, life is forever accumulating. Every passing event gets a noble value from the assurance that it gives us of God. This is the only real transfiguration of the dusty road, of the monotony and routine of living. It is all bright and beautiful if, in it all, God is giving us that certainty of Himself, by which we shall be fit to meet everything that we shall have to meet in this world and the world to come.

XX.

CHRISTIAN CHARITY.

" And there came a traveller unto the rich man; and he spared to take of his own flock and his own herd to dress for the wayfaring man that was come unto him." — 2 SAMUEL xii. 4.

I WANT to speak to you this morning of the relations between the rich and the poor in our city life; and these verses from the Old Testament suggest, in the way in which the Old Testament always suggests the New, in the way of metaphor and parable, the full gospel truth at which I hope that we shall be able to arrive.

The mixture of gold and clay of which our human nature is composed is nowhere so strikingly displayed as in the constant tendency of men to conceive lofty purposes and then to try to attain them by mean and sordid methods. We are so used to the sight of it, that we do not feel how strange it is. That a being should seek nothing noble, should live a brute's life through and through, that would be intelligible enough. That a being should seek high things and then refuse to take any low ways to reach them, should rather give up the hope of reaching them at all than seek them by unworthy ways; that too would be intelligible. But that men should seek the very highest, earnestly, zealously, genuinely seek it, and yet make the method of their search consist in acts which contradict the very essential ideas of that which they are seeking, this surely shows a strange condition of our human life. Men try to get more close to God by hating, persecuting, murdering, God's children. Men try to convert their fellow-men to what they know is truth by arguments which they know just as well are lies. Men are captivated with the idea of self-denial, and then they invent ingenious ways to make self-denial comfortable and easy. The high impulse and the low self-indulgent method are both real, and this same confused and contradictory humanity of ours is able to contain them both. Men do not seem to know that, however bright and strong they frame the golden gallery of their ambition, the only chance of their getting up to it must be in the strength of the stairway which they build. They are always building steps of straw to climb to heights of gold.

In this old story from the book of Samuel we have a picture of a hospitable man, a man who really wanted to help the poor traveller who came to him, but who wanted to help him with another man's property, to feed him on a neighbor's sheep. There is real charity in the impulse. There is essential meanness in the act. " He spared to take of his own flock and his own herd to dress for the wayfaring man that was come unto him." Here is real kindliness and real selfishness in the same heart; and not in struggle with one another but in most peaceful compromise. " I want to feed this guest of mine," the rich man says. " How fortunate that I am able to do it without encroaching on myself, without taking of my own flock and my own herd." And by and by there sits the guest before the smoking feast, and the host's sheep are all heard safe and bleating through the open windows.

22

I have said that this Old Testament story was a sort of parable of New Testament truth. It might be more than that. It might be traced into almost literal application. No doubt in these our modern days we do precisely what this strange mixed creature of the book of Samuel did. We feed the poor whom we pity on our neighbor's sheep. A great deal of our official charity, of our support of charitable societies which we urge other men to support while we are ready to disburse their riches with a patronizing condescension almost as if they were our own gift, comes very near the pattern of this ancient benefactor. But what I want most to speak of is not exactly that. There is what we may call perhaps a development, a refinement, of his self-deception, which escapes its grossness and yet keeps and repeats its essential vice. There is a sense in which it may be said that a man meaning to be charitable, and perhaps freely bestowing his money on the poor, still spares to take of that which is most truly and intimately his own to give to the wayfaring men who are always coming to him in the complications of our life. It is this sort of self-indulgence into which many most excellent people are always falling ; and it is this which our best thought and our newest plans about charity are feeling very deeply must somehow be changed before the relations between the rich and the poor, between the householders and the wayfarers, can be what they ought to be in a Christian land.

For one of the truths about the advancing culture of a human nature is that it is always deepening the idea of possession and making it more intimate. " My own " are always becoming more and more sacred words to

growing men. What is your own ? In the crude savage
state, in the intellectual and spiritual childhood beyond
which many men never get; it is your goods and chat-
tels, your money and your houses and your clothes.
They are your property. Then grow a little finer man,
and what succeeds ? You come to certain habits, certain
ways of life, the tokens and signs of certain privileges
which you have enjoyed. These mark your deepened
conception of your personality. You value yourself because of these ; the manners of a gentleman, the habits
of a man who has lived well and is well-bred. You look
down on the rich man, however rich he be, who has not
these. Mere wealth becomes to you only the garment
which sets off the habits of your cultivated life, and
which is yours only in the moderate sense in which the
garment ever is the man's. He might lose it or cast it
away, and yet still keep all himself. But by and by you
become yet a profounder man. Below the habits of
your life opens the world of thought and knowledge.
Ideas take hold of you. You take hold of ideas. And
when you have done that your ownership in them becomes so real and vivid, they are so truly a part of yourself, so intimately and really yours, that it seems as if
the previous ownerships had not deserved the name.
Riches are mere trinkets, and habits are mere tricks. Of
neither will the man say unreservedly, "This is mine,"
who has found a new sacredness in those words as he
has learned to use them of the truths which have become to him like very life. And then once more, when
life still further deepens, when in the gradual attainment
of character the man comes to count that his own which
he is, when to possess intrinsic qualities, to know him-

self brave, patient, self-respectful, humble, pure, becomes the satisfaction of the soul, then are not all the previous notions of possession once again made slight? Even the knowledge which his mind has won will hardly seem to be truly his own to the man who has realized with what far more intimate ownership his whole nature has taken possession of a character. What we know is like something lent to us, something that we may possibly forget, something that we may even throw away in fuller light. It is not ours forever like the thing we are, and which being it once we must be always through the eternities, unless in some eternity we cease to be ourselves.

These are the deepening degrees of ownership. You see how, as each one of them becomes real to a man, the previous ownerships get a kind of unreality. The savage owns his forest. The man of civilization owns his rich and complicated life, and his houses and fields are but the symbols of the higher life he has attained. The scholar, the thinker, has passed down and into a yet profounder property. He has come to that which no circumstances, no man, can take away from him. And then the seeker after character, he whom in Bible phrase we call the " saint," has gone into the inmost chamber, and counts money and company and even knowledge as only the means and assurances of the one thing which he really possesses, which is himself, his personal nature, his character.

And now is it not clear that with this deepening of the idea of property, the idea of charity must deepen also? I want to give a poor man what is mine. It is my duty and my wish to give. What shall I give him? If I have got no farther into the idea of property than the first stage, I am satisfied when I have filled his empty hands with dollars. But if I have gone farther than that, I cannot be content till I have bestowed on him by personal care something of that which dollars represent to me and without which they would be valueless, the noble and ennobling circumstances which civilization has gathered round my lot. But if I have gone deeper still and learned to count truth the one precious thing in all the world, I shall feel that I have "spared to take of my own" to give him, till I have at least tried to provide not merely for the body but for the mind. And then, to take once more the final step, as soon as I have come to think of character as the one only thing that I can really call my own, my conscience will not let me rest, I shall think all my benefaction an imperfect, crippled thing, until I have touched the springs of character in him and made him the sharer of that which it is the purpose and joy of my life to try to be.

I have dwelt long on this because I wanted to make clear the true philosophy of those convictions which have been growing stronger and stronger in the minds of charitable people of late years, and which have recently found expression in the most intelligent and conscientious efforts for the relief of poverty. Evidently it is by these convictions that all the best charity of the future is to be inspired. The sum of those convictions is that no relief of need is satisfactory, none meets the whole want of the needy man or answers the whole duty of the benefactor, which stops short of at least the effort to inspire character, to make the poor man a true sharer in what is the real substance of the rich man's wealth. And at the bottom of this profounder conception of charity there must lie, as I have tried to show, a deeper and more spiritual conception of property. The rich man's real wealth, what is it ? Not his money! He is a poor man to the end if he has nothing except that. And yet it is something associated with his money. It is something which his money may give him peculiar opportunities to win and keep. It is something which came to him in the slow accumulation of his money. It is a character into which enter those qualities, independence, intelligence, and the love of struggle, which are the qualities that make true and robust manliness in all the ages and throughout all the world; independence, or what the poet calls "the sweet sense of providing," the joy of self-support; intelligence, or the trained quickness to discern what is the true nature and what the true relations of the things about him; and love of struggle, the capacity of buoyant hope and of delight in the exercise of powers against resistance, — these are the substance, the heart, the core, of the rich man's privilege. And men are coming more and more to feel that the rich man does not do his duty by the poor man, the rich class does not really take of its own and give it to the poor class, unless by some outflow of itself it gives these qualities, and sends a perpetual stream of independence, intelligence, and struggle, down through the social mass, making the spiritual privileges of those who are living on the heights of life the possession and inspiration of the waiting, unsuccessful, discouraged souls that lie below.

And then, at once, one thing is evident, that this makes charity a far more exacting thing than it can be without such an idea. It clothes it in self-sacrifice. It requires the entrance into it of a high motive. I may feel it well to give a poor man money, or even to train him in the decencies of life, or even to give him knowledge, from very low motives; merely to save myself from importunity, merely that he may not offend my fastidious taste, merely that he may become less dangerous. But before I seriously undertake to make of him an independent, intelligent, struggling brother-man, to wake him from his torpor, to set him on his feet, to kindle in his soul that fire which keeps my own soul full of light and warmth, I must have something more than the impulse of a wise economy. This needs a sympathy which makes his life, with all its needs and miseries, my own. It demands of me to wrestle with his enemies, to undertake a fight for him which he is not yet ready to undertake himself, to sacrifice myself that I may make his true self live.

Perhaps this is more clear if we see how it is illustrated in all the profoundest gifts which men are called on to give to their fellow-men. The most sacred gift that any of us can try to give to his brother is Christian faith; and I am sure that if you have ever thought of it at all carefully, you have seen that just in proportion to the profoundness of the faith which you yourself possessed, has always been the profoundness of the act of giving it, and also the degree of struggle and effort and self-sacrifice with which the gift has been bestowed. Here too the conception of property measures the conception of charity. If faith to you meant nothing deeper than the holding of certain well-proved propositions, then the giving of faith to your brother-man meant only the presentation of those propositions to his intellect, all backed up with their unanswerable proof. And it was wholly an easy thing to do. You glibly told the argument which you had learned, and all your pride of partisanship stood eagerly waiting to see assent dawn in your pupil's face. But if faith by a far deeper experience had come to mean for you something far more profound, the resting of your soul on the soul of your Father, the full entrance of your nature into God's nature by grateful love, then how much greater was the boon you had to give. How much more earnest was your struggle with your disciple till he had received it. How you used the well-proved propositions only as the means of bringing these two hearts together, God's and God's child's. How you wrestled and watched and prayed. How at last, when your friend really was a believer, your joy was all generous and noble; fully and thankfully content that he should be a sharer of your faith, even though his views of truth and the propositions in which he stated it were very different from yours.

There is a more sacred illustration even than this. We all think of God as giving of that which is His own to us who are His children. Is it not true that according to our conception of God's ownership will always be our thought of His bestowal? Property and charity once more will correspond. If when we think of God, the great privilege of His perfect life seems to us to be that He is perfectly happy, that He can never suffer, then the great gift of God will seem to us to be mere happiness, immunity from suffering, reward to all His servants who have served Him well, and simply for-giveness, simply the lifting off of penalties from the sinners who have repented of their sins. And to such gifts we cannot well attach the thought of sacrifice without the shaping of some half-commercial theory such as long clung about the truth of Christ's atonement and still haunts that truth to the bewilderment of many earnest minds. But if, upon the other hand, God's great possession is His holiness, if the sublime prerogative of His perfection of which we always think is that He never sins, then His great gift will be holiness too. Not safety from punishment but purity from wickedness will be the promise which shines like a star before our spiritual hope. And in the giving of that supreme glory of His glorious life we can well see, by dim illustrations that our own life furnishes, how there not merely may be but there must be sacrifice. The mysterious intrusion of sorrow for us into the divine life, the surrender of incarnation, the tragedy of crucifixion; all this becomes not clear of mystery, but full of gracious possibility, as soon as, with the highest conception of God's possession, we have mounted to the completest idea of His salvation.

This last illustration gives me the chance to say distinctly what I have already intimated once or twice, that the deeper conception of benefaction, which will not rest satisfied with anything short of the imparting of character, still does not do away with the inferior and more superficial ideas. It uses the lower forms of gift still as means or types or pledges. When I think of God as the giver of goodness, I am led not less but all the more to thank Him for the forgiveness of my sin. But that forgiveness is not any longer an end in itself. It has become to me the means, the figure, the

promise, of the holiness, His own holiness, for which He
is trying to melt a way into my soul. When I try to
bring my friend to a spiritual faith in God, the arguments with which I try to meet his objections become
not less but more dignified and urgent because their
value lies not in themselves but in the new spiritual
condition for which they are laboring to make a way.
And so when you or I or a whole charitable community
conceives the profounder thought that the poor are not
merely to be rescued from starving but inspired and
built up into self-support, intelligence, and the love of
struggle, there is in such a new conviction no abandonment of the necessity of money-giving. The giving of
money becomes all the more necessary. Only it is
ennobled by being made the type of a diviner gift which
lies beyond. Sometimes the higher gift may be so
directly given that the type is needless. Sometimes the
modern benefactor may say like Peter at the temple-
gate, "Silver and gold have I none, but in the name of
Jesus rise and walk;" but the rule of life will be that
the type is needed for the full work of the reality; and
money must be given all the more richly and willingly,
the more transparent it becomes to show the higher
purpose lying in behind it.

We live, as I have said already, in the midst of a certain dissatisfaction with the methods of charity which
have long prevailed; in the midst of much misgiving
and wondering whether perhaps the work of almsgiving
men and women and of charitable societies, which have
poured out their benefactions freely in our great com-
munities, has not often done more harm than good. All
thoughtful citizens have welcomed the effort after a more

systematic and intelligent administration of charity of
which we have heard much, and of whose development
we hope to see a great deal more. We need to remember certain things as we think about it. First, that all
true organization helps spontaneity and does not hinder
it. The organization which discourages spontaneous action, and does not, by due direction and suggestion, simply
reduplicate its force and so encourage it, is worse than
worthless. And second, that the effort to help the poor
not merely out of starvation, but into character and the
self-support which can only come by character, is not a
relaxing but a tightening of the demands of charity. It
makes charity harder and not easier. It calls for profounder sympathy, and for more sleepless vigilance. To
the charitable man or the charitable community which
keeps both these truths in mind, which is on its guard
perpetually against the hardening of charity into a machine, and expects perpetually the opportunity of completer and completer entrance into the lot of the suffering
and needy, to such an one there looms up, I think, now
in the distance, a noble vision of what the relations of the
rich and poor in a great city may become. It is a vision
which has the same charm of soberness, thoughtfulness,
thoroughness, and infinite promise, that belongs to what
we may call the more rational and lofty Christian faith
which it seems as if God was opening before His church.
It is a vision not of money recklessly flung abroad in un-
discriminating relief of suffering; nor, on the other hand,
of tight, hard machinery, grinding forth help without
sympathy, from between the wheels of inflexible organization; but a vision in whose fulfilment there shall be something like the true kingdom of God on earth, in which no

soul shall be satisfied until, to some other soul which is
personally its care it shall be giving the best that God has
given it, making use of all lower gifts richly and freely,
but always with the purpose, never lost sight of, never
forgotten, of bringing character, the life of God, into the
life of one more of His children.

We, to whom the question comes of what the rich man
may and can do for the poor man, live in the midst of a
great city ; a city ever growing greater and greater, and
putting on more and more the character which belongs
to those vast aggregations of humanity which, according
to some men's judgment, are the frightful plague-spots
of the earth, and, in the judgment of other men, are the
crowns and glories of our planet. We have the poor man
before us not in the mere fact of his poverty, but as his
poverty is always being bruised and embittered and ex-
asperated in the life of a great city. Let us think for a
moment what it must be to be poor here in the midst of
these roaring and insulting streets ; how different the
burden of poverty must be here in the city from what
it is when a man has to carry it through quiet country
lanes, with all the sweet sights and sounds of nature in
his eyes and ears. Then we shall see something of the
wisdom and profoundness which the problem of charity
demands here in the city. The city poor man then, remember, lives in the sight of wealth which is continually
changing hands. There is no settled fixedness of property. Where one man flourished yesterday another man
is flourishing to-day, and the old prosperity has disappeared. Not in the city, as in the country, do the same
households hand their houses down for generations as
if they had some chartered privilege of security with

which no upstart aspirant must interfere. In the midst
of this pervading atmosphere of chance, of opportunity,
the poor man walks with a perpetually disappointed
hope which never can entirely die out in calm despair;
restless with a continual wonder that, in all this ceaseless change, none of the shifting fortune ever falls to
him. What condition of things could be more fit to
create discontent which never ripens into energy, a movement which can only fret and chafe. The city poor
man seems to live on the brink of a Bethesda which the
angel is forever troubling, but into which he learns
to peevishly complain that there is no man to put him
down at the right moment. Its waters seem to mock
and taunt him as they sparkle inaccessible in the sunlight.

And again, the poor man in a great city sees wealth
and wealthy men as a class. He does not know them
as individuals. And a class of men, known only as a
class, keeps all the exasperating qualities of personality,
but loses the graciousness which belongs to individual
relations. The political party which we hate is always
more hateful to us than the men of whom it is composed. The religious sect which we despise is always
more despicable to us than its individual believers.

And yet again, the city poor man is very apt to live
in squalid circumstances which, while they make him
wretched and embittered, disable at the same time the
powers of repair, and beget a dull and heavy carelessness. To the poor man in the country, however poor he
is, the bright skies at least bring unconscious influences
of order; and the fields, with their circling seasons, will
not let him totally forget that there is such a thing as

beauty. You cannot shut out the horizon with its hope from the most hopeless soul. He little knows how almost absolutely indestructible is the elasticity of the human soul, who thinks that poverty in the city loses nothing in being condemned to live in the midst of perpetual disorder, ugliness, and dirt.

And still, with all his enforced hopelessness, the stir of the great city keeps the mind of the poor man in its midst alive, awake. He never can become as torpid as the country clown. There is no opiate for him in the thin and eager air. He must lie upon his rack with senses all acute and active.

And yet, once more, the poor man finds himself of necessity made a servant and contributor to the very wealth which overbears him, and whose existence often seems to him an insult. In the complex existence where he lives, he cannot draw his life apart and till his little plot of earth and disregard the wealth which he cannot possess. He has to build up fortunes which are not his own. He seems to be the rich men's creature, used for their purposes as long as they require him;

> " And having brought their treasure where they will,
>   Then take they down his load, and turn him off,
>   Like to an empty ass, to shake his ears
>   And graze in commons."

And then, to name only one circumstance more, if, as so often is the case, the poor man in the city is one who once was prosperous, he is kept sore always by having to live in the presence of his old prosperity. He meets his old proud footprints stamped in the familiar streets. The ghost of what he used to be insults him everywhere. The memory of other days intensifies each misery. He cannot draw a curtain of forgetfulness about his altered lot, and fall asleep in dull content.

Now put all these conditions together in your mind, and then think what a tumult of unrest, of hopeless, blind, unreasonable, disorderly repining and complaint the poor man of the city carries in his heart. He does not analyze it into its elements, as I have tried to do, but it is all there; far more terrible in its unanalyzed completeness than any such enumeration of its elements can describe. He is no man of our imaginations, no mere lay-figure for a sermon. He is real. You meet him every day. His is the face that looks moodily at you as you hurry by him on the sidewalk, or throw the street's mud from your carriage wheels upon his coat. His is the hand that rings your door-bell in the dusk; and his the voice that whines and cringes to you in your hall, and curses you as he goes down your steps, with the memory of your glowing comfort before his eyes, and your quiet assurance that you have no money to give him in his ears, and the leaden load of wretchedness and disappointment heavier than ever at his heart. His is the house you hurry by in some back street, and wonder how a man can live in such a place as that. And O! be sure there do come to him hours when that horrible home seems to him every whit as hateful as it does to you. He is no fancy. He is terribly real. The streets reproach him with their boisterous prosperity and arrogant wealth. To us those streets are sympathetic. To prosperous men, full of activity, full of life, the city streets, overrunning with human vitality, are full of a sympathy, a sense of human fellowship, a comforting companionship, in all that mass of unknown and, as it were, generic men and women, which no utterance of special friendship or pity from the best-known lips can bring. The live and active man takes his trouble out into the crowded streets and finds it comforted by the mysterious consolation of his race. He takes his perplexity out there, and its darkness grows bright in the diffused, unconscious light of human life. But when activity beats low and life has lost its buoyancy, when the wretched man is miserably and desperately poor, then the streets and the crowds are no longer sympathetic; then the great sea which used to heave the strong ship on, whether it would go or no, opens its depth and drowns the broken wreck. Ah, how little do we know of how the great full city which is always enticing and encouraging and exhilarating us, is mocking and beating down and treading under foot some poor brother who walks along the pavement by one side.

What can we do about it, do you say? Ah, that is the question that our charity and charitable people are just coming to see that they must answer. Thank God, they are learning to look deeper for their answer than they have ever looked before. They will find the answer gradually. Some time or other they will find it perfectly. I certainly am not so foolish as to think that I can give it ready-made here in the hurried end of a sermon. Enough if I have set any of you to thinking that it must be found, and that the finding of it is no easy task.

But one or two things let me say before I close, that I may not seem to have spoken wholly unpractically. The first thing that men must do in order that they may really, thoroughly relieve the poor, is to profoundly recognize that there can be no complete and permanent relief until not merely men who have money shall have given it to men who have no money, but until men who have character shall have given it to men who are deficient in that last and only real possession. Not till you make men self-reliant, intelligent, and fond of struggle, fonder of struggle than of mere help, — not till then have you relieved poverty. If you could give every poor man in this town of ours a house, a wardrobe, and a balance in the bank to-morrow, do you think there would not be poor men and rich men here among us still? There must be, so long as there are some men with the spirit of independence, the light of intelligence, and the love of struggle; and other men who have none of those things, which make the only true riches of a manly man. And the second thing is this: the rich men of our community must be truly rich themselves, or they can have nothing worth giving to the poor; nothing with which they can permanently help their poorer brethren. Only a class of men independent, intelligent, and glorying in struggle themselves, can really send independence, intelligence, and the dignity of struggle, down through a whole city's life. This is the reason why your selfish and idle rich man, who has neither of these great human properties, does nothing for the permanent help of poverty. The money which he gives is no symbol. It means nothing. O let us be sure that the first necessity for giving the poor man character is that the rich man should have character to give him.

And then, lastly, the rich men, rich in character, must know that no man can give character to other men without self-sacrifice. Labor, personal effort, personal intercourse with the poor, these must come in before the work can be done. You cannot do your duty to the poor by a society. Your life must touch their life. You try to work solely by a society, and what does it come to? Is it not the old story of the book of Samuel? The traveller appeals to you, and you spare to take of your own thought and time and sympathy to give to the wayfaring man that is come to you. They are too precious. You say: "There is thought, time, sympathy, down at the charity bureau to which I have a right by virtue of a contribution I have made. Go down and get a ticket's worth of that."

The poor are always with us. The wayfarers come to us continually, and they do not come by chance. God sends them. And as they come, with their white faces and their poor scuffling feet, they are our judges. Not merely by whether we give, but by how we give and by what we give, they judge us. One man sends them entirely away. Another drops a little easy, careless, unconscientious money into their hands. Another man washes and clothes them. Another man teaches them lessons. Thank God there are some men and women here and there, full of the power of the Gospel, who cannot rest satisfied till they have opened their very hearts and given the poor wayfaring men the only thing which really is their own, themselves, their faith, their energy, their hope in God. Of such true charity-givers may He who gave Himself for us increase the multitude among us every day.

XXI.

THE MARKS OF THE LORD JESUS.

"From henceforth let no man trouble me, for I bear in my body the marks of the Lord Jesus."—GALATIANS vi. 17.

A MAN who is growing old claims for himself in these words the freedom and responsibility of his own life. He asks that he may work out his own career uninterfered with by the criticism of his brethren. He bids them stand aside and leave him to the Master whom he serves and by whom he must be judged. How natural that demand is! How we all long at times to make it! How every man, even if he dares not claim it now, looks forward to some time when it must be made. He knows the time will come when, educated perhaps for that moment by what his brethren's criticism has done for him, he will be ready and it will be his duty to turn aside and leave that criticism unlistened to and say, "From henceforth let no man trouble me. Now I must live my own life. I understand it best. You must stand aside and let me go the way where God is leading me." When a man is heard saying that, his fellow-men look at him and they can see how he is saying it. They know the difference between a wilful and selfish independence, and a sober, earnest sense of responsibility. They can tell when the man really has a right to claim his life; and if he has, they will give it

to him. They will stand aside and not dare to interfere while he works it out with God.

This was St. Paul's claim, and he told the Galatians
what right he had to make it. "From henceforth let
no man trouble me, for I bear in my body the marks of
the Lord Jesus." It is the reason for his claim of independence that I want to study with you. "I bear in
my body the marks of the Lord Jesus." He was growing an old man. Anybody who looked at him saw his
body covered with the signs of pain and care. The
haggard, wrinkled face, the bent figure, the trembling
hands; the scars which he had worn since the day when
they beat him at Philippi, since the day when they
stoned him at Lystra, since the day when he was shipwrecked at Melita; all these had robbed him forever of
the fresh, bright beauty which he had had once when he
sat, a boy, at the feet of old Gamaliel. He was stamped
and marked by life. The wounds of his conflicts, the
furrows of his years, were on him. And all these wounds
and furrows had come to him since the great change of
his life. They were closely bound up with the service
of his Master to whom he had given himself at Damascus. Every scar must have still quivered with the
earnestness of the words of Christian loyalty which
brought the blow that made it. See what he calls these
scars, then. "I bear in my body the marks of the Lord
Jesus." He had a figure in his mind. He was thinking of the way in which a master branded his slaves.
Burnt into their very flesh, they carried the initial of
their master's name, or some other sign that they belonged to him, that they were not their own. That
mark on the slave's body forbade any other but his own

master to touch him or compel his labor. It was the
sign at once of his servitude to one master and of his
freedom from all others. So St. Paul says that these
marks in his flesh, which signify his servantship to
Jesus, are the witnesses of his freedom from every other
service. Since he is responsible to his Master he is
responsible to no one else. "From henceforth let no
man trouble me, for I bear in my body the marks of the
Lord Jesus."

It is a vivid, graphic figure. I hope that we shall find
that it may be as true of the life of any one of us as it was
of the life of Paul. We see at once with what a pathos and
a dignity it clothes the human body. It makes the body
the interpreter of the spiritual life that goes on within
it, the register of its experiences. A very clumsy and imperfect interpreter of the soul indeed the body is, and
yet we all know that it gets its real interest from what
power of interpretation and record it does possess. A
scar upon the face recalls some time of pain and peril,
and lets us know of a soul that has undergone the discipline of danger. Whether the pain came and was met
nobly or meanly, whether it was the peril of the soldier
or the peril of the burglar, the dumb scar cannot tell.
The quiet peaceful smile upon the face declares the soul
at rest; but whether the rest be idle self-indulgence, or
the satisfaction of a soul at peace with duty, only he
who reads behind the smile into its subtlest meaning
is able to discover. Yet in its clumsy, halting way the
outer is the record of the inner life. The body tells the
story of the soul. We bear in our flesh the marks of
our masters. The hard hand of the laborer tells that he
is the servant of unpitying toil. The knit brow of the

merchant declares what master sits over him in his
anxious office.   The serious forehead of the thinker reveals his service to his master, Truth.   And when we lay
a human body in the ground at last there is a reverence
or a pity which starts within us as we see the coffin-lid
close on the marks of noble or ignoble servantship which
years have left written on the face.

This is the principle on which rests St. Paul's description of himself.   And now let us see how that same description may be true of men to-day ; how they still may
bear in their bodies the marks of the Lord Jesus, the
very brands, as it were, which declare them to be His servants, His property.   Here is a man whose body shows
the signs of toil and care.   I will not read the long familiar catalogue.   The whitened hair, the cautious step, the
dulness in the eye, the forehead seamed with thought ;
you know them all, you watch their coming in your friend,
you feel their coming in yourself.   What do they mean ?
In the first and largest way they mean life.   The difference between this man and the baby, in whose soft flesh
there are no branded marks like these, is that this man
has lived.   But then they mean also all that life has
meant ; and life, below its special circumstances, always
means the mastery in obedience to which all the actions
have been done and all the character has taken shape.
" Who is your master ? " is the question that includes
all questions.   And if a man tries to push that question
aside ; if he says, " Nay, but my life cannot be judged
so, for I have no master," still he answers the question
which he rejects.   He answers it in rejecting it.   He
declares that he is his own master.   And then he bears
in his body the marks of himself ; the faded colors and

the scars mean only wilfulness and selfishness. But now suppose that life has meant for that man, from the beginning, the claiming of his soul by a higher soul; suppose that every new experience has seemed in its heart, its meaning, its spirit, to be only a little closer overfolding and embracing of the will by the Supreme Will; suppose that as the result of all, as the blended and completed issue of all this living, the life is Christ's life, uttering His wishes, seeking His purposes, filled and inspired by His love, reckoning its vitality by the degree of conscious and realized sympathy with Him; suppose all this, and then it will be true that every outward sign in which those inward experiences are recorded will become a mark of the Lord Jesus, a sign of that occupation of the nature by His nature, of the ownership of the man by Him, which is what it has meant for this man to live.

For instance, here among the white careworn features there are certain lines which tell, beyond all misunderstanding, that this man has struggled and has had to yield. Somewhere or other, sometime or other, he has tried to do something which he very much wanted to do, and failed. As clear as the scratches on the rock which make us sure that the glacier has ground its way along its face, so clearly this man lets us know that he has been pressed and crushed and broken by a weight which was too strong for him. What was that weight? If it were only disappointment, then these marks are the marks of simple failure. If the weight were laid on him as punishment, then these marks are marks of sin. If it were a weight of culture, then the marks are marks of education. If the weight was the personal hand of the Lord Jesus Christ teaching the man that his own will must be surrendered to the will of a Lord to whom he belonged; if the Lord Jesus Christ has been drawing him away from every other obedience to His obedience; then these marks which he bears in his body are the marks of the Lord Jesus. It is as if a master, seeking for his sheep, found him all snarled and tangled in a thicket, clinging to and clung to by the thorns and cruel branches. He unsnarls him with all tenderness, but the poor captive cannot escape without wounds. He even clings himself to the thorns that hold him, and so is wounded all the more. When the rescue is complete and the master stands with his sheep in safety, he looks down on him and says : " I need not brand you· more. These wounds which have come in your rescue will be forever signs that you belong to me. No other sheep will carry scars just like them, for every sheep's wanderings, and so every sheep's wounds, are different from every other's. Their pain will pass away, but the tokens of the trials through which I brought you to my service will remain. They shall declare that you are mine. You shall bear in your body my marks forever."

And then what follows? Freedom! "I bear in my body the marks of the Lord Jesus ; therefore let no man trouble me." I think that we have all seen how there are two classes among experienced and world-worn men. Some men with their scars and wrinkles and wounds grow timid, cringing, and spiritless. Their only object seems to be to get through the rest of life with as few more shocks and blows as possible. They apologize for living. They try to keep out of other men's

way and so are always open to their criticism, and
slaves of their whims. Poor broken creatures they are.
And then there are other men, whose hard experience
of life has evidently lifted them away from any anxious
care about what other men may think of them, given
them an independent self-contained life, and made them
free. What is it that makes the difference? Does it
not all depend on this: on whether the experience of
life has given a man any new master whom he trusts
and serves; on whether the "marks in his body," the
scars and bruises, are the ownership marks of any recognized and trusted Lord; or whether they are only the
unmeaning records of an aimless drifting hither and
thither among the rocks? The master may be more or
less worthy. If there only be a master, the man is free
from all other servitudes. His marks are signs of liberty. It may be only that he has made his own passions his lord. In self-indulgence and self-admiration
he may have settled down to the mere service of himself. But even in selfishness there is freedom. The
man of fixed contented selfishness is liberated from a
hundred cares about what other people think of him, or
what they have a right to ask. But let the new master
which life has given us be a principle, a cause, even a
petty conscientious scruple, and then how clear the
freedom from our fellows' tyranny becomes. "From
henceforth let no man trouble me, for I must do my
duty; I must work out my study; I must maintain my
cause." Very hard and sullen and cruel often grows
the independence that is born of such a mastery. But
now suppose that not one's self, and not some abstract
cause, but the Lord Jesus is the Master to whom the

body's marks bear witness. The strongest and yet the gentlest of all masters! The gentlest yet the strongest! Then comes an independence which is complete and yet which has no bitterness. There is no crude and weak contempt of fellow-men, while yet there is a calm and complete assertion that no fellow-man must hinder or intrude upon our life.

Indeed there is, in all the independence which the Christian as the servant of Christ claims with reference to his fellow-men, this subtle element which always redeems his independence from indifference or cruelty, — that the first duty which his new Master lays upon him is to go and serve and help those very fellow-men from whom he has plucked away his life, that he may give it completely to this loftier service. This is the noble poise and balance of the Christian life. Christ rescues the soul from the obedience of the world in order that in His obedience it may serve the world with a completer consecration. The soul tears itself away from slavery to the world and gives itself to Christ; and lo, in Him it serves the world for which He lived and died, with a devoted faithfulness of which it never dreamed before. Paul was never so busy working for men as in this very day when he cried out, "Let no man trouble me." His cry was primarily a demand that no man should dare to question his apostolical commission, because Christ had adopted him; but the more earnestly that he refused to let men question that deep transaction which lay between his soul and his Master's, so much the more completely did he give himself up to the service of the men who he insisted should not be his judges or his lords.

One principle you see lies at the bottom of all that we are saying, of all that Paul says in this verse. It is that no man in this world attains to freedom from any slavery except by entrance into some higher servitude. There is no such thing as an entirely free man conceivable. If there were one such being he would be lost in this great universe, all strung through as it is with obligations, somewhere in the net of which every man must find his place. It is not whether you are free or a servant, but whose servant you are, that is the question. This was what Jesus said. "No man can serve two masters." "Ye cannot serve God and mammon." It was always a choice of masters to which He was urging men. The Son who was to "make them free so that they should be free indeed," was to be one to whom they should show their love by "keeping His commandments." To know this truth is the first opening of the gates of life to a young man. It is not by striking off all allegiance, but by finding your true Lord and serving Him with a complete submission, that you can escape from slavery. "I will walk at liberty, for I keep Thy commandments," said David. This is the universal necessity of faith, which is but the obedience of the complete man, soul as well as body. This is the everlasting and fundamental difference between two inquiring and seeking souls. One of them is looking for some door which shall lead out into absolute freedom. The other is asking with free-eyed earnestness for its true Master. Before the one there can be nothing but vague restlessness and endless discontent. The other shall certainly some day arrive at peace in believing and obeying. O my dear friend, look for your master. Be satisfied with none until you find Him who by His love and His wisdom and His power has the right to rule you. Then give yourself to Him completely. Let Him mark you as His by whatever marks He will. Count every such mark a privilege. Find in His service the charter of your freedom. Resist all other men's intrusion on your life, because your life belongs to Him. Be jealous for it as your Lord's domain. That is the real emancipation of the soul of a child of God, its total consecration to its Father.

It is not only in the duties of active life that a man receives the mark of Christ and enters into the liberty which He bestows. The same liberation sometimes comes by sickness and the incapacity for work. I can speak perhaps more clearly if I picture to myself some one here in my congregation on whom that calamity has fallen. For years you have been doing your part in the world. You have held your own. You have asked nothing, you have taken nothing, from your fellow-men. But suddenly, it may be, the blow has fallen on you. Sickness has come. You cannot work. You are dependent where you used to trust only in yourself. How terrible it is ! How it seems as if now all liberty were gone. You must stretch out your hand in your blindness for somebody to lead you. You must open your helpless mouth for somebody to feed you. Life seems all slavery and uselessness. What can release you ? If it could come to pass that by your pain you should be brought into a personal knowledge of Him who can console your pain ; that by your weakness you could be brought to a personal reliance on His strength ; and so your pain and weakness could become to you profoundly

and inseparably associated with your allegiance to Him,
— then see ! Would they not be transformed ? Still you
must rest on others for what you would gladly do for
yourself. But it would be no enfeeblement, no demor-
alization of your life. The higher meaning of your
pain would swallow up its lower meaning. The association which it made for you with God would overrule
the association which it made for you with your brethren.
Through Him on whom it made you able to rely, you
would be strengthened so that even those on whom you
rested physically every day would feel your strength
and spiritually rest on you. That would be freedom
for you.

Such sicknesses there are. Such we have sometimes
known ; some men or women, helpless so that their lives
seemed to be all dependent, who yet, through their sickness, had so mounted to a higher life and so identified
themselves with Christ that those on whom they rested
found the Christ in them and rested upon it. Their sick-
rooms became churches. Their weak voices spoke gospels.
The hands they seemed to clasp were really clasping theirs.
They were depended on while they seemed to be most
dependent. And when they died, when the faint flicker
of their life went out, strong men whose light seemed
radiant, found themselves walking in the darkness ; and
stout hearts on which theirs used to lean, trembled as if
the staff and substance of their strength was gone. A
noble freedom certainly is this in which the arm that
holds you up is really held up by you ; in which, while
others think they are supporting you, you really are
supporting them ; and this noble freedom may come to
any weak and wounded life whose wounds and weak-

ness have become the signs and tokens that it belongs to Christ.

But I must not seem to speak as if it were only the sick and wounded in the great army of life upon whom the great Captain's mark is set. There are too many young eager, hopeful lives here before me who belong in the very van of that army, and whose strength and health find no worthy and sufficient explanation, unless we see in them the marks by which the Lord of our humanity would claim the choicest of our humanity for his own. Remember what the Incarnation was. "The Word was made flesh and dwelt among us." Then were the capacities of our human flesh declared. Then in the strong and healthy life of Jesus it was made known to what divine uses a strong body might be given. And since everything in this world properly belongs to the highest uses to which it may possibly be put, the strong human body was there declared to belong to righteousness and God. Thenceforward, after Jesus and His life, wherever human flesh appeared at its best, wherever a human body stood forth specially strong, specially perfect and beautiful, it had the mark and memory of the Incarnation on it. It might be totally perverted. It might be given to the Devil. But, since the work that Jesus did, the life that Jesus lived in a human body, the human body in its fullest vigor has belonged to the high work which He did in it, the service of God and help of fellow-man. Its vigor is His mark upon it. Feel this, and then how sacred becomes the body's health and strength. It is no chance, no luxury. God means that in it you should do work for Him. By it He claims you for His own. He to whom God has given it, is bound to have strong convictions, a live conscience, and intense earnest purposes of work.

Let a young strong man feel this and then he claims the proper freedom of his youth. "Let no man trouble me," he says, "for I bear in my body the marks of the Lord Jesus." I have tried to show you what those words mean when an old man says them out of the heart of his experience, with the bruises and scars of a hard life all over him. Even more solemn and full of meaning they are when a young man says them in the conscious vigor and full consecration of his youth. "You must not hamper and restrain me," he asserts. "You must not turn me from my way to yours. You must not coldly criticise all that I try to do. You must not ask me to conform to all the traditions which your cautiousness marks out. You must let me risk something of repute, of fortune, of comfort, of life itself, to do my duty. You must not think me arrogant or self-conceited if I disregard both your anxiety and your sneers, and go the way, the new way, the strange way, that is clearly set before me." It is a noble thing when out of all the jealousy, out of all the anxiety and love of older men, a young man thus quietly and firmly claims his life; but the nobleness only comes when he claims his life because Christ has claimed him, and because the full vigor and health in which he glories are to him marks of the Lord Jesus. To give one's life up timidly to the traditions that demand it on the one hand, and to assert one's independence in pure wilfulness on the other; both of these are perversions of the purpose for which we were made. To insist that we must have our lives to ourselves, that their own power may be worked out freely because we belong to Christ, that is the perfect scheme of existence, the sanctification of liberty, the transfiguration of ambition.

It is not hard, I think, to believe that something of this sort of symbolic consecration, this consecration of the spirit under the body's symbols, may pass over into the other life, and so may last forever. St. Paul tells us that in heaven we are to have a spiritual body in place of the natural body which we wear here. The privilege of that spiritual body must be to express with perfect clearness the experiences of the spirit which will then be the master. And if the great experience of the soul must always be redemption, redemption remembered in its beginning here, and ever going on to its completion through eternity, then certainly the body, which in some mysterious way will bear the record of that process, cannot fail to speak of Christ the Redeemer. The unimaginable perfectness which will belong to every organ will forever utter Him. Every perfection will be a new mark of the Lord Jesus. And since each saint's belonging to the Savior must be forever different from every other's, each saint will have in his spiritual body his own "marks of the Lord Jesus;" the signs of how his Lord has claimed him with a discriminating love that is entirely his own, different from that with which every other saint in all the millions has been saved.

In such a thought as that there opens before me all the social life of heaven. It is all liberty. No redeemed spirit shall ever have the power or the wish to encroach a hair's breadth upon the development of the redeemed life in any other. Each shall grow free and straight towards its own perfectness. And yet between these free lives, which never invade one another, there will always be the complete sympathy of a common dependence upon the one Source and Savior of them all. They will be all one, because they all belong to Christ, and yet the separateness of each shall be kept perfect because each is claimed with its own peculiar claim and marked with its own special mark. In all the solemnity of personalness and all the sweetness of brotherhood, the celestial life shall flow along its ever deepening way.

And must we wait for that until we get to heaven? O my dear friends, in this world, full of crude self-assertion and of feeble conformity, in this society where men invade each other's lives, and yet where, if one man stands out and claims his own life, his claim seems arrogant and harsh and makes a discord in the feeble music to which alone it seems as if the psalm of life could be sung; how sometimes we have dreamed of a better state of things in which each man's independence should make the brotherhood of all men perfect; where the more earnestly each man claimed his own life for himself the more certainly other men should know that that life was given to them. Must we wait for such a society as that until we get to heaven? Surely not! Even here every man may claim his own life, not for himself but for his Lord. Belonging to that Lord, this life then must belong through Him to all His brethren. And so all that the man plucked out of their grasp, to give to Christ, comes back to them freely, sanctified and ennobled by passing through Him who is the Lord and Master of them all.

For such a social life as that we have a right to pray.

But we may do more than pray for it. We may begin it in ourselves. Already we may give ourselves to Christ. We may own that we are His. We may see in all our bodily life, — in the strength and glory of our youth if we are young and strong, in the weariness and depression of our age or feebleness if we are old and feeble, — the marks of His ownership, the signs that we are His. We may wait for His coming to claim us, as the marked tree back in the woods waits till the ship-builder who has struck his sign into it with his axe comes by and by to take it and make it part of the great ship that he is building. And while we wait we may make the world stronger by being our own, and sweeter by being our brethren's; and both, because and only because we are really not our own nor theirs, but Christ's. Such lives may He give to us all!

University Press: John Wilson & Son, Cambridge.